Coming of Age in Wexford GAA
(1983-2004)

Best wishes,

Jim Mc Govern.

Coming of Age in Wexford GAA

(1983-2004)

Jim McGovern

Published by Ballinulty Publishing,
Killurin, Enniscorthy, Co. Wexford.

Front Cover Photograph:
Action Photograph from 1989 Wexford Senior Football Semi-Final,
Glynn-Barntown V Clongeen.
Back Cover Photograph:
New Clubhouse at Glynn-Barntown GAA Club.

Editors: Jim McGovern, Bernadette McGovern and Philip Higgins

Printed by
The Leinster Leader Ltd.
Main Street, Naas, Co. Kildare.

Contents

Contents   v

Acknowledgements   vi

Preface   vii

Foreword   x

Introduction   1

1. Starlights Serenade   6

2. The Purple and Gold Experience   23

3. The Glynn-Barntown Years – Punctuated   63

4. Gaelic Games in CBS Enniscorthy   104

5. Putting Something Back   120

6. Fixtures Frustration   143

7. A Chairman's Life   165

8. Glynn-Barntown on Tour   174

9. The Purple and Gold Stars   188

10. Some Things on my Mind   197

11. My Best Fifteen   215

12. Epilogue   223

Acknowledgments

In addition to main sponsor J.S. Bolger, Oylegate, I would like to express my sincere thanks to the following for their generous contributions towards the costs of printing and publishing this book:

Albert Randall, Killurin
J. Donohoe (Motors) Ltd., Enniscorthy
Gerry McGovern, Internet Consultant, Dublin
Hugh McGovern, Bovi Genetics Ltd., Kildare
Paddy Kehoe, Ceiling Contractor
Paul Roche, Net Communications, Enniscorthy
Sam McCauley, Chemists Ltd.
Alcast Company Ltd., Enniscorthy
John Kavanagh, Nursery & Fancy Goods, Enniscorthy
Ibar Carty, Photographer, Enniscorthy
Bristol-Myers-Squibb
Wexford Farmers Co-op (WFC), Enniscorthy
Wexford Creamery
Ned Buggy Sports, Wexford
Crosbie Brothers Ltd, Wexford
Hore's Stores Ltd, Wexford
Pettitt's Supermarkets, Wexford

Thanks also to all the various photographers whose pictures I have used, especially Ibar Carty and Paddy Murphy, Enniscorthy, and Ger Hore, Wexford, and to anyone else whose material I may have quoted from, especially those whom I was unable to contact for their permission.

Preface

This book is about my personal experiences in Wexford GAA in the period 1983 – 2004 inclusive. I have tried to remain true to myself in recounting these and have used newspaper reports and snippets to further authenticate my account. As Shakespeare said: *"to thine own self be true, and it must follow, as the night the day, thou canst not then be false to any man."* Let me get one thing straight from the beginning: this is not the story of a gifted player who won All- Ireland medals and All-Star awards; rather it is about an average player who strove very hard to make the most of his ability. Over the last few years the thought has kept recurring that I should do this book and it just wouldn't remain unwritten! So it's a story I felt I had to tell if only to put the record straight on a few issues. I really landed on my feet when I came to Wexford and feel very fortunate to have met a lot of tremendous people through my involvement in the GAA and this, of course, was a major factor in helping me integrate into the community at a time of great uncertainty in my life when I was weighing up, carefully, whether I would return to the Irish College in Rome to continue my studies for the priesthood or carve out a career in teaching.

I was very fortunate to be able to join one of the top senior clubs in Wexford on my arrival and to win a senior championship medal in my first year with them. I then went on to play for Wexford for several years and it was indeed a privilege to wear the purple and gold. I had played little or no inter county football with Longford (in fact they were showing no interest in me as I left for Wexford in September 1982) and to get an opportunity to do so with the Model County was for me just marvellous and something I was not going to miss out on. I was twenty eight when I played my first championship game for the county which was very late in inter county terms but I was very driven and fiercely determined to get as much out of it as I possibly could and the harder the training the more I liked it. I played on a very good Wexford team that came within a whisker of getting into Division 1 in the mid 1980s beating some of the best teams in the country in the process and also running then Leinster champions, Dublin, to a few points in the Leinster quarter final of 1986.

However, I don't think I ever did myself full justice playing with Wexford as, not being from the county and to justify my place on the team, I really felt I had to play out of my skin in every game and, as a result, probably put myself under too much pressure at times. Nevertheless I will always treasure my involvement with the county, and the number fourteen jersey which I was given to keep (the same applied to everyone else) after we beat Dublin at Croke Park in February1985 will always remain one of my proudest possessions. I was very keen to 'put something back' so to speak and did so through my involvement with Wexford underage teams but, if I have one regret about that, it is perhaps that I got involved while I was still an active player and this may have curtailed or indeed wrote *'fini'* to my senior inter-county career, at a time when I was playing the best football of my life with Glynn-Barntown. But I certainly found my work with the underage teams very fulfilling and was very glad that I did it.

Perhaps another regret I have is that I did not come to the county a few years earlier, as I feel sure I could have made a much bigger impact. I had to work extremely hard to succeed at inter county level as I had received little or no formal coaching growing up. For instance, I was never encouraged to work on my weaker right foot but soon realised that, if I was to make the grade, I would have to become proficient with both feet. To that end I worked constantly on my right and finally reached a stage where I favoured it more than my left at least in terms of accuracy if not power. I was well aware of my limitations (I knew I was no Mick O'Connell or Jack O'Shea) but always tried to have a positive attitude. I'd like to think Wexford people saw me as ebullient rather than arrogant and that they will regard this book in the same light.

I never liked playing full forward for Wexford and there would have been many who would have been critical of me at times, and rightly so, for not passing the ball. This tendency to hang onto the ball could have stemmed from my time playing in Longford where, as part of a junior team, I tended to carry the ball a lot. However, I do believe that the Wexford team I was part of could have done with the services of a *'forwards coach'* to help us play better as a unit. Had that happened, I feel we could have achieved a lot more as we had very good individual players. In no way did I want to be seen as being selfish as I got as much pleasure out of giving a good pass as I did out of making a high catch or getting a score. I was very conscious that there is no *'i'* in team but then again I tended towards not doing the obvious. I was however a completely different player out at midfield, where I had far more room to express myself, and greater freedom of action. I played for Wexford in three different positions: midfield, centre and full forward, but the bottom line is, even though I eventually became exasperated with the full forward position, I would have played anywhere just to be on the team.

I am very much indebted to everyone who assisted me in any way with the writing of this book. A word of thanks to Seamus Keevans who helped me jog my memory with regard to players and positions as I tried to select a team from the period in question. I am particularly grateful to my teaching colleagues Terri Talbot and Dympna Gartland, and also to Liam Griffin and Martin Codd Jnr. who took time out of their busy schedules to read over the manuscript and offer suggestions. Further thanks to Liam for writing the foreword. Thanks also to the staff of Wexford Library. My greatest thanks though, goes to my wife, Bernadette, my typist, my guide and editor of first and last resort, who has been such a huge help to me from day one. Of course I cannot forget our three daughters, Claire, Susan and Eimear who showed great forbearance as I commandeered their 'den' halfway through the writing of the manuscript. My heartfelt thanks to all four of you for your extraordinary patience and understanding, and for giving me the time and space to research and write this book. You can have *'the den'* back now girls.

Wexford has been very good to me over the past twenty one years. It is a beautiful part of the country and I feel privileged to live here with my family among friendly people. I have been involved with club, school and county, and generally it has been a very enjoyable and rewarding experience. I would like to donate all profits from this book towards the provision of a modern stand and floodlighting facilities at Glynn-Barntown GAA club, and the development of Gaelic games at CBS Enniscorthy.

Foreword

Behind every extraordinary player you see on the playing fields of Ireland there is a story of ordinary men. The talented player, particularly if he is well decorated at national level, will have a willing audience for his story. The ordinary man, however, will not tell his story for fear of many things real and imagined.

Jim McGovern spoke to me a few years ago and asked my opinion on his intention of writing a book. Jim occupies an uncrowded place in the GAA world, as he is a sensitive and gentle soul who, like all of us, fears rejection. Of course Jim McGovern should tell his story; we may learn more and gain more from the stories of ordinary men than we ever could from people who have seen the dizzy heights. It should be remembered that most players who make it in the GAA do so by accident of birth.

Born into a strong senior club in hurling or football gives a player a massive head start. When that club is in a strong county, it is a further major advantage. Jim started out his adult playing life from a then junior club, Mullinalaghta, in Co. Longford. He was later to become chairman of Glynn-Barntown – one of Wexford's most progressive hurling and football clubs, and is now in his seventh consecutive year at the helm. During his time as chairman, Glynn-Barntown undertook some of the most progressive developments by any GAA club in County Wexford or beyond. The club is one of the most respected in County Wexford and are widely regarded as fair and honest. I can honestly say from experience it's always a pleasure to meet them on the playing fields, irrespective of the results. This of course is down to the fine leadership and the many respected families in the area.

Nicky Rackard won his first county medal playing underage hurling for Glynn. He did so as an *'isolated player'* as there was no minor hurling team in Rathnure in 1939. Jim McGovern was lucky to find the parish of Glynn, the luck was mutual.

From a football point of view I can't make up my mind as to whether or not Jim was lucky or unlucky to have attended St. Mel's of Longford. Read the book and make up your own mind. What I do know, however, is that during my schooldays, St. Mel's was regarded as one of the finest Gaelic football colleges in the land. The schoolboys of County Wexford and Enniscorthy in particular can be grateful to Mel's as Jim turned out to be a teacher with a strong GAA commitment. Teachers and the clergy have, in fact, made the GAA what it is today; they will never be repaid, we can never thank them enough.

Jim's playing story is interesting and varied. The benefits of a strong club are evident here. From a county senior medal with Enniscorthy Starlights, to the privilege of playing in the purple and gold of Wexford, Jim McGovern appreciates it all greatly. He has shown appreciation in practical terms by serving as a mentor with various county, club and school teams. The profits from this book will be given to the Glynn-Barntown GAA Club and CBS Enniscorthy. No surprise there.

Sadly, Jim never had the opportunity to play hurling, an accident of birth! It should never happen in a country like Ireland of course. The GAA has a case to answer here. Hurling is our national game, don't forget.

It has taken almost 50 years, from Ballinulty in Co. Longford to Glynn-Barntown in Co. Wexford, for this story to develop. Yes, it's the story of an ordinary man, but where would we all be without them. The book is worth reading, the causes worth supporting.

Liam Griffin

Introduction

I was born in Longford on the 15th of June 1956, and brought up in the townland of Ballinulty in the parish of Colmcille in North Longford. It is also the parish of top GAA journalist Eugene McGee. My local town would be Granard, which is about five miles from my home. It is a place made famous by Michael Collins and Kitty Kiernan. In fact, Collins, being on the run at the time, often walked down through our, and other neighbours, fields on his way to Granard to see his beloved Kitty. And, according to my grandfather, took refreshment on more than one occasion from our spring well!

Granard is also the birthplace of famous international showjumper Eddie Macken, and former RTE sports commentator and international athlete, the late Brendan O' Reilly. I attended St Joseph's National School at Purth, which is less than a mile from my home. The school itself is directly opposite the home of the great champion jockey Frank Berry. Sadly, it closed its doors many years ago and is now the property of the Berry family. I enjoyed my years in the school, but was never taught the basics of Gaelic football (or indeed hurling), there, something I felt was always to my disadvantage in my subsequent attempts to master the game. We had good teachers in Mrs Rodgers and Mrs Smyth, but I don't think I was receptive to being taught much, and was continually coming home late in the evenings, preferring instead to loiter around Lough Gowna's lovely shores just across from the school, and, in the process, escaping some chores at home. This of course was much to my mother's annoyance and eventually she could take it no longer. She pleaded with the President of St. Mel's College, Monsignor Lennon, to take me in as a boarder as I had her heart broken. The only snag about it was that I was only in fifth class and knew next to nothing!

Nevertheless my mother could be very persistent and persuasive and, eventually, the president agreed to give me a chance and so I entered St. Mel's College in September 1968. Football in the county was on a high at the time, the Longford team having just lost gloriously to Kerry in the All Ireland semi final the previous month, and I was certainly looking forward to playing a lot of It in Mel's, but more about that later.

Not having done sixth class, I found the first year in the college extremely tough going, receiving very poor results (a number of 0% results actually) in my Christmas and summer tests. Slowly but surely however, I got to grips with the situation, worked extremely hard and left the college in June 1973, having been made Head Prefect in my final year. I entered Maynooth College in September '73 to study for the priesthood, and three years later, having completed a degree in history and philosophy, was sent by my bishop to study at the Gregorian University in Rome. I left the *eternal city* in late January 1979, initially intending to take a couple of years out to consider my future and to experience a bit of the world, as I had been in a very sheltered environment up to that point.

Soon, I was doing a course in Personnel Management and when that was completed, I headed off to Denmark for a few months to earn some money. I was back in Ireland in November 1979 and took up a temporary position teaching Religion and History in January 1980. I returned to Maynooth in October of that year to complete the B.D. degree in Theology that I had started in Rome some years earlier. I took my Higher Diploma in Education in 1982, and during that summer actively sought a full time teaching post, though still not one hundred per cent sure what I wanted to do with my life.

Now, as that wonderful wordsmith Con Houlihan might say, read on!

It was the summer of 1982, Britain had won the Falklands War, Israel had invaded the Lebanon, Michael Fagan had invaded the Queen of England's bedroom and Italy was triumphant in the World Cup. And what was I doing? Well, as I said, I was looking for a full time teaching post, and my search took me to Co. Wexford, where I had applied for a job at Wexford Town Vocational College. In due course I was called for interview and so I headed down from my home in Longford to the model county. It was a long but interesting journey, travelling through some places I had never been before, until ultimately I arrived in Wexford town. I did what I considered a good interview (I was subsequently offered the job), and then went for something to eat.

To pass the time I purchased an Irish Independent and, out of curiosity, went to the jobs section where I noted that a job was available in C.B.S. Enniscorthy for a teacher of History and Religion, which happened to be my subjects. I decided to enquire about the job on my way back through Enniscorthy. This I duly did and spent about an hour speaking with the Principal, Brother Flannery. Before I was back home my mother had received a call from the Brother to say I had got the job if I wanted it. I didn't need much persuading to take up the offer, a bird in the hand being better than two in the bush, and so I started work in Enniscorthy in September 1982, really looking forward to the challenge.

The first evening I arrived, I stayed in a Bed and Breakfast outside the town. The following morning, to clear my head, I decided to walk to school. I was about halfway there, when a local farmer stopped and offered me a lift. Not wishing to decline local hospitality, I accepted. We started talking and naturally the subject of the GAA came up. I was keen to hear what the local senior teams were like, and he assured me that the local town club, Starlights, were on the verge of something big, while a team a few miles from the town, Duffry Rovers, had great potential.

I was very keen to play senior football as I had only participated in the junior and intermediate grades in Longford. My involvement in football (to my great regret I never had the opportunity to play hurling) was greatly curtailed due to the fact that I was a student in Rome from 1976 to 1979. I had made every effort to help my native parish, Colmcille, attain senior status but it was not to be. So when I arrived in Wexford, my number one aim sports wise, was to play senior football and hopefully win something too. I did seriously consider giving it one final shot with my home club, but eventually decided against it, primarily because of the amount of travel involved, but also because I saw sport as a way of helping me integrate into the Wexford community.

I found the staff in the C.B.S. to be very friendly, and in due course sought out those who had a particular interest or involvement in the GAA. Two in particular stood out: Josie Murphy as she was then - she is now Josie Foley, and Michael Carty. Josie was prominent with the Duffry Rovers GAA Club, while Michael was a lynchpin of the Castletown GAA Club in North Wexford. Both had already made tremendous contributions to the GAA, Josie as an administrator and Michael as a player. Josie had been county treasurer for several years (the first lady to hold the position), and was later to become chairperson of her club. Michael was an outstanding inter-county footballer and had also played on the great, all-conquering U.C.D. teams of the 1970s, a team that included household names such as Pat O'Neill of Dublin, John O'Keefe of Kerry, Gerry McEntee and Colm O'Rourke of Meath and Tony McManus of Roscommon, to name but a few. Michael Carty could more than hold his own in such company, and in fact Eugene McGee (who managed those teams) is on record as saying that the Castletown man was the most dedicated player he had ever come across.

So naturally, over time, I sought their advice as to what club I might join. (I should point out that, at this stage, I had moved into Enniscorthy town and was sharing a flat with a Limerick man, Donal O'Brien, who had also just joined the staff.) The general thrust of their advice was to join the club where you are living and that would have been the local Starlights club; but, having come from a rural club in Longford, my preference would have been for a similar one in Wexford, and this I related to Josie who in turn passed it on to her club, Duffry Rovers. The only drawback was that, to be legal, I would have to live in their parish for twenty-eight days at least. While they were in the process of sorting out accommodation for me, Starlights must have got wind of what was happening for who should appear at the school but Pat Hall, a prominent member of Enniscorthy Hurling and Football Club (as they were called) with a transfer form in his hand. I just decided there and then that I would sign for Starlights as I knew they had a good team and the thoughts of having to move house again didn't really appeal to me. Given the success that Duffry Rovers later enjoyed I occasionally wondered if I had made the right choice!

Nevertheless Starlights it was, but since it was still only the autumn of '82, I continued to return to Longford to play league games with my club. I eventually informed them that I would be leaving and one in particular pleaded with me to stay one more year. That person was Dr. Peter Heraty, our medical officer, and a prominent member of the club. Sadly, he died years later at the very young age of fifty-one and was a huge loss to the club and the local community.

However my mind was made up, but I did promise the good doctor that I would return for at least a year at some future date, in spite of the travel involved, but more of that later.

I can clearly recall the first hurling game I went to in Co. Wexford. It was a senior championship game, Buffers Alley v Geraldine O'Hanrahans, and it took place at Bellefield, Enniscorthy. Why it remains so clearly in my mind is because it was the first hurling game I saw in the flesh so to speak, but more importantly the first time I witnessed the great Tony Doran 'live', having heard and read so much about him, and having seen him of course on TV. There was a huge crowd there that day, and a great air of expectancy any time the slio-thar went in the vicinity of the great Tony. I was intrigued by this and parked myself opposite the twenty-one yard line to get a good close-up of the action. I was so fascinated by the flame haired man from Monamolin that I went to the other end for the second half and did the same. I must say that in all my time in Wexford I have not come across another player who excited crowds in quite the same way as Tony did. Perhaps Martin Storey and Matty Forde have come close.

The first football game I saw was a senior championship encounter between Castletown and Sarsfields, also at Bellefield. Both teams were going well at the time, Castletown having won the Championship in 1981, and Sarsfields going on to win it in centenary year 1984.

The rest of '82 really flew by as I immersed myself in my work as a teacher; I particularly enjoyed giving a hand with the school teams. Of course I also needed to keep myself fit, and to that end I sought and received permission from county football team manager, Tony Dempsey, to train with the county football panel, which was training in St. Patrick's Park, Enniscorthy, at the time. I think he might have regretted the decision as, in the words of Gusserane's Tadgh Foran, who was on the panel at the time, I *"hit the place like a tornado, and was dumping fellows on their backsides all over the place"!* This train-ing certainly kept me fit, as I prepared for 1983 and my debut with the famed Starlights.

Chapter 1

Starlights Serenade

"Each venture is a new beginning" T.S. Eliot

I think it must have been in early January1983 that I wrote to Michael Doyle then, as now, chairman of Enniscorthy Hurling and Football Club, thanking him for giving me the opportunity to play with the club, and looking forward to ultimate success in 1983. I knew that the Starlights were there or thereabouts every year and I was determined to play my part in helping them win a senior championship. I was almost twenty-seven years of age, and realised that I had no time to waste. I felt very driven and was prepared to put in any amount of hard work to succeed. We started training in February under former Wexford player, Phil Wilson. We did a lot of hard stamina work at the start and Phil, although then in his forties trained with us. He was a hard task master but he didn't ask us to do anything he wasn't prepared to do himself, and therefore you felt you had to make a big effort as he led by example.

The first game I played in Wexford was a senior challenge v Castletown in Bellefield. Castletown had won the championship in '81 and, although their team was getting old, they were still a force to be reckoned with. I had also heard that they had a tough reputation and took no prisoners. It was an evening game and I was delighted to be at last playing for Starlights. One thing I can clearly remember from the game is, pulling on a ball on the ground about forty yards out from the Castletown goal and sending it straight over the bar, something I had never done before or since! Then again, it wasn't always wise to go down on a ball against the north county men! I enjoyed the game and felt I had played well. The following day at work Michael Carty, who played against me that evening, remarked that I seemed to be out to prove a point. And indeed I probably was, as I knew that if I could do well against what was regarded as the toughest team in Wexford, I would fear nobody else.

I now looked forward with great eagerness to the start of the championship. The competition was run on a league- championship basis then and we were in a group with Ballyhogue, Rathgarogue-Cushinstown and Duffry Rovers. My first competitive game in Wexford was against Ballyhogue at Wexford Park. I could not wait to play my first match in the county grounds but was a bit disappointed when I discovered I was lining out full forward, as I much preferred midfield. Nevertheless, I was very glad to be even on the team and I thought I did okay even though I was marked by former Leinster player Pat Leacy who, in fairness, was probably past his considerable best at that stage. We won the game by six points to four and I got a point from play, so I suppose it was a satisfactory enough debut. We had got our championship campaign off to a winning start and with training going well, we looked forward to our next game against Duffry Rovers, the club I could have joined. The general consensus was that this would be a tough game for us but we won it quite easily by 1-11 to 0-4. It was four points to three for the Duffry at half time but, given that they had played with a very strong wind, it didn't seem enough. And so it proved. We added 1-8 to our tally in the second period while keeping our opponents scoreless in the process. I was quite happy with how I played, scoring three points and received a further boost in the *'People'* Paper the following week when one of the *'Gaelograms'* snippets stated that: *'Starlights looked great in their senior football championship win over Duffry Rovers and most critics rate them championship favourites. Newcomer Seamus McGovern is proving a great addition. The Stars must easily be the biggest team in the county'.*

The team's confidence was quite high now, but amazingly we had to wait over two and a half months for our next championship match v Rathgarogue Cushinstown. While marking time we tried to keep ourselves sharp by playing challenge and tournament games. I had the added difficulty in that, being a secondary school teacher, I was on my summer holidays and was travelling up and down from Longford for training and matches. Our match against the New Ross district side eventually took place on Saturday 31st July, and we won quite easily on a scoreline of 3-18 to 0-3. It was certainly our best display to date, but the winning margin flattered us in that Cushinstown were short a number of their regulars through injuries and holidays and had very little chance of qualifying for the knock-out stages before the match. I was very pleased with my own display getting five points from play and received glowing references in the *Enniscorthy Echo* the following week when, in the course of his match report, writer Ger Walsh stated that: *"one of the big strengths of the Starlights attack comes not from the Cathedral town at all, but from Co. Longford. Jim McGovern, a schoolteacher, has made a tremendous difference since his introduction at full forward. McGovern has the strength and size to cause problems for even the most effective defences"*. Two weeks later a snippet in the *Wexford People's 'Gaelograms'* said that: *"a knowledgeable follower in Enniscorthy is convinced that Seamus McGovern, the Starlights full-forward who is playing superb stuff right now is well worthy of his place on the county senior football panel for the National League. Club mate Jim Rigley is another one worth watching"*. Talk about *"Mol an óige agus tiocaidh sé!"*

Naturally we were all on a high after such an easy win, but I think we realised the opposition had been very weak and we certainly were not going to let all the media attention go to our heads. We were now through to the quarterfinals of the championship where we were picked to play George O'Connor's club, St Martin's. Had the game been played a week or two after the Cushinstown game, I believe we would have won with a bit to spare as we had built up a great deal of momentum but, as it was, it didn't take place until the 2nd October, over two months after our last game. We tried, as before, to keep ourselves in shape for the fixture by playing challenge and tournament games, but while they are fine in themselves, they are no substitute for the real thing. One game I clearly remember was the final of the Spellman Park Tournament, against Castletown, hosted by Kildavin GAA Club in Co. Carlow on Sunday 11th September 1983. The reason I can recall it so clearly is because of a major *'dust up'* that happened half way through the second half. It involved everybody bar the Castletown goalkeeper, full back, and myself. Since it happened at the other end of the field we felt it was just too far away to get involved! Whatever about winning the fight, we won the game on a scoreline of 1-6 to 1-4!

The *'Echo'* had a very brief report on the game which went as follows. *"Two superlative goals by Tommy Masterson and Jim McGovern*

8

(my first goal for Starlights) *were highlights of a very tough and hard fought final of the Spellman Park Tournament in Kildavin on Sunday afternoon, won by the Enniscorthy side with Dan Jordan voted 'man of the match'."* I had played with strained ankle ligaments and now decided to rest for a couple of weeks to be ready for the quarter final which eventually took place on Sunday 2nd October at Wexford Park. This was a game we certainly would not have won but for the excellent play of our goalkeeper Billy Morrissey who saved two certain goals and the brilliant free taking of Jim Rigley who scored seven out of our eight points from frees (we won by 8 points to 6). One of Jim's points from an almost impossible angle on the sideline was one of the finest frees from the ground I have ever seen. We felt we got out of jail in this game and were most relieved to progress. St. Martin's were a fine team and played some excellent football, but they did not score enough when they had the wind in the second half, (we only led by a point at half time and the signs seemed ominous). The Piercestown men squandered a lot of chances including a couple of easy frees. They did get to the senior hurling final later in the year, which was some consolation I suppose.

We were now into the penultimate round of the championship and were drawn to face reigning champions Half Way House, Bunclody, who had won the title for the very first time the previous year, and had given Portlaoise a really serious run for their money in the Leinster Club Championship, despite having had a player sent off. (The Laois club later went on to win the All Ireland Title). We won a low scoring game by six points to five and can thank our defence for putting us into the final. Writing in the *'People'* Newspaper, reporter Mervyn Moore offered the following: *"for a game that was close, tough and sometimes downright rugged, the Enniscorthy side gave one of the best defensive displays ever seen at the venue to hold the title holders to a lead of three points at the break … No praise is too high for the manner in which the Starlights defence controlled the first half (when they played against a near gale force wind). Take into consideration the fact that the ball often curled its way back to the kicker because of the wind and you'll agree that to hold Bunclody to just three points before the break was nothing short of incredible".*

Most instrumental in repelling the Bunclody charge in that first half were right corner back Sean Nolan and full back Ed Doran. Both were absolutely superb, not just in the first period but right throughout the game, and in over twenty years in Wexford never have I witnessed a better display of defensive defiance and all done with a touch of class.

It was, then, looking good for us at the interval, being only three points down with a very strong wind to assist us in the second half. However it was Bunclody who scored first on the resumption, increasing their lead to four points and now we knew we really had a game on our hands.

I kicked a point over my shoulder (a speciality of mine!) after about five minutes to register our first score. Jim Rigley, whose freetaking wasn't as immaculate as it had been in the quarter final, further reduced the deficit. I got another point a few minutes later and then Jim O'Sullivan levelled matters with twelve minutes to go. Three minutes later I put Starlights into the lead with one of the most unusual points I have ever scored. I won a ball out close to the sideline at the town end on the stand side. I headed for goal but was forced out towards the corner flag by a Bunclody defence that was now every bit as defiant as ours had been in the first half. Close to the endline now, and under severe pressure, I tried another kick over my shoulder, and to my delight it sailed between the posts.

When Pat Neville added another minor a couple of minutes later it looked like we might pull away, but Bunclody were not going to give up their title easily, and put our defence under a lot of pressure in the last few minutes but, as in the first half, our rearguard was more than equal to it with 'man of the match' Sean Nolan particularly outstanding. Bunclody did reduce the deficit to a single point two minutes into injury time, but the final whistle went on the kickout and Starlights were into another county senior football final.

For me this was a dream come true: my first full year in Wexford and I was about to play in a county senior football decider. An added bonus arising from the game was that I was also called into the county senior football panel, but I was not yet eligible, not having declared for Wexford on my transfer form; I hadn't been so presumptuous!

The final was fixed for Sunday, November the thirteenth, so we had about a month to get ready for it. I had picked up an injury in the semi-final, which required specialist treatment, and meant that I missed about two weeks of training. Of course at that time of year prepara-tions were going to be restricted anyway because of the short evenings, and any daylight work would have to be done at weekends. Our opponents in the final would be Wexford District, (a team drawn from Junior and Intermediate Clubs), who had beaten 1979 county champions St. Fintan's in the other semi-final by 1-6 to 0-6. We were installed as warm favourites, but none of us were under any illusions about the task ahead of us. We knew the district team would be for-midable opposition with all bar one of their team having represented Wexford at some level or other, many of them at senior. So we were fully aware of the danger posed by the district combination and, while quietly confident, we knew that we would have our work cut out to win. And so it proved as we emerged victors by just a one-point margin in a low scoring game (0-8 to 2-1). But really we should have won by much more.

The report of the game in the *Irish Independent* the following day (Monday 14th November) gave an accurate summary of the proceed-ings: *"a point one minute into injury time from a Jim Rigley free gave Starlights a single point victory over Wexford District in a disappoint-ing Wexford senior football final at Wexford Park yesterday. Starlights have no one to blame but themselves for allowing Wexford District to remain in contention to the end. They dominated the game over the hour but poor finishing nearly cost them the title in the end. Wexford District were a sore disappointment. Outplayed at midfield, the defence was under tremendous pressure over the hour, but full cred-it to their defensive quality for keeping their side in the game right to the final whistle. The Starlights who led 0-3 to 0-1 at the interval, had their best players in Sean Nolan, Ed Doran, Padge Courtney, Mick Millar, Nicky Sweetman, Pat Neville, Jim McGovern and Jim Rigley. For the losers Noel Barry, Eamonn O'Connor, Nicky Jones and Sean O'Shea were best."*

And so we had won our first senior championship in 46 years, and afterwards there was a great sense of joy, elation and indeed relief, not least because we knew that Wexford District could have caught us in the end. Pat Neville received the *'man of the match'* award but Nicky Sweetman, who gave a towering performance at midfield, must have run him very close. I was reasonably happy with my own per-formance winning a lot of possession from the very tenacious Jack O'Leary and finally shaking him off late in the second half to score

11

what proved to be a vital point. But really and truly it was a team effort and all involved played their part.

Tho team that lined out in the final was as follows: Billy Morrissey, Sean Nolan, Ed Doran, Mossy Rigley, Mick Millar, Padge Walsh, Padge Courtney, Pat Creane, Nicky Sweetman, Jim Sullivan, Pat Neville, (0-1), Jim Rigley, (0-5), Dan Jordan, Jim McGovern, (0-1) and Pat Goff. The substitutes were Michael Farrell, R.I.P., Joe Rigley, (brother of Mossy and Jim), Seamus Whelan, Joe Moorehouse and Tom Doyle. Michael Farrell replaced Dan Jordan in the course of the game.

Wexford District lined out as follows: Ger Turner (St. Mary's, Rosslare), Noel Barry (Kilmore), Jack O'Leary (St. Brigid's, Blackwater,), Pat White (St. Anne's), Michael O'Leary (St. Brigid's, Blackwater), Jim White (St. Anne's), Eamonn O'Connor (Volunteers), Michael Walsh (Glynn-Barntown), John Creane R.I.P. (St. Mary's, Maudlinstown), Sean O'Shea (St Brigid's Blackwater, 1-0), John Doran (St. Mary's Maudlinstown), Matt Furlong (St. Brigid's, Blackwater 1-0), Paddy Murphy (St. Brigid's Blackwater), Ger Howlin (Dan O'Connell's) and Nicky Jones (Volunteers 0-1). Subs. used were: T. Wade (St. Mary's, Maudlinstown) for M. O'Leary, Willy White (St. Anne's) for Walsh and I. Power (St. Anne's) for Doran.

To make the day truly memorable for the club, our junior *'B'* footballers recorded an easy win over Adamstown to claim the county title. No team deserved a championship more, as they had to play eleven games (their opponents played just four) and one period of extra time (in the county semi-final) to reach their objective. Speaking of the county semi-final, this game (against St. Martin's) developed into one of the longest running sagas in the history of Wexford GAA. It took three games and a period of extra time before the Starlights finally triumphed. That they won the final so convincingly (3-8 to 1-1) was perhaps entirely fitting, given the hard road they had to tread to get there.

The junior *'B'* team and substitutes were as follows: Liam Murphy, Michael Foley, Joe Murphy, Pat Sinnott, Owen Tyrell, Vincent Daly, Padraig Doyle, Donal O'Connor, Ger Franklin, Paddy Farrell, Murt Dempsey, Paul Nolan, Frankie Farnan, Jim Tyrell, and Pat 'Junior' Hanley. Subs used were: Willy Newe for Sinnott, Billy Dwyer R.I.P. for

Hanley and Tom Murphy for Farnan. Also on the panel were: Philip Murphy, Brendan Cahill, Jim Breen, Gerry McKenna, John Donnelly, Niall Wall and Larry McDonald.

What a marvellous achievement for the club on that November day in 1983! But let's not forget the backroom teams who played no little part in the wins. The senior selectors were: Larry Byrne, Tony Ennis, John Doyle and Michael Donegan (RIP) and, as mentioned earlier, the team was trained by Phil Wilson. The junior selectors comprised: Noel Matthews, Roy Tierney, Pat Hall and Michael Doyle.

The senior team was now into the Leinster Club Championship but only just! Forced to compete just three days after our county final victory because of the very late finish to our own championship, we had to give way to a fresher Rathvilly side (Carlow champions), in a game played at Dr. Cullen Park, Carlow. Getting off work on a Wednesday to play the match was certainly a novel experience, although many of the players had taken the week off from work to celebrate anyway!

And so, a very tired (and perhaps hungover!) Starlights team journeyed to Carlow to play its first ever game in the Leinster Club Football Championship. We suffered a severe loss even before the game began with the news that Pat Neville, *'man of the match'* in the county final, could not start due to injury. This led to a reshuffle, with captain Padge Walsh being moved to centre forward, Seamus Whelan coming in at corner back and Sean Nolan moving to centre back.

As in the county final we dominated the game for long periods but just could not translate our superiority into scores, whereas Rathvilly scored virtually every time they attacked our goal. It was four points to two at half time in favour of the Carlow team. They got well on top early in the second half adding two quick points and they really put themselves in a winning position when they secured a goal from an obvious square ball infringement, the score being allowed to stand despite one of the neutral umpires ruling against it. From then on the Carlow side were in the driving seat and even though we put on a lot of pressure, it was almost impossible to make headway against a packed home defence. I was a bit unlucky for a goal near the end when I shot from the end line and hit the butt of the far post; unbelievably the ball came straight back to me but I was immediately surrounded and nothing came of it. Rathvilly went on to win the match by

1-7 to 0-5. And so our adventure in the Leinster Club Championship ended almost before it had begun. It was certainly a pity we didn't have time to prepare for it.

Nevertheless we had won our first county senior championship since 1937, and that was going to be celebrated for some time to come! Indeed it was, in song and verse, as evidenced by the poem written by England resident Tommy Monaghan, formerly of the Shannon, entitled *'A Starlight Serenade'*:

"It was a great Starlights win that put the town in good cheer.
Christmas had come early for they were all drinking beer.
They talked of the game and told tales of the past,
But 'twas the bould Jim Rigley who kicked the ball last.
There were tales of the midfield, whose two were supreme.
They said Sweetman and Creane were the best ever seen,
Sullivan and Neville, they also played well,
And whatever passed Mossy was going like hell.
Sean Nolan was good – Millar, Doran and the Padges two.
With Morrissey in goal, that deflection turned him blue,
Pat Goff was unlucky not to be given that goal,
With McGovern and tough Jordan doing what they were told.
Nearly fifty years have gone by since the Great Team had fame,
Dan Kennedy, Paddy Monaghan, Patsy Goff, Peter Hayes ... Ah sure!
What's in a name?
Those were a few of the stars of the past,
They were honest and plucky, skilful and fast."

1984 dawned with a genuine desire to successfully defend our title. This became quite apparent at our dinner dance in March, when we were presented with our senior championship medals by Dublin foot-ballers Tommy Drumm and Mick Holden. But the reality was different. The commitment was not as good as it had been the year before and there was probably a greater emphasis on hurling which could be seen as fair enough when you consider that we were a dual senior club and, naturally enough, many people in the club would now be anx-ious to win a senior hurling title. But, with Wexford senior hurlers hav-ing had a tremendous win over Kilkenny in the Leinster semi final (Tony Doran scored an unforgettable clinching goal with a couple of minutes to go), one had no real idea when our first championship game (it was now knockout) would be played.

Being a secondary school teacher I now had my summer holidays and had returned to my home in the midlands. I was not in a position financially to hold onto my accommodation in Enniscorthy during the summer months. I did try to commute for some training and challenge/tournament games but I found the 280 mile round journey a bit much at times; on one occasion I got up bright and early one Saturday morning to travel down from Longford for a challenge game to find that we could only muster nine players at the Bellefield assembly point, so the game had to be cancelled.

This further indicated to me that the commitment to win a championship was not going to be on a par with the year before. On my way back to Longford I had a good long hard think about the situation. I had a lot to consider: I mightn't have a championship game with Starlights for another six weeks particularly if Wexford's senior hurlers continued to progress and I also felt the need to do some work to keep myself occupied. Bearing everything in mind I made a decision to go and work in Germany for a few weeks, not being willing to even look for a second job in Enniscorthy or elsewhere given the unemployment situation then. I went to work in Stuttgart where I had worked before as a student in 1980, but I resolved to keep myself in good condition. I lived in student accommodation after a while, and was able to train on a nearby soccer pitch.

I kept in touch with events at home and when Wexford hurlers suffered a surprising defeat to Offaly in the Leinster final, I knew our championship game v Sarsfields could well be on the horizon soon. It eventually took place on Saturday evening, 28th of July and Starlights brought me home for the game. That was the second time this had happened, as my club in Longford, Colmcille, had done the same for a championship game in 1980. We played a draw with Sarsfields (10 points each), and were relatively lucky to do so as it took a wonderful long range point from Padge Walsh in injury time to earn us a second bite at the cherry. I was naturally disappointed we didn't win but I thought I had paid my way with two points from play and generally showed up well. But the star of the show was undoubtedly Paddy Barnes of Sarsfields whose free taking (we felt that there were some very questionable frees awarded against us) was superb. Starlights officials informed me after the game that the replay would probably not be for a few weeks but they were not really sure when. On that basis, and having regained my appetite for football, I returned to

Germany and decided to step up my training, although it is difficult to train with any great intensity when you are training on your own.

You can imagine I was very taken aback when, in the course of a telephone call to a friend in Enniscorthy a week later, I was informed that the replay had been played and that Sarsfields had put us out of the championship after extra time on a scoreline of 1-11 to 1-9! Had Starlights informed me of the game I would have paid my own way home, as they had already done so before and might not have been in a position to do so again, or alternatively, I would have tried to come home early as I was due back soon anyway. It was all so, so disappointing and made all the worse when Sarsfields later went on to win the Championship. Perhaps the outcome might well have been the same, but who knows? At least I would have taken part.

We had a resounding victory over Castletown (2-10 to 0-8) in the first round of the 1985 championship and were considered favourites for ultimate honours that year, but surprisingly came a cropper against St. Martin's in our next match on a scoreline of seven points to five. The Piercestown men seemed to be fitter and more determined and had an ace free taker in George O'Connor who contributed four points of their total. We were extremely disappointed and the deafening silence in our dressing room after the game told its own story. I had played reasonably well in both games but I would have to say that my confidence was at a low ebb after the Dublin debacle in June, (see chapter 2 – The Purple and Gold Experience). Bunclody went on to win their second title that year beating Gusserane in a final replay. My main memory of those games is of two wonderful long-range points, kicked from the terrace side of Wexford Park by Bunclody's Noel Swords.

After being sent off (for two bookable offences) playing full forward for Wexford in the 1986 championship against Dublin, I was really out to prove a point in the local championship. That point being that I was a far better midfielder than *'edge of the square man'*. I had two of my most memorable games for Starlights in that domestic campaign. The first was against Sarsfields at Monamolin, a game that we won by 0-15 to 1-6. Padge Walsh and myself scored eight points between us in that encounter, *'The People'* report stating that: *"they (i.e. Starlights) had one or two players who provided that little bit extra and, in this respect, the performances of Padge Walsh and Jim McGovern marked them as players apart. Walsh was commanding at centre back while McGovern was outstanding at midfield; the fielding of both was superb and they also got forward enough to kick eight points between them".* In fairness it was an overall good team effort with Sarsfields themselves contributing in no small way to a fine open game of football. The teams lined out as follows:

Starlights: George O'Connor, Sean Nolan, Pat Creane, Joe Newe, Billy Dwyer, Padge Walsh (0-4 2frees), Padge Courtney, Jim McGovern (0-4), Michael Farrell (0-1) , Pat Hanly (0-1), Mick Millar (0-2), Paul Nolan (0-2), Paddy Farrell (0-1), Pat Goff, Jim Rigley (0-2).

Sarsfields: John Doyle, Billy Keeling, Noel Doyle, Larry Roche, Billy Walsh, Tony Walsh, Ger Halligan, John Harrington (0-1), Willy Murphy, John Walker (0-1), John Curtis, Kevin Carty (0-1), Billy Dodd (0-3), Jim Roice, Nicky Murphy (1-0).

Referee: Jack O'Brien (Monamolin).

The championship then, of course, was back to a league basis and we knew that if we could win our next game against Gusserane, we would qualify for the county semi final. A continuation of our impressive form saw us win this game by 0-14 to 0-8. *'The People'* reported: *"The hunger in both sides was evident from the start with the game played at a fast pace. After the sides had swapped early points to level at 0-2 each after ten minutes, Starlights established a bridgehead at midfield, where the fielding of their 'big men', Nicky Sweetman and Jim McGovern was both impressive and beneficial. McGovern was particularly outstanding, and in addition to notching a couple of points himself, set up a host of chances for his team mates, and it was primarily due to his prompting that Starlights led by 0-7 to 0-4 at half time."*

This victory installed us as one of the favourites for the championship and we were all wondering who we would draw in the penultimate round. As luck would have it Gusserane were again our opponents. The other semi final brought together Duffry Rovers (still seeking that elusive first title) and Bunclody, now going for two in a row. The preview in the *'People'* favoured the latter saying: *"Bunclody must be fancied. Their greater experience will be an asset and if they can bring it to bear they also seem to have a better balanced side".* In relation to our game it said: *"when the sides met recently in a make or break league game, the Enniscorthy side had six points to spare. They are taken to repeat the result on this occasion but maybe not as emphatically. Gusserane performed on that occasion with a depleted side and if, as reported, both Liam and John Cullen are available for this match, it could well put a different complexion on things."*

And it certainly did as the Cullen brothers both, it must be noted, established inter county footballers, turned out in the centre of the field for Gusserane and were very influential as the New Ross District side completely reversed the earlier result in securing a nine point victory (2-8 to 0-5). The game was really over as a contest at half time when we were 2-6 to 0-1 in arrears and, although we improved in the second half, there was only ever going to be one result.

I have to say that, like the rest of the lads, I was very deflated after the game. Personally I thought I had played reasonably well but had sincerely hoped that pre-match publicity had not affected my game. For example there were comments such as:

A: *"The brilliant performances being turned on by county full forward James McGovern at midfield for his club in the senior championship in which they are undefeated could well influence the county selectors to place him in that position for the national league"* (snippet from the *Wexford People* 12/9/1986).

B: *"Starlights strength on that occasion (earlier group game v Gusserane) stemmed from their towering midfield partnership of Jim McGovern and Nicky Sweetman. McGovern, in particular, is revelling in his new found freedom, and the towering Longford school teacher looks the most complete player in the county this year".* (Excerpt from preview to county semi final v Gusserane, *Wexford People*, 26/9/1986.

Being human like everyone else, I have to say I was pleased to get such recognition, as I had worked extremely hard virtually every day during the summer months of 1986 to improve my game, and make myself an alternative viable midfielder for the county. That also included a month spent in Chicago at the invitation of the McBride's club, where I rubbed shoulders favourably with some of the best players in the game. These included T.J. Kilgallon and Peter Forde (Mayo), John

O'Keefe (Kerry), Ciaran McNally and Jim McCorry (Armagh) and Paul Earley (Roscommon).

That was an enriching experience which gave my confidence a huge boost when returning to play club football in Wexford, as really, when it all boils down to it, its all about that particular commodity and its corollary, genuine belief in your own ability. After all, as the old saying goes: *'if you don't believe in your own ability it doesn't matter what ability you have'.*

The teams that lined out in that county semi-final at Wexford Park in October 1986 (the game was postponed for a week as a mark of respect to the Millar family, Enniscorthy, on the death of their father) were as follows:

Gusserane: Brendan Duffin, Michael Keevans, Peter Culleton, Donie Whelan, Pat Culleton, Michael Caulfield, Eddie O'Connor, John Cullen (0-1), Liam Cullen, Kevin Kehoe (0-2), Laurence Keevans, Tadgh Foran (0-2), Liam Whelan, John Culleton (0-1), Seamus Cullen (2-0). Subs: Kieran Cullen (0-2) for L. Whelan, J. Roche for L. Keevans.

Starlights: George O'Connor, Sean Nolan, Pat Creane, Vinny Daly, Padge Courtney, Padge Walsh, Billy Dwyer, Nicky Sweetman, Jim McGovern (0-3), Paul Nolan, Michael Farrell, Jim Rigley (0-1), Billy Sinnott, Pat Goff, Paddy Farrell (0-1). Subs: Donal O'Connor for M. Farrell, Joe Rigley for P. Farrell.

Referee: Jack O'Brien.

Footnote: Duffry Rovers went on to beat Gusserane in the final thereby starting a run of success that did not end until Kilanerin put a stop to their gallop in 1993. But it took a brilliant individual goal from eighteen-year-old John Hegarty to end their dreams of winning eight titles in a row.

Our defeat to Gusserane, but more so the manner of it, seemed to have a detrimental effect on the team, and this was borne out in poor attendances at training in early 1987. In addition, the club seemed to be putting a much greater emphasis on hurling as it endeavoured to win a first county senior title since 1978.

The indifferent attitude to training was reflected in poor early results. In May we struggled to beat St. Mary's, Rosslare by eight points to six at Wexford Park. However, in early July we were well beaten by Taghmon-Camross (2-8 to 0-8) at the same venue. There was a bit of a shake up after that game, and we recovered to beat St. Martin's 1-10 to 0-3, also at Wexford Park at the end of July.

A month later we followed that up with a very comfortable 2-9 to 0-3 win over Castletown at Monamolin. You might have thought we were well in contention for the championship at this stage, but due to the vagaries of a league - championship system we had to beat Duffry Rovers in our next game to remain in the race for honours. As I saw it, that was a very tall order given that the Duffry were reigning county champions and full of confidence. They were also in superb physical shape, their English born trainer Bob Brakewell having seen to that. In contrast, due to poor attendances at training, particularly the early stamina phase, we would not have been in the same shape at all. And so it proved in early September 1987 at O'Kennedy Park, New Ross, when Duffry had a comfortable five point winning margin over us (0-9 to 0-4). Seamus Fitzhenry's class shone out like a beacon among those around him and he was the key difference between the sides, obviously having fully shaken off the hamstring injury that made him a very late withdrawal for the Leinster championship game v Kildare in May.

I played with Starlights until 1988 and I would have to say that they were as fine a bunch of fellows as you could wish to meet. They made me very welcome at a time of great uncertainty in my life and helped me to integrate into the Wexford scene. I really think that the team of '83 was a team of all the talents that never reached its full potential. In my opinion it had everything going for it: size, strength, skill, power, fitness and a great attitude. It should have dominated Wexford football for a number of years, and had it got over the Sarsfields hurdle in 1984, I believe it would have gone on to do so.

I would like to share a few thoughts on that team of '83. Billy Morrissey was goalkeeper and a good one at that. He had great reflexes and saved us on a number of occasions, particularly against St. Martin's in the quarter-final. Sean Nolan was a classy right corner back and was always constructive in his clearances, ditto with Ed Doran who could have had a very successful inter county career but for a troublesome back injury. Left corner back Mossy Rigley was a very tenacious player, and very little got by him. Mick Millar was a stylish right wing back, who had reverted from wing forward, had great pace and got forward to help his attack on a regular basis. Centre back and captain was Padge '*Skinner*' Walsh; an inspirational player in every sense of the word, who often notched up important scores from this pivotal position. He showed his longevity by winning further senior medals as a panel member in 2002 and 2004. Padge Courtney filled the left half back position, and did so with distinction; he had great pace and often electrified crowds with his great ball carrying ability. Pat Creane and Nicky Sweetman formed the midfield partnership and they complimented each other very well. Pat was a very hard working player and very strong under the high ball; he was also brave and fearless in picking up the breaks. Nicky was a formidable force, being over 6 foot 6 inches tall; he reserved his best performance for the county final. It is perhaps not that well known that, but for a neck injury, Nicky could have played international rugby for Ireland. He had only taken up Gaelic football four years previously.

Jim Sullivan slotted in at right wing forward, and was an extremely fit, skilful and hardworking player; his exploits as a boxer are, of course, legendary. Pat Neville was centre forward, and had tremendous natural ability; he played extremely well in the final. To his left was Jim Rigley, a brother of Mossy's. Jim was indispensable to our success, and his five points in the final were absolutely vital; he had a very high skill level. Dan Jordan was right corner forward, probably not his best position, as he was a great man to get possession out the field. Nevertheless, Dan was very skilful and versatile. Full forward was yours truly, while left corner forward was Pat Goff, also noted as an excellent goalkeeper. Pat was unlucky not to be given a goal in the final and was a strong, powerful player; he was also a more than useful rugby player.

The substitutes were also accomplished footballers, and included Joe Rigley, a brother of Mossy and Jim. Joe provided excellent cover for the back-line and was a fast, skilful player. Well-known referee Seamus Whelan, also provided a back-up for the rearguard, and was a tough, no nonsense player who had already won a senior championship medal in Carlow. Joe Moorehouse was a fast and tenacious wingback. The late Michael Farrell was a fast, powerful, incisive forward, who was also capable of playing midfield; he was also a very good rugby player. Finally, Tom Doyle was another option for the forward line and was a very fast, skilful player. He was also an excellent soccer player. The vast majority of the panel had played for Wexford at one level or other, and really it was a group of players that should have won much more.

ENNISCORTHY STARLIGHTS
1983 Senior Football Champions

ENNISCORTHY STARLIGHTS – 1983 SENIOR FOOTBALL CHAMPIONS
Back Row, Left to Right: P. Creane, P. Walsh (Capt.), E. Doran, N. Sweetman, J. McGovern, J. O'Sullivan, P. Goff, S. Nolan.
Front Row, Left to Right: P. Neville, P. Courtney, B. Morrissey, M. Millar, J. Rigley, M. Rigley and D. Jordan.
Mascot: Keith Whelan

Chapter 2

The Purple and Gold Experience

'Hold fast to dreams for if dreams die,
Life is a broken-winged bird that cannot fly.'
Langston Hughes.

Growing up in Longford in the 1960's I was, of course, besotted by the exploits of the Longford senior football team, particularly from 1965 onwards. But Wexford also held an interest for me as I was fascinated by the purple and gold jersey. Of course 1968 was a great year for both counties, Longford winning its first ever Leinster senior football title while Wexford won its fifth All Ireland senior hurling crown. It must have been around that time that the Sunday newspapers started publishing coloured pictures of the teams on All Ireland final day, for I can clearly recall cutting out the picture of the Wexford team and putting it up on my bedroom wall. Little did I realise then, that some sixteen years later, I would be wearing that very famous and unique geansaí, and very honoured to do so as well.

As I mentioned earlier, I was asked to join the county senior panel after the county semi final in October 1983 but since we (Starlights) had qualified for the final, and because there was also a question about my eligibility, I decided to concentrate all my efforts on helping Starlights win the county title.

Having secured that elusive crown and after our brief foray into the Leinster Club Championship, I could now give my all to my adopted county. In spite of the very long year at club level, I was delighted and indeed quite privileged to be involved, and really determined to make an impression. Of course I knew a lot of the lads already having trained with them from September 1982, when I first came to

23

Wexford. Now I was officially on the panel and with a group of players who were doing very well having just beaten highflying Mayo, Willy Joe Padden and all, in Division Two of the National Football League!

My first official involvement with Wexford was as a substitute for their league game v Louth which was played in Dundalk on Sunday 4th December 1983. The model county recorded an excellent away win on a scoreline of 2-5 to 1-5, and my abiding memories of the game are of two excellently taken goals by Billy Byrne, who nowadays is much better known as a top class hurler, but who was also a lovely stylish footballer, and of two brilliant points under pressure by the classy Seamus Fitzhenry.

The Wexford team lined out as follows: Vincent Murphy (Davidstown-Courtnacuddy), Tom Foley (St. Mary's, Sligo), John O'Gorman (Taghmon-Camross), Mick Caulfield (Gusserane), John Curtis (Sarsfields), Garry Byrne (Ballyhogue), Liam Cullen (Gusserane), Padge Walsh (Starlights), John Fitzhenry (Duffry Rovers), Billy Byrne (Gorey), Seamus Fitzhenry (Duffry Rovers), Seanie O'Shea (Blackwater), Martin Hanrick (Bunclody), Michael Carty (Castletown) and Eddie Mahon (Gusserane). Subs: Ger Turner (Rosslare), Rory Deane (Bunclody), Billy Rowsome (Monageer-Boolavogue), Matt Furlong (Blackwater), Noel Barry (Kilmore), Jim McGovern (Starlights), John Creane RIP (Maudlinstown), Tadhg Foran (Gusserane), Arthur O'Connor (St. Martin's) and Michael Walsh (Glynn-Barntown).

Naturally there was great delight with the win afterwards, the now defunct *Irish Press* stating in its report of the game the following day: *"Wexford's hopes of promotion to Division One of the National Football League were considerably boosted following their unexpected, but well deserved win over Louth yesterday in Dundalk. As they set out again on their long trip home, team manager Tony Dempsey and his crew were surely already rubbing their hands in anticipation of their home games against Galway and Cavan when the league resumes in the Spring".*

It was with these games in mind that Tony Dempsey organised a weekend away in Offaly in early January 1984. We were to play 1982 All Ireland Champions Offaly in two matches, one on Saturday and one on Sunday, but were lucky to get away with one on the Saturday due to the blizzard like conditions that prevailed in the midlands at

WEXFORD TEAM V DUBLIN CROKE PARK SUNDAY 10th JUNE 1984
Back Row, Left to Right: Garry Byrne, Noel Swords, Padge Walsh, Jim McGovern,
John O'Gorman, John Curtis, Martin Quigley.
Front Row, Left to Right: Tom Foley, Eddie Mahon, Martin Hanrick, Liam Cullen,
Vincent Murphy, Seamus Fitzhenry, George O'Connor, Mick Caulfield.
Mascots, from left: John Murphy, Ruairi Quigley

that time. Offaly reporter, Eddie Rogers titled his piece: *'Offaly reserves blitzed in a blizzard'*, and it was no exaggeration. In fact the game should probably not have been played at all but, since we had made such a long journey (before the worst of the weather had set in), it was decided to go ahead with it. Conditions were so bad that Offaly team manager, Eugene McGee, could not attend the game because of impassable roads in the region of his home in Longford.

It was my first full game for Wexford and we recorded a resounding 2-11 to 0-8 win. Of course it was impossible to judge anyone in those conditions, but I was quite pleased with my own display, given the fact that I was marking the highly experienced Mick Fitzgerald. Our team that day was virtually a second string with only three players remaining from the Louth league game before Christmas. Of course the 'A' team was to play the following day but, as I said earlier, that was ruled out due to the heavy snow.

Those who braved the elements for Wexford were: Martin Fitzhenry, John Fitzhenry, Arthur O'Connor, Jack Swords, John Creane, Liam Cullen, Padge Courtney, Michael Walsh (0-1), Tadgh Foran (0-1), Sean O'Shea (1-3), Noel Barry (0-1), Rory Deane, Michael McGee (0-2), Jim McGovern (1-2), and Matt Furlong (0-1).

A notable feature of the trip was that we paid for our own hotel accommodation in Tullamore, something I'm sure that would not be countenanced nowadays! The following week the *'Gaelograms'* man was again on my case, this time as gaeilge! : *"Fuair Seamus Mac Samhrain (Na Réiltíní) a chéad sheans le fhuireann peil sinsear an Condae an Sathrain seo caite v Ubhaile agus thóg sé an sheans lena dhá láimh. Fuair sé 1-2 ón imirt ar All-star. Tá sheans eile tuil aige anois."*

Having commenced training on January 3rd we now continued our twice weekly sessions and played Cork at Dungarvan in a challenge game the following Sunday. The Leesiders fielded eleven of the team that had won the Munster Championship the previous year. It was a really good workout with a late Tom Mannix goal giving Cork victory on a scoreline of 2-8 to 1-9. I had won a lot of aerial possession on Christy Ryan but my finishing and distribution left something to be desired.

A week later we played another challenge game against Wicklow in Gorey, winning in a torrential downpour by 1-10 to 0-11. At this stage I didn't feel my chances of making the team for the National League game v Galway were great, as experienced players such as Michael Carty and Eamonn Kehoe were well ahead of me in the pecking order for the full forward position.

I was right, and Wexford lined out as follows against a Galway team, most of whom had contested the previous year's All Ireland final: Vincent Murphy, Tom Foley, John O'Gorman, Michael Caulfield, John Curtis, Garry Byrne, Liam Cullen, Padge Walsh, John Fitzhenry, Noel Swords, Seamus Fitzhenry (0-2), Billy Byrne, Martin Hanrick, Eamonn

Kehoe (0-1) and Eddie Mahon (0-4). Galway's greater experience and class told in the end, winning the game by 11 points to 7 and leaving Wexford's chances of promotion, with one game left, rather slim.

Cavan were next up in New Ross the following Sunday and it was a game we had to win to have any hope of promotion. The selectors made four changes with Rory Deane, Padge Courtney, Tadgh Foran and Michael Carty coming into the team, the latter crying off with injury just before the game to be replaced by Eamonn Kehoe. I made a brief appearance towards the end of the game, which ended in a draw, Wexford 0-9, Cavan 1-6. It was a game we could have won and could have lost so a draw was probably a fair result. The point gained was not enough to earn us promotion, but it did mean that we maintained our Division 2 status and could now look forward to the championship. Training was now intensified with some of it held on Curracloe beach as the championship came on the horizon!

1984 was, of course, the centenary of the association and to honour the occasion the GAA instituted a new competition called the Centenary Cup. Our first game in it was against Armagh in Lurgan, a really formidable task given that the orchard county men were well nigh unbeatable at that venue. The *'People'* newspaper in its preview of the game stated that: *"Wexford's task here looks rather hopeless because they face a full strength Armagh side, eager to do well in this knockout competition with a team that hasn't had a game since drawing with Cavan in the last of the league series ... the best we can hope for is that they avoid a drubbing".*

Well we did more than that, much more; in fact we won the game by 3-3 to 0-6! This was my first full competitive game for the county and I thought I acquitted myself quite well, winning a lot of possession at full forward. We came onto the field to shouts of 'where are your hurleys' from some of the Armagh supporters. There was none of that talk, however, as we marched proudly off the field at the end of the game, I hasten to add. Seanie O'Shea came on as a substitute and scored an absolutely wonderful goal. He carried the ball at great pace down the right wing for about fifty yards, cut in cleverly and stuck a glorious shot in the back of the net past the experienced Brian McAlinden. As good a goal as you could wish to see! My other abiding memory of that day is of seeing John O'Gorman stride majestically forward from full back, take a pass from Eddie Mahon and stroke over a glorious point. We were well aware that the northern venue had proven to be a graveyard for many counties over the years but we were fiercely determined to do well, as epitomised by Seamus Fitzhenry who played despite a nasty mouth injury received in a recent hurling game. He wore a special mouth guard for protection.

There was a brilliant feeling of elation after the game as no one had expected us to win, but we had done what teams like Kerry and Dublin couldn't do, i.e. beat Armagh in their impregnable fortress of Lurgan. It should also be noted it was achieved without the services of Padge Courtney, Billy Byrne and George O'Connor, all accomplished footballers but who that very day were assisting the county hurlers in the National League Final against Limerick in Thurles. (Unfortunately they lost by 3-16 to 1-9).

The Armagh team was quite a formidable one containing as it did most of their Ulster winning side of 1982. It lined out as follows: B. McAlinden, D. Stevenson, T. Cassidy, J. Donnelly, B. Canavan, J. McCorry, K. McGurk, K. McNally, C. McKinstry, B. McCabe (0-1), J. Kiernan, F. McMahon (0-1), P. Rafferty (0-4), G. Houlihan and M. McQuillan. Subs used: B. Hughes for K. McGurk, P. Coleman for B. McCabe.

The victorious Wexford team was: V. Murphy, T. Foley, J. O'Gorman (0-1), M. Caulfield, J. Curtis, R. Deane, L. Cullen, N. Swords, P. Walsh, S. Fitzhenry (1-0), G. Byrne, T. Foran, M. Hanrick (1-0), J. McGovern and E. Mahon (0-2). Sub used: S. O'Shea (1-0) for T. Foran.

We drew Westmeath in the next round and managed to get a home venue (Wexford Park), and also had George O'Connor back in the team. George proceeded to play brilliantly as we romped to a runaway victory on a scoreline of 3-10 to 0-4; a win all the more merited when you consider that we had Rory Deane dismissed after about twenty minutes of the first half. While I was naturally delighted we won, the game did not go well for me personally and I was taken off just after half time. It was a learning experience and an eye opener for me in terms of the demands of inter-county football. I felt I had allowed myself to be pushed around too much, and resolved in future to be much more streetwise and use my height and strength to my advantage. Despite being extremely disappointed with my performance I, along with my Starlights colleague Padge Walsh and Gusserane's Liam Cullen and Mick Caulfield, journeyed to Piercestown later that evening to play a senior football league game between Starlights and Gusserane, which Starlights won by 2-6 to 1-3. I managed to play reasonably well, scored a goal and got the Westmeath game out of my system.

We were pitted against Cavan in the quarter final of the Centenary Cup and it was a game I was really looking forward to, not least because Cavan are our next-door neighbours up in Longford. I faced an anxious wait to see whether I would be picked on the team but thankfully I did get the nod and was really determined to do well and get into the game from the word 'go'. After our great wins against Armagh and Westmeath we started favourites and commenced the game really well when Seamus Fitzhenry made a great run through the Cavan defence, his shot was half blocked and I was on hand to grab the ball and sidefoot it to the net. That score, and the unhurried manner in which I felt I took it, gave my confidence a great boost. However, Cavan went on to dominate after that and they led by 1-5 to 1-2 at half time.

Midway through the second half they were still ahead by 1-7 to 1-3, but a great rally from us tied the scores at 1-7 each. The game was in the melting pot now, but Cavan pulled away in the final minutes with two clinching points. It was a game we certainly could have won as we missed quite a few chances particularly in the second half and it was a great disappointment not to be able to play in a national semi-final in Croke Park. One notable aspect of the proceedings was the tremendous vocal support that Cavan enjoyed. Writing on the game in the *Anglo-Celt* the following week, the Cavan reporter had this to say: *"Cavan went into the game as underdogs, but a tremendous Cavan following travelled to the game, intent on encouraging their side to victory. Even when things were looking bleak for a period in the second half, it was the fanatical support of the Breffni fans which helped the team overcome a stiff challenge to finish strongly to book their passage to the semi-final. If Cavan needed any encouragement to win something this year, they certainly got it from the fans, who travelled by bus and car in their hundreds, and their enthusiasm was strong throughout".*

Wexford People reporter Michael Heverin wrote: *"It was interesting to note the attitude to the game of the respective supporters and administrators at home. It was like a home game for Cavan so strong was their support. Busloads travelled to Newbridge and they roared themselves hoarse from start to finish. The small Wexford contingent could never match them vocally. And while Sunday was a closed day in Cavan, as their team played in a national quarter final, games went on in Wexford at four venues. Coach Tony Dempsey and his team were certainly serious about the game but one wonders how highly it was rated by the hierarchy in the county."*

Certainly you could feel it on the field. Cavan's scores got a terrific reception while the response to ours was just about audible and that is casting no aspersions on the dedicated Wexford fans that did travel. However, I honestly believe that, in a close game, good vocal support can drive a team on to victory and so it proved with Cavan.

The Wexford team comprised: V. Murphy, T. Foley, J. O'Gorman, M. Caulfield, J. Curtis, P. Walsh, L. Cullen, G. O'Connor (0-1), N. Swords, S. Fitzhenry (0-2), G. Byrne (0-1), B. Byrne, M. Hanrick (0-1), J. McGovern (1-1) and E. Mahon (0-1). Subs: P. Courtney for Curtis, S. O'Shea for Swords.

Cavan lined out: D. O' Reilly, E. Kiernan, J. McAweeney, M. Bouchier, B. O'Grady, J. Dillon, J. Reilly, S. King, M. McEntee, Kevin Óg Carney, F. McDonagh, R. Cullivan, D. Donoghoe, D. McDonnell and P. McNamee. Subs: P. Faulkner for F. McDonagh, B. Tierney for K. Óg Carney.

The referee was Seamus Aldridge, (Kildare).

Meath beat Cavan the following Sunday and went on to win the Centenary Cup, and it was the start of their great run under Sean Boylan. Who knows what might have happened had we beaten the Breffni men on that May day in Newbridge in 1984.

Footnote: Revered journalist Con Houlihan featured the game in his popular column on the back of the Evening Press and in the course of his report referred to an incident involving myself halfway through the second half. I had caught a high ball on the end line, and was immediately surrounded by at least three Cavan players; under severe pressure I attempted to punch the ball across the goalmouth but got a push as I did so, and only succeeded in punching it over the bar. The score was immediately disallowed as in those days you could not punch a point. Con felt this was wrong and took from the game, and later on, the punched point was restored.

We now turned our attentions to the Leinster Championship and training was stepped up considerably. A number of challenge games were also played including one against a highly rated Mayo side in Athlone, which we won convincingly. I actually played centre forward in that game, marking a certain John Maughan. Our final challenge game before we played All Ireland Champions, Dublin, in the first round of the championship turned out to be a bit of a fiasco as a bus carrying a number of Wexford players to the venue (the game was against Offaly), got lost on the way to the ground and the game got under way with only 13 Wexford players and two players from Offaly completing the team. We did have a full team later but Offaly got off to a very good start and had a comfortable victory in the end. It didn't augur well for our chances against the mighty Dubs a week later, but we certainly could approach that game with some confidence given our performances in the league and the Centenary Cup.

The great Martin Quigley made a welcome return to the team at right full forward after an absence of more than four years, and I was lucky enough to be chosen beside him at full forward. The prospect of playing in Croke Park really excited me. Growing up in Longford in the 1960's when, as I mentioned earlier, my native county had a really good football team, my dream was to emulate players like Jimmy Hanniffy, Jackie Devine and Brendan Barden and play on the hallowed turf. Now, almost twenty years later, I would be getting my first opportunity to play there, not wearing the blue and gold of my native county but rather the purple and gold of my adopted county and relishing the prospect. Dublin had won a controversial All Ireland in 1983 when their *"twelve apostles"* gained a magnificent victory over fourteen Galway men and they named their All Ireland winning team for their opening defence of their Leinster title against us.

As it transpired they needn't have bothered, as they coasted to victory on a scoreline of 4-12 to 0-9. We were certainly expected to put up a much better show but found the Dubs too hot to handle and were really up against it at half time when we trailed by 2-5 to 0-3. We were 2-8 to 0-5 in arrears when Garry Byrne, arguably our best player on the day, brought a brilliant save out of John O'Leary (he subsequently won *'save of the season'* for it) and that was that as far as we were concerned.

I have two main memories of my first appearance in Croke Park, that is apart from nervousness and finding it hard to settle into the match for a while. The first occurred after 10 minutes when George O'Connor floated in a free kick which goalkeeper, John O'Leary and myself contested. I kept my eye on the ball all the way and managed to finish it to the net. However, the score was disallowed as I was adjudged to have fouled the goalkeeper who was subsequently detained in hospital overnight suffering from concussion. It should be noted however that John O'Leary resumed action after a couple of minutes treatment, and later made that brilliant save from Garry Byrne that I referred to earlier. In his official biography *'Back to the Hill'* John says of the incident: *"it isn't a game I recall with fondness, because I ended up concussed. Wexford full forward, big Jim McGovern ran into me in the first half, flipping me over like a coin. My head hit the ground and I can't remember a whole lot about the game from there on, except that I won 'save of the season'. I have no recollection whatsoever of making the save. What was that about goalies being mad? I had made a great save, apparently, while in a state of concussion!"*

I have to say that I had great respect for John O'Leary and very much regretted that he was concussed. I never had any intention of injuring him.

My second memory is not a pleasant one either! I was moved to midfield. I think it was midway through the second half; the issue was decided at this stage and Dublin had eased off a bit. Nevertheless, I was delighted to be playing in my favourite position and in Croke Park too! It was something I had always dreamed about! I won a couple of balls in the air and was feeling good. Another high ball came my way; I jumped for it and the next thing I know I am in agony on the ground, a Dublin player having thrust his two knees into my stomach while I was totally focussed on catching the high ball. It was quite a cowardly thing to do and the most agonising blow I ever got in my life but I would not stay down. I was out at midfield and I was going to keep going! I walked around in agony for a couple of minutes but was able to finish the game subsequently. So it wasn't just the heavy beating I remember.

Wexford's line out that day was: Vincent Murphy, Tom Foley, John O'Gorman, Michael Caulfield, John Curtis, Padge Walsh, Liam Cullen, George O'Connor (0-2 frees), Noel Swords (0-2), Garry Byrne,

Seamus Fitzhenry, Eddie Mahon (0-2 frees), Martin Quigley (0-1), Jim McGovern (0-1), Martin Hanrick (0-1). Sub: Padge Courtney for Michael Caulfield.

Dublin fielded: John O'Leary, Mick Holden, Gerry Hargan, Ray Hasley, Pat Canavan, Tommy Drumm, P.J. Buckley, Jim Roynane (0-1), Brian Mullins (0-1), Barney Rock (2-4), Tommy Conroy (0-2), Ciaran Duff (1-2), John Caffrey (0-1), Anton O'Toole, Joe McNally (1-1). Sub.: Mick Kennedy for P.J. Buckley. The Metropolitans of course went on to reach the All Ireland final where they were beaten by Kerry.

However, all was not doom and gloom for Wexford on that 10th day of June 1984. In the curtain raiser to the senior game, Wexford junior footballers won their first provincial title since 1963 with an eight points to six points victory over Louth. The victorious Wexford team was as follows: Philip Walsh (Bannow-Ballymitty), Brendan Murphy (St. Joseph's), Jack O'Leary (Blackwater), Eamon O'Connor (Volunteers), Luke Finn (Craanford), Ger O'Brien (Realt na Mara), George Foley (Fethard), John Creane RIP (Maudlinstown), Pat McGrath (Bannow-Ballymitty), George Hearn (Horeswood), Pat Barden (Adamstown), Sean O'Shea (Blackwater), Seamus Kennelly (Realt na Mara), Michael Walsh (Glynn-Barntown), Nicky Jones (Volunteers). Subs.: Eugene O'Brien (Realt na Mara), for McGrath, Matt Furlong (Blackwater) for M. Walsh.

It was now back to club action, but inter county activity resumed on September 15th when we met Offaly in a senior football tournament at a County Carlow venue. The game marked the official opening of the William Dobbs GAA Park at Ballinabranna, a village close to the Wexford/ Carlow border. The game retains a special place in my memory as it was the one and only time I captained Wexford, and to victory I might add! Arrangements for the game were excellent and there was even a band playing. I felt so proud and honoured as I led the team in the parade before the game. According to the match programme the teams lined out as follows:

Offaly: M. Furlong, L. Groom, L. O'Connor, M. Fitzgerald, P. Fitzgerald, R. O'Connor, S. McEvoy, T. O'Connor, P. Dunne, S. Tuckler, P. Spollen, A. O'Halloran, B. Lowry, J. Mooney and K. Kyley.

Wexford: V. Murphy, M. Caulfield, J. O'Gorman, D. Whelan, L.

Cullen, G. Halligan, J. Curtis, N. Swords, J. Lacey, B. Byrne, N. Barry, P. Courtney, E. Mahon, J. McGovern and M. Hanrick.

I was very pleased to be moved to midfield for the second half of this game and thought I did well, fielding a number of high balls and distributing them well. We won on a scoreline of 1-7 to 1-3, and I was delighted to accept the John O'Brien Memorial Cup on behalf of Wexford.

It was now down to serious training for the National Football League. We operated out of Division II, but it was a very competitive division consisting of Mayo, Offaly, Roscommon, Donegal, Louth, Monaghan, Dublin and ourselves. Our first match was against Mayo in Crossmolina. Wexford had beaten them in Enniscorthy the previous year, so obviously they would be all out to exact revenge, and it was going to be a very difficult fixture for us. With seven minutes left in the game we were five points in arrears but a great fight back saw us earn a share of the spoils. I managed to prevent a high ball going wide knocking it down to the waiting Padge Walsh, who had come on as a substitute earlier, and he buried it in the roof of the net. Eddie Mahon followed up with two points from frees to tie the match. Probably the turning point of the game was a brilliant penalty save by Vincent Murphy from current RTE analyst Kevin McStay. I scored 1-2 and was very happy with my performance, particularly as I was marking a very good full back in current Galway manager, Peter Forde, but the backs were quite outstanding despite being under severe pressure at times. It was a major achievement to go to Mayo and, before a big (and might I say appreciative) home crowd, take a point back to Wexford, and what a return journey it was!

Having stopped for a meal and a couple of drinks along the way, everyone was in high spirits and conversations raged throughout the bus. Undoubtedly, the highlight was a philosophical debate between John Curtis and myself as to who was the better philosopher: the Dane, Soren Kierkegaard or the German, Hermann Hesse. John spoke in favour of the latter while I defended the Dane. It was hilarious as all the lads chipped in with their contributions. Kierkegaard was even accused of beating his wife even though he never married! Bunclody's John Dunne chaired the debate and was very fair to both sides. The debate was interrupted as we reached Carlow, where Mayo midfielder Sean Maher got off (we had given him a lift back as he was working in Carlow at the time). The bus stopped at a place adjacent to a building site, and while Sean was getting his gear out of the boot of the bus, I suggested to Chairman Dunne that the debate was becoming a bit abstract, and what we needed was a more concrete one. Well, John took me at my word as he spotted a concrete mixer on the building site, jumped out of the bus and, being a builder, had it going almost immediately. Now, we had plenty of concrete ideas for the rest of the debate which John eventually declared a draw!

The teams on that day in Crossmolina were:

Wexford: V. Murphy, T. Foley, J. O'Gorman, M. Caulfield, J. Curtis, J. Dunne, L. Cullen, J. Lacey, G. Halligan, E. Mahon (0-2 frees), N. Swords, S. Fitzhenry (0-1), M. Hanrick, J. McGovern (1-2), B. Byrne. Subs: E. Cleary for Lacey, P. Walsh (1-0) for Swords.

Mayo: G. Irwin, J. Monaghan, P. Forde, D. Flanagan, F. Noone, J. Byrne, J. Finn, S. Maher (0-2), P. Brogan, T.J. Kilgallon, H. Gavin (1-2), A. Finnerty (0-1), K. McStay (0-1), T. Byrne (0-2), J. Bourke.

Footnote: Virtually that same Mayo team went on to win the Connacht title in 1985 and took Dublin to a replay in the All Ireland semi final, Padraig Brogan scoring the goal of the season.

We had to wait three weeks for our next game against Offaly who had won that unforgettable All Ireland against Kerry two years previously and, though losing their Leinster and All Ireland crowns to Dublin in 1983, were still a formidable outfit. In absolutely dreadful conditions in Wexford Park we shocked the Midlanders by winning 3-5 to 1-8. It was one of the last games that the great Matt Connor played for his county; he scored five points. I was credited with 2-1, but always felt that Padge Walsh may have got the final touch on one of them. However, I was annoyed that I had another goal disallowed for allegedly stepping out over the endline after fielding a high ball and blasting it past Martin Furlong from an acute angle.

We were now in great spirits with three points out of a possible four but faced a tricky trip to Monaghan next. Here, a superb display from midfielder Louis Rafter saw us lead by 1-4 to 0-2 at the interval, but sadly just before half time Louis picked up an ankle injury and had to be replaced. He was a huge loss to us. I was moved to midfield. Now normally I would have been delighted to be brought out to my favourite position, but if there was ever an occasion when I did not want to be moved to that area, then this was it. I felt rotten, with the symptoms of 'flu', but with my confidence on a high since the Offaly game, I just wanted to play. It was a mistake! The previous night I had roomed with county secretary Sean Ormonde and a couple of others, and I must have kept them awake most of the night with all the coughing and spluttering I was doing. As the American saying goes: *'I should have stood in bed'*. However, team manager Tony Dempsey was very keen that I should play and I felt I couldn't refuse him.

These flu symptoms really got me down when I was playing for Wexford. It seemed as if I had a flu every other week and it was playing hell with my training and my confidence. I tried training right through them, but felt weak as a result and, anyway, I knew that was no long-term solution. It wasn't until early 1989 that I found the remedy. An alternative healer in Tullow, Co. Carlow diagnosed an allergy to dairy products and a host of other triggers. Having tried everything else I felt I had nothing to lose. It worked like a dream, and during the years 1989-91, I probably played the best football of my career with Glynn-Barntown.

But I digress; we eventually lost that game to Monaghan (the eventual League winners as it turned out), by 0-10 to 1-6. Some very strange refereeing decisions, and of course the injury to Louis cost us dearly that day. We soon got back to winning ways in our next game, when we hammered a Roscommon team that contained many of their unlucky All Ireland Final team of 1980. The match was played at Bellefield and the final score was 1-9 to 0-4. Their team manager, Sean Young, was very irate afterwards and complained bitterly about the size and state of the pitch but we had no problem with it.

We followed that up with a 1-10 to 0-8 win over Louth in Gorey. This game was much more difficult than anticipated with a goal by Seamus Fitzhenry in the first half being critical to the outcome of the game. I was pleased about my part in that score. I was playing full forward and came out to win the ball about sixty yards from the Louth goal. Out of the corner of my eye I saw Seamus dashing past me at great speed. I turned and managed to plant the ball straight over his head and right into his path; he did not have to break stride as he finished the ball to the roof of the net in a very clinical manner. It was one of the finest passes I'd ever given and I only wish I could have given more of them while playing full forward for Wexford. And so we ended the year on a winning note with seven valuable points in the bag and more than a fighting chance of making the knockout stages of the National League and promotion to Division I. We received further encouragement in an article in the Sunday Press on the 23rd December 1984 when sports writer Martin Breheny ranked us 11th in an assessment of the 32 counties.

The league would resume in February with two away games against Dublin and Donegal, and we were determined to step up our training and get something out of these difficult fixtures. The whole panel received the following letter from team manager Tony Dempsey just before Christmas 1984:

'Just a note to wish you all a happy Christmas and a successful 1985 and to inform you of my plans for our remaining league campaign. Mick O'Dwyer the Kerry trainer has drawn up a programme, which he feels, would be necessary if we're to win our next games. It entails running around the pitch many times. It would help then if you would keep yourself in shape over Christmas by doing this exercise on your own. There's a pitch near everyone. Down you go, put on a tracksuit and spend 45 minutes at least lapping the pitch ...'

To hear that the legendary Mick O'Dwyer had mapped out a programme for us and would be visiting us later for a training session was music to my ears. I wasn't getting any younger and I was prepared to do whatever it took to be successful. We put in a huge effort for the Dublin game in February, following Micko's instructions to the letter. Starting on December 30th we trained three times a week, doing forty laps of St. Patrick's Park in Enniscorthy during each training session. And it all paid off in glorious fashion on Sunday 3rd of February in Croke Park when we downed the mighty Dubs on a scoreline of 1-5 to 0-7, in a game which was absolutely vital to both sides in terms of promotion to Division I. And the scoreline did not nearly reflect our superiority, given the vast amount of possession we secured. I would have to take some of the blame for that since I won a huge amount of ball from Gerry Hargan but didn't put enough of it to good use. Nevertheless, I played my part and we were all elated after the game. Its not every day you beat the Dubs in a competitive game in Croke Park, in a match they were really keen to win; (before the game they were on six league points while we were on seven).

We got great coverage in the national press the following day. An excerpt from the *Irish Times* report ran as follows: *"Dublin's weary and disconsolate footballers were indicted by their warmest supporter, coach, team manager and guiding light, Kevin Heffernan, in their Croke Park dressing room after seeing their National league hopes rudely snatched by a determined Wexford side in front of 6,779 well rewarded spectators ... Wexford's front six tried relentlessly to establish penetration and often looked very dangerous. James McGovern, a tall and strong full forward, threatened to inflict real damage whenever he got possession and gave Gerry Hargan a most anxious afternoon. Once he foot-rushed past Hargan and Mick Holden like a big bustling rugby forward and was unlucky not to round off with a classic goal, the ball slipping just wide of the far post".*

But, naturally, the most comprehensive account appeared in the *Wexford People* courtesy of the late Mervyn Moore. Given that it was such an historic victory (it was the one and only time Wexford had beaten the Dubs in a National League game in Croke Park), I will recount his report in full. Entitled *"Footballers down the Dubs with super show"* it went: *'Tony Dempsey summed up this Wexford performance in just three words minutes after the final whistle: 'you were magnificent', he told his charges as the dressing room under the Hogan Stand threatened to burst with euphoria. How true! And how understandable the celebrations after a superb Wexford performance against the Leinster champions and All Ireland runners-up, one that consigned Dublin to another year in Division II and virtually assured Wexford of a place in the NFL quarter finals and more importantly, a spot in Division I next season.*

The win was narrow (1-5 to 0-7), and Wexford's goal may have been of the fortunate variety, but there is no question as to which was the better team on the day. They never gave Dublin an opportunity to produce the sweet, free flowing movements that had proved so shattering six months ago in the championship. Wexford were led just twice over the hour but at one stage were four points clear and might have been in an uncatchable position with a little more luck.

They silenced the intimidating whistlers on Hill 16 as early as the 15th minute when a speculative lob from Garry Byrne ended up in the net. And the Dublin fans were totally mute as Seamus Fitzhenry skimmed the bar with a fierce shot; Martin Hanrick hit an upright and Jim McGovern watched a perfect square ball skim across the Dublin goal line needing just a breath to push it over. He also saw John O'Leary make a great save from him, from a hard ground shot. Seldom has a Wexford football team produced such determination. Youngsters, John Lacey and Louis Rafter were superb at midfield and the entire team showed such purpose that it was obvious from early on that 'The Dubs' were in trouble. Wexford deservedly led by three points at half time (1-3 to 0-3), and although the opposition appeared more determined on the resumption, Wexford still played with abandon, blocking down with such purpose that the much vaunted Dublin forwards seldom had an open shot at goal.

Throughout the second half Garry Byrne and Eddie Mahon proved a tremendous back-up for the defence while up front, McGovern, Fitzhenry and Hanrick provided Dublin with a real test. They scored just two points in a nail biting second half but the efforts of Hanrick and Fitzhenry proved vital as the improvement expected from Dublin materialised. Twice in the second half referee Paddy Collins ignored blatant fouls on Garry Byrne as he was heading for goal.

Indeed, one wondered what Wexford had to do to attract his attention, although Dublin's Brian Mullins appeared to have little difficulty in gaining his favour. Full back John O Gorman was majestic. And this is reflected in the fact that Dublin changed their full forward three times but neither Ciaran Duff, Barney Rock nor Brian Mullins could make an impression on the Taghmon man. For one so young John Lacey fitted into midfield like a veteran and with Louis Rafter formed a superb partnership. Tom Foley, Vincent Murphy (goal), Mick Caulfield, John Dunne and Liam Cullen, all played their part while the doggedness of Garry Byrne and Eddie Mahon also contributed.

Seamus Fitzhenry's speed caught Dublin on the hop regularly and he was backed up well by Martin Hanrick. Dublin full-back, Gerry Hargan, had a nightmare hour trying to keep tabs on Jim McGovern, and if the big full-forward's finishing had been as good as his other attributes, this game might have been wrapped up well before the end.

After the game both Tony Dempsey and county chairman Simon Kennedy, visited the Dublin dressing room to commiserate with the *former All Ireland champs. It wasn't a gesture which was returned however; sportsmanship apparently is not one of Dublin's trademarks. Of course, Dublin are not accustomed to being beaten by Wexford.'*

Wexford: Vincent Murphy, Tom Foley, John O'Gorman, Michael Caulfield, John Curtis, John Dunne, Liam Cullen, John Lacey, Louis Rafter, Seamus Fitzhenry (0-1), Padge Walsh, Eddie Mahon (0-1), Martin Hanrick (0-2), Jim McGovern (0-1), Garry Byrne (1-0). Sub: Noel Swords for Padge Walsh.

Dublin: John O'Leary, Mick Holden, Gerry Hargan, Declan McGrath, Pat Canavan (0-1), Tom Byrne, David Sinnott, Tommy Conroy, Brian Mullins, Barney Rock (0-2 frees), Joe McNally, P.J. Buckley, Tom Cassin (0-1), Kieran Duff (0-1), Maurice O'Callaghan (0-2). Sub.: Jim Ronayne for P.J. Buckley.

Referee: Paddy Collins, Westmeath.

We were allowed to keep the jerseys after the game and it felt like we had won an All Ireland but, we had to remind ourselves that we had only won a single league game and had no silverware to show for it. To be sure of a place in the quarter finals and promotion to Division I, we had to travel up to Ballyshannon to play Donegal the following Sunday and take at least a point from the fixture.

On one of the most bitterly cold days I have ever experienced, Donegal beat us comfortably by 1-12 to 0-6. We could never get into the game due in no small measure to the brilliance of Martin McHugh who scored eight points of the Donegal tally. All of McHugh's points were greeted rather emphatically by my marker Martin Griffin with the words: *"Good wee mon Máirtín!"* In retrospect, we were on too much of a high after the Dublin game and could have done with an extra week to prepare. Mick O'Dwyer had warned Tony Dempsey that it would be very difficult to bring us down to earth in such a short space of time. The Ulstermen were very highly motivated as they were battling against relegation, and their play seemed to have a much greater urgency than ours. They were also far more used to the arctic like conditions that prevailed that day!

We were now in a play off with Roscommon, having trounced them in an earlier league game but who, rather surprisingly, went to Mayo and beat them in their final league game. Our game formed part of a double header in Athy; the hurlers played Laois before us but unfortunately lost. By the time the football game started, the pitch resembled a mud bath and was certainly not conducive to good football. We started well and, due mainly to the brilliant long range free taking of Louis Rafter, were ahead by 5 points to 4 after 24 minutes. Then I won a ball about fifty yards out from the Roscommon goal and spotted Eddie Mahon breaking in behind his marker, Harry Keegan. I managed to stick the ball straight onto Eddie's chest but, unfortunately, his well struck shot from ten yards out hit the butt of an upright and was scrambled to safety. This was a crucial incident as a goal at that stage could well have put us on the road to victory. Sadly it was not to be, and Roscommon gained promotion to Division I, and a league quarterfinal spot against Down on a scoreline of 11 points to 7.

We now had to pick ourselves up for the championship, and that was going to be a major task given the disappointing end to our league campaign, a campaign that had promised so much. And who were we going to be playing in the first round of the championship? My native county Longford of course!

Please be so kind as to let me digress for a little while, as I tell you about my native county's glory days during the mid to late 1960's. It was during this period in the county's history that Longford produced a group of players, the vast majority of whom could more than hold their own against the very best at inter county level. It helped of course that several of the most prominent players, such as Jimmy Hanniffy, Bobby Burns, Tom Mulvihill, Sean Donnelly and the late Sean Murray R.I.P. were playing with and against some of the best footballers in the country at university level, and were quite at home in such company. This gave them great confidence and belief in their own ability when they pulled on the *'blue and gold'* jersey of their native county.

Another major factor in the revival was the appointment of Fr. Philip McGee (brother of Eugene) as team manager. The Colmcille priest initially trained and coached the team but in early 1965 he secured the services of Cavan great, Mick Higgins, to act in that capacity. It was a masterly move, as Higgins was seen, particularly around the midlands, as being one of the all time greats of Gaelic football (he had won three All Ireland and eight Ulster medals). It was also a huge boost to the morale of the Longford players to have a person of Higgins' stature involved with them. Incidentally, Higgins is on record as stating that Wexford's Billy Goodison was the best footballer he ever played against.

Success was not long in coming for the Longford lads. The team reached the Leinster senior final for the first time ever in July 1965 with merited victories over Offaly, Laois and Meath respectively. However, nothing went right for them in the final against Dublin, and they lost by a margin of six points (3-6 to 0-9). But many would feel they threw the game away as they missed a penalty after seven minutes, and then Dublin went down the field soon after to register a quite fortuitous goal. The city men secured two further goals in the second half to emerge victorious, but it was a very flattering scoreline for them. Nonetheless, Longford had shown great promise and this was further exemplified when they won the O'Byrne and Gaelic Weekly Cups before large crowds later on in the year.

An all out effort was now to be made in the National League where Longford operated out of Division II. They proceeded to beat Cavan, Sligo, Leitrim and Meath to qualify for the Division II final, where they again overcame Cavan. This latter game posed a real dilemma for Mick Higgins as he was also coaching the Breffni men; naturally enough he decided to stay with the county he had played with (he was actually born in New York) but all to no avail as Longford won by eleven points to seven. They were now into the league semi final proper where Donegal was overcome on a thirteen points to eleven scoreline. Longford had now reached their first ever League final where they would be opposed by, without question, the greatest team of that decade, the all conquering Galway combination who had won the All - Ireland in '64 and'65 also adding the league title in '65 for good measure. League finals were major occasions in those days and a crowd of well over 45,000 people turned up to see Longford's "David" face Galway's "Goliath".

Whatever about the biblical outcome most people could see only one result here: a comfortable Galway victory. But they hadn't reckoned on a marvellous Longford backline who blunted the, up to now, almost invincible Galway forward line, the brilliant midfield play of Jimmy Flynn and the superb score taking of Longford full forward

42

Bobby Burns who accounted for all but one point of his teams total. Longford had an interval lead of seven points to five but, like true champions, the Tribesmen fought back to level the game as we entered the last quarter.

There followed, in sporting terms, the most tense fifteen minutes I have ever experienced. Only one point was scored during that period, when Bobby Burns pointed a free with eleven minutes to go. This of course, turned out to be the decisive score of the game, as Longford hung on to win by nine points to eight, but my abiding memory is of a heroic display by the Longford defence as the Galway attack threw everything at them, but could not break through. There were scenes of wild jubilation as the final whistle sounded. The famine was over, well not quite as the team still had to play a robust New York team over two legs to win the title outright, which they duly did in October by an aggregate margin of four points (1-18 to 0-17).

An interesting anecdote from the time concerns a story told to me by my teaching colleague in CBS Enniscorthy, Galway man, Michael Deegan. Michael had been at the final and stayed overnight in Dublin. The following evening he came across a delighted Longford supporter at the hotel bar, reading all the daily and evening newspaper reports of the match over and over again, and obviously relishing the experience! And what did some of those reports say? Well, in the *Irish Press* Mick Dunne stated that: *"Longford have, at long last, broken through proudly and deservedly, to join the elite of the game"*. Paddy Downey in the *Irish Times* opened with: *"Galway, all conquering champions of the game for the past two years, were blown from their pedestal with the explosive impact of Nelson's crash"*. While J.D. Hickey in the *Irish Independent* said: *"The laurels truly rest where they belong, and their win clearly established them for what they are – a great side!"*

A great side with serious championship ambitions but, sensationally, they were dumped out of the Leinster Championship by Louth a couple of weeks after their League triumph. Perhaps the game had come too soon, as obviously there was still a lot of celebrating going on, but whatever the reason it was a terrible let down for all Longford supporters. People just couldn't figure out what had happened. There were all sorts of conspiracy theories floating about. One that gained ground was that the players' soup had been spiked before the game!

Incidentally, Galway went on to win the All-Ireland that year thus completing a marvellous three in a row. It took Longford a long time to recover from that defeat, but they finally got it right in 1968, when wins over Dublin and All-Ireland Champions, Meath, before a massive crowd of 20,000 people in Mullingar (including yours truly) put them into a Leinster final against a tough Laois side, who they beat convincingly (3-9 to 1-4) to record their first ever Leinster senior football title.

Longford were now into an All-Ireland semi final, and excitement in the county was at fever pitch. Their opponents were the mighty kingdom of Kerry (containing all time greats Mick O'Connell and Mick O'Dwyer), but Longford, showing scant regard for the lofty reputations of the Munster men, raced into a four point lead after just five minutes play. However, Kerry gradually got to grips with the situation and went on to lead by 2-7 to 0-6 at the interval. Longford moved Jimmy Hanniffy to midfield for the second half and this inspired a marvellous comeback, one of the finest seen at Croke Park, which resulted in the midland county leading by a point (2-10 to 2-9) with just eight minutes to go. Unfortunately that great effort had taken its toll, and Kerry used their greater experience to good effect in the remaining minutes to win by 2-13 to 2-11. It must be pointed out though that Longford had to start the game without two of their best players, midfielder Jimmy Flynn, and corner forward Sean Murray, both of them having sustained injuries in the Leinster final. Flynn was one of the finest midfielders in the country at the time (he had turned in a brilliant performance in the League final v Galway in '66) and was a majestic fielder of the ball, while Murray was a proven top class scoring forward. In addition to those blows, Longford suffered a further one midway through the first half when the tenacious Pat Burke had to retire with an injury. As a small county, with a population of just 30,000, we simply did not have the strength in depth to deal with such setbacks.

In spite of all that, with a little more coolness and cuteness in those final minutes I firmly believe we could have beaten Kerry and, with a full strength team available for the final, we would have gone on to win the All Ireland that year. In fact, if memory serves me correctly, I recall the great Sean O'Neill of Down, the eventual winners, saying before our semi final with Kerry that he would prefer to meet the Kingdom in the final. This was lent further weight when Longford beat Down by six points (3-9 to 0-12) in a teak tough Grounds

Tournament semi final in October of that year. Eamon Mongey B.L., Esq., of the Sunday Press did a fouls analysis of that game on the 20th of October 1968 and found that Down conceded twenty fouls while Longford gave away only thirteen. Now, it has always been my contention that the team that is finding it difficult to cope with the opposition resorts to fouling, although it's interesting to note that the foul count then was nothing as excessive as it is today.

Anyway, Longford remained a force at inter county level for several years afterwards but sadly the halcyon days of 1966 and 1968 were never repeated. They did however get their revenge on Kerry in a league game at Tralee in November 1972, when they scored a superb, eleven points to eight win over the Kingdom. Quite a remarkable incident happened in this game when a huge hole became apparent close to the Longford goal, and it took twelve cement blocks and four barrows of sand to fill it. Play was held up for about fifteen minutes while this was taking place, but the stoppage didn't affect Longford, who went on to record a famous victory. I read the reports of that game with great relish in Longford hospital (now closed) where I was getting an ingrown toenail removed!

Being such a fanatical supporter of my county, naturally I longed to wear the blue and gold jersey and try to emulate those heroes of '66 and '68 (I was inconsolable when we lost to Kerry in '68) but apart from very brief appearances at U21 and senior level, it was not to be. Now I would be lining out for my adopted county against Longford in the championship. It was all very hard to take in and I was certainly having mixed emotions.

It took us a long time to get over the demoralising defeat to Roscommon in the league play-off, but gradually we got ourselves back on the rails again with some tough training sessions and a series of challenge and tournament games. It was during one of those games in early April 1985 (it marked the official opening of the pitch and dressing rooms at Bunclody G.A.A. Club) that I sustained a serious Achilles tendon injury, which left me very doubtful for the clash with Longford. My colleague in Enniscorthy CBS, Michael Carty, had a similar injury some years previously and told me it was very difficult to shake off; it would seem OK and you would return to train only for it to flare up again. So naturally, despite receiving a lot of physiotherapy, I was rather pessimistic about being fit.

Padraig O'Brien from the Longford Leader rang me the Saturday week before the game and in the course of an interview I told him that due to the injury I was extremely doubtful. Two days later, Monday, I was put through a fitness test and was passed fit to play. I was absolutely delighted, but on Tuesday morning my delight turned to despair when the heel felt very sore and stiff upon awakening. I kept this to myself and, for the rest of the week, went every day to a local stream that was reputed to have amazing curative properties, and immersed my ankle in it for long periods. Whether it was the rest or that stream, the heel improved as the week went on and I was able to take my place on the team, but still very anxious as to whether the injury would hold up or not. In fact, it was a nerve racking experience running onto Pearse Park, for a number of reasons, not least being the fact that I had not trained properly for seven weeks, and I was wondering if I could possibly do myself justice against my own native county in the circumstances. I had a horror of playing badly and being taken off, and how would I ever live that down. The only thing I had in my favour was that I was reasonably familiar with the pitch, having played there in Longford club competitions a number of times down through the years.

There was a very strong wind that Sunday 26th of May 1985 and Longford had first use of it. They opened the scoring in the fourth minute with an excellent point from Eugene McCormack. We equalised four minutes later, when Eddie Mahon pointed a free, and then I combined well with Martin Hanrick for the latter to score a fine goal. Eddie Mahon added a point soon afterwards and things were now looking good. However, Longford took over after that and played some absolutely brilliant football to lead at the interval by 0-11 to1-2. Some of their points, particularly from John McCormack, were simply breathtaking and from the vantage point of the full forward position, one could only stand and admire. We were certainly very relieved to hear the half time whistle and were looking forward to the assistance of the wind in the second half.

However, things didn't get any better on the restart, with Longford adding two quick points. With 25 minutes left my native county still led by 8 points and were looking odds on to win. One could even sense a celebratory mood among the Longford supporters! But we kept plugging away and what happened next would probably be best summed up in the acronym made famous by Dr. Conor Cruise O'Brien,

GUBU: grotesque, unbelievable, bizarre and unprecedented, at least as far as Longford people were concerned! Eddie Mahon pointed a free, and then we got the goal we so badly needed. A long clearance out of defence found the unmarked Martin Hanrick close to the end-line, the Bunclody man crossed the ball expertly to Seamus Fitzhenery who finished it to the net. Worse was to come for Longford when a terrible kick out from Longford goalkeeper, John Martin, was intercepted by that man Hanrick again, who kept his nerve to coolly finish the ball to the net. There was now only a point in it and it was anybody's game. Longford wasted a couple of chances and then we had 4 wides in quick succession before Eddie Mahon levelled the game with a superb sideline kick. Eight minutes now remained, and Longford seemed to be shell-shocked. Kevin O'Rourke had a bad wide for them, before Martin Hanrick put us into the lead for only the second time in the game, and we clinched victory with further points, from Louis Rafter (a massive sixty metre free), and yours truly, or as the report in the *Longford News* described the score: '*... and to rub salt into the wounds, McGovern dealt the final blow to his native county with a point in the dying seconds*'.

It was truly an unbelievable turn around and it was hard to take it all in. I was just pleased to have got through the game with my Achilles tendon holding up reasonably well. I didn't think I had a great game, but I had set up the first goal, was fouled for a free that was scored and kicked the final point of the game. Of course I had mixed feelings about helping to beat my native county whom I had fanatically supported from my youth. But I was absolutely committed to my adopted county now. Longford players and supporters alike were stunned at the outcome, as this was a fine team of whom there were high expectations. John Donlon, now news editor of *The Star* newspaper, summed it all up well in the introduction to his report on the game: "*How could it have happened? What went wrong? These were the questions, numbed Longford supporters in the 4,000 crowd mumbled between expletives, as they trooped downheartedly from Pearse Park on Sunday last, having witnessed an unbelievable Wexford victory in the Leinster senior football championship.*"

There is no doubt that Longford played some wonderful attacking football and were probably the better footballing side, but they lacked the killer instinct when they had us totally on the rack in the first ten minutes of the second half. Donlon put forward another reason for their defeat, *"...the failure of many Longford players to show enough commitment to winning the 50-50 ball, in short, many lacked what Eamon Dunphy calls 'bottle'; they shunned the ball when the going got really tough; they tackled half-heartedly; they didn't wade in. It is something that the least skilful of players can have in abundance. Therefore the lack of it is inexcusable at county level. Wexford had it in abundance."* We may have had but I think Donlon is a bit unfair on the Longford players, who were superb for much of the game. Certainly players like Kevin Hughes (tragically killed in an accident a few years later, RIP), Sean O'Shea, Liam Tierney, Mick Casey, Dessie Barry, John McCormack and Mickey O'Hara could more than hold their own in any company.

The teams on that never to be forgotten day were:

Wexford: John Roche, Jack O'Leary, John O'Gorman, Michael Caulfield, John Curtis, John Dunne, Liam Cullen, John Lacey, Louis Rafter (0-1 free), Eddie Mahon (0-4 frees), Seamus Fitzhenry (1-0), Martin Hanrick (2-1), Ger Halligan, Jim McGovern (0-1), Garry Byrne (0-1). Subs: Tadgh Foran for Lacey, Padge Walsh for Halligan.

Longford: John Martin, James Keegan, Kevin Hughes, Sean O'Shea, Liam Tierney, Philip Kiernan, Michael Casey, Gerry Clarke, Matt Duggan (0-1), Dessie Barry (0-1), Frank McNamee (0-2), John McCormack (0-2), Eugene McCormack, Kevin O'Rourke (0-3), Mickey O'Hara (0-1). Sub: Mark Mimnagh for E. McCormack.

Footnote: The last championship meeting between Wexford and Longford had been sixteen years earlier in 1969. It produced a sensational result with the then Leinster Champions being dumped out at the first hurdle by the unranked Slaneysiders. *"Wexford's shock victory, Longford flop badly and surrender title"* **ran the headline in the Longford Leader the following week. It went on to say that:** *"Almost throughout the field Wexford held the whip hand and particularly at midfield where Longford could make little impression even with a complete new pairing after only twenty minutes of the first half. There were weaknesses in the Longford defence right through the hour, and the Longford attack carried some passengers on this occasion."*

"Outstanding in Wexford's sensational victory were Pat Leacy, Davy Rowe, Larry O'Shaughnessy and Denis Asple in defence, midfielders Joe Foley and Andy Merrigan and forwards Jack Berry, Sean Sheridan and Phil

Wilson." "Brendan Barden turned in a superb display at centre half back for Longford. Jim Hanniffy also did everything possible to swing the game while others to play reasonably well were Seamus Flynn, J.P. Reilly, Sean Donnelly and Jackie Devine. John Donlon, who substituted in goal for the injured John Henaghan, and Seamus Lee also showed up well."

The teams that lined out at Croke Park on that Sunday 8th June 1969 were:

Wexford: W. Howlett, J. O'Neill, P. Leacy, D. Rowe, J. Berry, D. Asple, L. O'Shaughnessy, A. Merrigan, J. Foley, G. Rankins, Jack Berry, P. Wilson, L. Howlin, P. Cleere, S. Sheridan.

Longford: J. Henaghan, S. Flynn, L. Gillen, P. Barden, M. Garraghan, B. Barden, J.P. Reilly, T. Mulvihill (0-1), M. Kenny, J. Devine (1-0), J. Hanniffy, P. Macken, P. Burke, M. Hopkins, S. Donnelly.

We were now through to a quarter final with Dublin and had three weeks to prepare. We knew that we would have to improve beyond all recognition if we were to be in with a chance of beating the reigning Leinster Champions. But we had beaten Dublin in the league in February and that was going to give us a certain amount of confidence at least. Of course the city men would be thirsting for revenge and we would really have to be up for the game. We stepped up our training and the Sunday before the big game we were invited to participate at the official opening of the Pete Coughlan Memorial Park at Beaufort in Co. Kerry. We were delighted to play the All Ireland champions and after quite a competitive game we managed to defeat them on a scoreline of 1-7 to 0-8. John Dunne kicked two great points from centre back while others to score were; Seamus Fitzhenry(0-1), Paul Harrington(0-1), Eddie Mahon(0-2), Jim McGovern(1-1). We were treated royally by the Beaufort GAA club and were presented with beautiful plaques for winning the game. Prior to that match apparently, Wexford had not beaten Kerry for close to half a century and the last time the teams had met in a competitive senior football game was on the 1st November 1964, when the Kingdom scored a 2-11 to 1-8 victory over the model county in the National League at Bellefield.

The Wexford team that day was: A. Doyle, W. Foley, J. Roche, J. Furlong, E. Walsh, N. Asple, P. Doyle, S. Keevans, T. Nolan, M. Bergin, Joe Foley, D. Asple, S. Sheridan, L. Swan, L. O'Shaughnessy. Subs:

Joe O'Shaughnessy for S. Sheridan, John Kennedy for J. Furlong. Kerry lined out as follows: J. Culloty, Donie O'Sullivan, N. Sheehy, D. Lovett, Denis O'Sullivan, P. O'Donoghue, T. Sheehan, M. O'Connell, G. O'Riordan, B. O'Callaghan, M. O'Dwyer, P. Griffin, S. Burrows, J.J. Barrett, Denis O' Shea.

Following the victory over Kerry and having scored 1-1, my confidence was at an all time high and I just couldn't wait for the Dublin game seven days later. As usual I made sure I had very early nights the week of the game. Come the night before the match however, I just couldn't sleep, and when I was still awake at 3 am I decided to take a sleeping tablet to see if it would help. I woke again at 7 am however and tossed and turned for several hours, until eventually getting up around 10 am to go to Mass. But I felt sluggish and sleepy, and it was preying on my mind that I had not got enough sleep for such an important game. It also worried me that the effects of the sleeping tablet would not wear off in time. The whole thing affected my confidence and I knew I just wasn't right for the match.

It certainly didn't help that we met a really fired up Dublin team hellbent on revenge for their league defeat at our hands at Croke Park in February. As I went to take up my position at full forward, I could actually sense the air of determination among the Dublin players not least my own marker, Gerry Hargan. There was real tension in the air, and our wingback Liam Cullen was the first victim of that, when he received a black eye before the ball was even thrown in!

The match itself was a disaster for us, as apart from the first few minutes when we took a two point lead, we were never in it. Dublin were dominant all over the field, and ended up completely crushing us on a scoreline of 4-13 to 0-6. Unfortunately that massacre took place before one of the biggest crowds ever seen at Wexford Park: the official attendance was given as 17,000 but most people felt there were at least 20,000 people there, with a number getting in free. In fact I heard a story of one man who did a thriving business with a ladder, letting people in for a fee behind the Clonard-end goal! Of course another group who did a thriving business that weekend was the Wexford town business community, who certainly benefited from the thousands of Dublin supporters in town for the game. So you could say I suppose, that it's an ill-wind that blows no good.

I've always admired the Dublin wit and a story I heard just recently illustrates it well. As the second half of our match against Dublin wore on and the result became a foregone conclusion, one Dublin supporter behind the town end goal had enough and lay down to go to sleep. Sometime later he was aroused from his slumber, took a look up at the scoreboard, saw a scoreline something like 4-11 to 0-5, and proclaimed: *"Jeez, is that the score or the time!"*

So 1985 had ended in a terribly disappointing fashion for us, with many Wexford people swearing they would never go to a Wexford football game again. The general view was that the disastrous defeat had put the game in the county back at least ten years. But, in mitigation, a few points need to be borne in mind. I suppose the major thing that needs to be said is that we had put a huge effort into getting into Division 1, beating some of the best teams in the country and only losing by a single point to Monaghan, who went on to win the League outright. As stated earlier, that was a game we were extremely unlucky to lose and would not have lost had Louis Rafter not had to depart the field injured after only twenty minutes, at a stage when we held a five point lead. We had trained incredibly hard for that League campaign particularly after Christmas, following a severe stamina programme laid out for us by Kerry legend Mick O'Dwyer. The result, unfortunately, was that we had little left in the tank when it came round to the championship. I am not saying that the latter was unimportant to us, far from it, but really we had set our hearts on getting to Division 1, knowing that playing there regularly against the top teams in the country would improve our game no end, but it was not to be, and really we were on a psychological downer after that, however we tried to convince ourselves otherwise

Going up to play Longford we were a tired team (in spite of another visit from Mick O'Dwyer to New Ross, a visit incidentally which caused a lot of controversy as it was held behind closed doors) and had a superior Longford team the killer instinct, they would surely have beaten us that day, but it was really only postponing the inevitable as the Dublin defeat proved. New faces were tried for the '85 – '86 National League, but we ended up losing every game and being relegated. Being pointless at Christmas, The "People" newspaper decided to ask four dedicated supporters from different parts of the county to pick the team they would like to see facing Mayo (away) when the League resumed on the first of February.

First up was **'Russian Man'** who selected the following team for the game: V. Murphy, L. Kelly (Bunclody), J. O'Gorman, J. Dunne, Jack Swords, G. Byrne, L. Cullen, L. Rafter, J. Dalton (Ramsgrange), S. Fitzhenry, G. O'Connor, J. Curtis, J. Culleton (Gusserane), J. McGovern, Jay Codd (Duffry Rovers). Subs: N. Swords, M. Hanrick, M. Caulfield, G. Turner, E. Kehoe, J. Mernagh (Duffry Rovers), A. Stafford (Marshalstown). Commenting on his team *'Russian Man'* stated: *"Liam Kelly was the best corner back in the county championship during the year while Jack Swords was a star county man until injury. He is now back to his best and should be recalled."*

'Always There' was next and this was his selection: G. Turner, L. Cullen, J. Dunne, E. Kehoe, G. Byrne, J. O'Gorman, P. O'Gorman (Taghmon), G. O'Connor, L. Rafter, S. Fitzhenry, K. Brennan (Rosslare), T. Foran, J. Harrington (Sarsfields), B. Furlong, E. Brennan (Rosslare). Subs: B. Duffin, G. Foley, N. Swords, M. Hanrick, P. Byrne (Kilmore), B. O'Gorman, Pat Culleton (Gusserane). His comments included: *"backs are waiting for the ball to come to them and not getting out in front. No plans in the forward line, no one making space. Eamon Kehoe is a natural back who is always played in the forwards or at midfield. Young lively men needed in the forwards, thus I include Harrington and Eugene Brennan. Kieran Brennan showed great potential in drawn Intermediate County final."*

"Over the Bar" weighed in with this team: G. Turner, L. Cullen, J. O'Gorman, M. Caulfield, J. Swords, T. Foley, J. Curtis, L. Rafter, J. Lacey, S. Fitzhenry, G. Halligan, G. Byrne, M. Hanrick, J. McGovern, N. Swords. Subs: J. Roche (New Ross), C. Jevens, P. Barden, J. O'Leary, J. Dunne. His comment was: *"I am constantly amazed at the teams that are picked. Putting a man on a county team does not make a county man of him."*

'Bullring Man' gave his team without a comment. It read: B. Duffin, T. Foley, J. O'Gorman, M. Caulfield, L. Cullen, J. Dunne, J. Curtis, L. Rafter, T. Foran, S. Fitzhenry, G. O'Connor, G. Byrne, M. Hanrick, J. McGovern, E. Mahon. Subs: P. Walsh (Bannow-Ballymitty), G. Foley, B. O'Gorman, P. Courtney, L. Keevans, K. Kehoe, Eugene Brennan.

Taking an overall look at the selections, only five players were picked on all four teams. Those were Liam Cullen, Garry Byrne, John O'Gorman, Louis Rafter and Seamus Fitzhenry. I was honoured to appear on three of them. *'Always There'* didn't pick me and I noted his comment about no plans in the forward line and no one making space. When the championship came round I was determined, while still acting as a target man, to create more space around the goal for lively forwards such as Martin Hanrick, Garry Byrne and Seamus Fitzhenry. Our first championship match was against Kildare at Wexford Park on Sunday May 18th 1986. It was actually a very special day for our family as, while I was lining out for Wexford in Wexford Park, my brother Gerry was making his debut for Longford in the championship against Louth in Drogheda (my other brother, Hugh, a very skilful forward, had played for Longford some years earlier). What made the day even more unique was the fact that Richie Culhane, another man from my own parish Colmcille, was lining out for Louth. It must have been highly unusual for a GAA club to have three former members playing Leinster Senior Championship Football for three different counties on the same day. And, of course, we couldn't all be on the winning side!

We won on a 1-11 to 1-8 scoreline (Longford lost). We had built up a big lead by half time, wind assisted, and withstood a strong second half rally by the Lilywhites to emerge victorious. Martin Hanrick was man of the match giving an exhibition of attacking play and finishing the game with a personal tally of 1-7. His vital first half goal in particular was quite superbly taken.

That victory earned us a crack at reigning Leinster Champions, Dublin in the quarterfinal. It was the third time in three years we had met them; they had beaten us by fifteen points in 1984, nineteen points in 1985, what would the outcome be in 1986? Very few people gave us any chance before the game and this was reflected in the very poor attendance from the county for the Croke Park clash. We had conceded a total of eight goals in our two previous meetings and our team management was determined that there would not be a repeat of that on this occasion, and so, any time Dublin used their ploy of a third midfielder, we left our man back in the full back line to cover off. It worked to the extent that Dublin scored no goals, and although they did win, it was only by five points on this occasion (17 points to 3-3). It was 2-2 to 0-8 at half time with our two goals being quite superbly taken. The first one came from Seamus Fitzhenry after a brilliant solo run that saw him finish sublimely to the top right hand corner of the net. This score subsequently got the RTE goal of the year. While the goal just described was a great individual effort, our second, two minutes before half time was the result of some great teamwork. Louis Rafter, who had an outstanding game despite a long lay-off due to injury, fed centre forward, Pat Barden with a fine pass down the wing, he in turn put a very intelligent ball into the path of Gary Byrne who applied a really clinical finish despite the close attentions of two Dublin defenders and the despairing dive of goalkeeper John O'Leary.

Dublin replied with a point to leave the sides level at half time. The fact that we were still level at this point gave us great encouragement for the second period and we left our dressing room full of confidence. Dublin, however, made a bright start to the second half with two quick points; I reduced the deficit to the minimum, with a point over my head from an oblique angle and then we struck for our third goal. Louis Rafter played in a high ball, which I flicked on to the unmarked Seamus Fitzhenry who, in turn, found Martin Hanrick in glorious isolation in front of the Dublin goal. The Bunclody man had proven himself coolness personified in such situations in the past, and so it proved on this occasion, as he rounded the advancing John O'Leary with consummate ease, to register our third goal. Who would have believed it? We were now doing to Dublin what they had done to us in our previous two meetings: scoring goals with gay abandon. Could we now go on to win the game? Sadly not. In the last 17 minutes the Metropolitans reeled off six unanswered points to emerge victorious. In truth the winners probably did move up a gear in the final quarter while we seemed to run out of steam, giving away too many needless frees, and gifting possession to the opposition on several occasions.

Nevertheless, we had still put Dublin to the pin of their collar and gone a long way towards erasing the memory of the previous year's drubbing. We had shown tremendous fighting spirit and restored pride in the jersey. Everyone had given of their very best with Louis Rafter probably our best player until he tired. On a personal level I was reasonably happy with my display, being responsible for all of our points, the first I was fouled for, the second I made Mick Kennedy overplay the ball for a free in, and the third I scored myself. I was also instrumental in our third goal and did my level best generally to create space in front of goal, by taking Gerry Hargan away from the edge of the square. I think its only fair to point out that Pat Barden also played a very intelligent and unselfish role at centre forward by taking their centre back out of the centre, thereby creating space through the middle.

Unfortunately, the day did not have a happy ending for me. I was sent off along with Dublin's Shay Fleming with eight minutes to go. Team manager Tony Dempsey had continually stressed the need to close down the Dublin backline to prevent them getting in good clearances, and I think we managed to do that to a large degree, for the most part anyway. It was while trying to do this that I was booked for what I considered to be, at most, a very innocuous late tackle on Dave Synnott. The second 'bookable' offence occurred when Shay Fleming was coming clear with the ball along the Hogan Stand side, I was with him all the way and was tackling him pretty vigorously I will admit (but no more so than any Meath forward would!) when suddenly he turned around and caught me with his elbow in the throat. The referee arrived on the scene and sent the two of us off, with yours truly subsequently receiving a two week suspension while the Dublin man got a month. It was not a nice feeling being sent off in Croke Park, and one I'd much prefer not to have experienced. On that June day in 1986 the teams lined out as follows:

Dublin: John O'Leary, Shay Fleming, Gerry Hargan, Mick Kennedy, P.J. Buckley, Noel McCaffrey (0-1), Dave Synnott (0-1), John Kearns, Jim Bissett, Declan Sheehan (0-1), Joe McNally (0-3), Sean Kearns (0-2), Barney Rock (0-6), Tommy Carr (0-1), Charlie Redmond (0-1). Subs: Paul Clarke for J. Kearns, Ciaran Duff (0-1) for Sheehan.

Wexford: Ger Turner, Cormac Jevens, John O'Gorman, Michael Caulfield, Ger Halligan, John Dunne, Liam Cullen, John Cullen, Louis Rafter, Bernard O'Gorman, Pat Barden, Garry Byrne (1-0), Seamus Fitzhenry (1-0), Jim McGovern (0-1), Martin Hanrick (1-2). Subs: John Creane for B. O'Gorman, Eddie Mahon for Creane, and Vincent Tighe for Byrne.

Referee: Seamus Aldridge (Kildare)

In late 1986 I was appointed a county minor football selector and, after having shown very good form at midfield with my club Starlights in the local club championship, I told senior football manager Tony Dempsey that I would prefer not to be considered for the full forward position any longer, but wanted to fight for a place at midfield. I didn't get a real opportunity to stake a claim there apart from coming on as a substitute from time to time. I suppose I was also a bit distracted by my duties as a county minor selector. Ironically, though, had I started the game at full forward against Kildare at Newbridge in May 1987 we may very well have gone on to win it. That was the opinion of most Wexford supporters at the match, my colleague, Michael Carty, informed me at work the following day. Louis Rafter dominated midfield in the first half and presented the forwards with a host of chances most of which were not availed of. Sean Óg O'Ceallacháin summed it up well in the following day's *Evening Press* when he wrote: *"the writing was on the wall for Wexford after the opening half, during which stage they shot ten very bad wides, most of them from good scoring ground."* As it was, I was brought into the team at half time and scored 1-1, as we almost caught a superior but far from great Kildare team at the end.

My recollection of my goal is quite clear: as against Dublin the previous year, I was doing my very best to drag the full back away from the edge of the square to try and create some space in front of goal. On this occasion I dragged him out to the left corner as we attacked. The ball was played to Martin Hanrick and I made my way in along the endline calling for a pass. Martin, to his credit, put the ball straight into my path and, with what seemed like half the Kildare defence hanging out of me, I remained totally focussed and buried the ball in the roof of the net, giving as Sean Óg stated in his report *"the Kildare goalie Sean Sergent no chance in the world"*! But unfortunately it was not enough as Colm Moran made victory safe for Kildare with a clinching point. The final score was 0-14 to 2-6. Of course, the loss of Seamus Fitzhenry with a hamstring injury just before the game was a real hammer blow, as he was central to the game plan. Wing back Ger Halligan was also a late withdrawal with a broken toe, and the absence of the Sarsfields man was also felt, as he had become a well established member of the team. His loss was exacerbated by the fact that his direct replacement, John Casey of Duffry Rovers, got an absolute roasting from *'man of the match'* Mark Shaw, a player whom I would have played with at university. Shaw scored five points from play. So, having run the then Leinster Champions, Dublin close the previous year in Croke Park, we had now lost to a moderate Kildare team. We seemed to be going backwards. On that Sunday 24th of May 1987 in Newbridge the teams lined out as follows:

Wexford: Ger Turner, Cormac Jevens, Padge Walsh, Mick Caulfield,

John Casey, John O'Gorman, Jim O'Donohue, Louis Rafter (0-1), John Nolan, Ml. Mahon, Pat Barden (0-1), Garry Byrne, Bernard O'Gorman (0-1), Jim Byrne (0-1) Martin Hanrick (1-1). Sub: Jim McGovern (1-1) for Nolan.

Kildare: Sean Sargent, Sean Dowling, David Malone, Paddy O'Donohue, Sean Ryan, Bill Sex, Brian Donovan, Ml. Moynihan, Anthony McLoughlin (0-2), Paul McLoughlin, John Crofton, Mark Shaw (0-5), Declan Kerrigan (0-1), Colm Moran (0-1), Brian Nolan (0-4). Sub: Liam McLoughlin (0-1) for P. McLoughlin.

Tony Dempsey and his selection team of Patsy Farrell, Larry O'Shaughnessy and Tom Foley (the late Michael Deane had also been a selector for several years and was replaced by Tom who had retired from inter-county football), stepped down after the Kildare defeat; in fairness they had achieved a lot over previous years and brought a new respectability to Wexford football. Team manager Tony was a great trainer and motivator and, knowing that coaching was not his forte, was quite prepared to take advice in this area. During his term in the hot seat he had Eugene McGee, Kevin Heffernan and Mick O'Dwyer conduct coaching sessions with us in Wexford. The outgoing management was replaced by a five-man selection team, which comprised: Kevin Power, Seamus Keevans, Paddy Wickham, Pat Hanrick and Senan Lillis. The team was now trained and coached by Good Counsel teachers Aidan O'Brien and Brian Teague. We had quite a good league run reaching the Division Three South play off where our opponents were Longford. This game was played at Portlaoise and resulted in a narrow one point win (1-5 to 0-7) for my native county.

Again, I was introduced at half time going straight into midfield where I felt I made an immediate impression. The report in the *Wexford People* seemed to agree when it read: *"Wexford stepped up their performance in the second half and the introduction to midfield of Jim McGovern played no small part in that. The Glynn man certainly turned it on against his native county and it is a matter of pure conjecture to wonder what might have happened had he been on from the start".* We had been 1-2 to 0-1 down at the interval but launched a determined fight back to level the game at 1-3 to 0-6 with fourteen minutes left. Longford went ahead again with a point from wingback Cathal Lee and a minute later Billy Dodd was unlucky not to goal for us when he pulled on a loose ball outside the square only to see it cannon off the crossbar and rebound to safety. Longford breathed a huge sigh of relief and a minute later they were two points to the good when, after a sweeping move, that man from my own parish, Cathal Lee, pointed again. Realising that there was little time left I fielded the resultant kick out and embarked on a sixty yard solo run that took me to within twenty yards of the Longford goal but, just as I was picking my spot in the top right hand corner to the net, I was tripped from behind and we were awarded a free in on the fourteen yard line. Billy Dodd took it quickly and tried for a goal but it was deflected out for a fifty, which Louis Rafter pointed to leave the minimum between the sides. Mick Mahon had a chance to level the game and bring it to extra time but his snap shot from the left of the goal went wide and that was that.

Gerry McCarthy probably summed up proceedings best in the *Irish Press* the following day when he stated: *"so a game that Wexford might have won, and will probably claim they should have won, went to Longford simply because the Midlanders took their chances"*. The forwards engaged in wholesale squandermania particularly during the first half and we would almost certainly have won had Seamus Fitzhenry been available. The Duffry man, now more focussed on hurling, informed the selectors the Tuesday night before the game that he was not travelling. The teams lined out that day as follows:

Longford: J. Halligan, J. McCabe, J. Toher, L. Tierney, C. Lee (0-2), S. O'Shea, M. Harkins, F. McNamee, D. Flanagan (0-1), B. Lennon (1-1), J. Keegan, D. Rowley (0-1, M O'Hara, G. Clarke, C. Gilmore.

Wexford: G. O'Connor, C. Jevens, J. O'Gorman, M. Caulfield, B. O'Gorman R. Deane, G. Halligan, L. Rafter (0-2), E. Mulrooney, J. Power (0-1), J. Roche, M. Mahon (0-2), M. Hanrick, J.J. McCormack (0-2), B. Dodd. Subs: Jim McGovern for Halligan, Barry Kirwan for Mulrooney.

Referee: P. Kavanagh (Meath).

Losing to Longford was a real downer and it was very hard to pick up the pieces for the championship. Training lacked something, not least the under twenty-one members of the panel who were having a great run in the Leinster Championship. In addition, a number of players were struggling with injury, with Ger Halligan, Martin Hanrick, J.J.

McCormack and Billy Dodd being of greatest concern. We were drawn to play Offaly in Tullamore and it was Wexford's first ever senior championship appearance at the venue. Sadly it was one that few of us involved will want to remember as we got a right hammering from the Faithful county, eventually losing by 1-18 to 1-7. Personally, it was a game I had prepared for meticulously as the indications were, after the game against Longford, that I would be partnering Louis Rafter in the middle of the field for the championship. This was the opportunity I had always wanted, indeed craved for, to play centre field for Wexford in the Leinster Championship. For at least three months before the game I trained virtually every day and sometimes twice a day on days when I would have had collective training with the county panel. I would go out on my own with footballs and work on my high fielding, soloing and kicking with both feet.

In a high fielding duel with Dublin full back Gerry Hargan, Leinster Quarter Final 1986

The more I did, the more confident I became and I just could not wait for the game to take place. Then, inexplicably, on the morning of the match I had a crisis of confidence. I didn't believe myself capable of effecting the simplest catch or of kicking a ball straight over ten yards, something that would be normally child's play to me. In the hours before the game I tried to accentuate the positive and get rid of the negative thoughts but it made little difference. I was in the wrong frame of mind for the game and I found it terribly frustrating.

Wind assisted, Offaly started the game in whirlwind fashion and were six points ahead of us before we knew it. Louis Rafter and myself were finding it extremely difficult to come to terms with the dominant Offaly pairing of Dave Kavanagh and Peter Brady. Kavanagh in particular, was playing out of his skin as was alluded to in the *Wexford People* report of the game: *"Typical of their problems on Sunday was the inability to curb Offaly midfielder Dave Kavanagh. Both of Wexford's midfield men, Jim McGovern and Louis Rafter tried to mark him in the first half; the obvious choice, John Harrington, was also taken out from the full forward line to try, and the musical chairs ended with McGovern reverting to his original position long after the game was lost".*

Kavanagh had trained with the Wexford panel at one stage, his work having taken him to the Wexford area. From that experience I knew that both Louis and myself were well capable of marking him but it just didn't work out on the day. Very few of us played well in that game but full back John O'Gorman was an exception; he restored a bit of Wexford pride by coming forward from full back to score two fine points.

The Wexford team was: George O'Connor, Cormac Jevens, John O'Gorman (0-2), Michael Caulfield, Donal Caulfield, Ger Halligan, Bernard O'Gorman, Louis Rafter, Jim McGovern, Pat Barden (1-0), John Roche, Mick Mahon (0-2), Noel Fitzhenry, John Harrington (0-1), Martin Hanrick (0-3). Subs: J.J. McCormack for Roche, Michael Dillon for Michael Caulfield, Barry Kirwan for Jevens.

Offaly lined out as follows: D. O'Neill, S. McEvoy, M. Brady, K. Rigney, M. Lowry, A. Stewart (0-1), J. Stewart, D. Kavanagh (0-3), P. Brady (0-2), S. Lynam (0-4), R. Connor (0-2), V. Claffey (0-2), B. Flynn (1-2), P. Mollen (0-1), P. Cushen (0-1).

Footnote: To complete a truly miserable day for the county, the minors were also beaten in the curtain raiser by the same opposition on a scoreline of 1-8 to 2-3. One fundamental lesson I learned from the senior game is that 'its all on the day' and while proper preparation is all important if you can't produce it on the day that matters, it counts for little. Subsequently I tried to apply this to my man management of the county minor and under twenty-one teams. In a nutshell, it was all about taking control of the game when the pressure comes on!

I didn't think I'd experience another day like June 1985 in Wexford

Park again, but the Tullamore experience came pretty close; it was a real nadir for me in terms of my inter-county career, and I never played senior championship football for Wexford again. I was still on the panel for the National Football League in the autumn, but only made sporadic, if quite effective appearances, eventually withdrawing from the panel in January 1989.

Before leaving 1988 however, it would be remiss of me not to mention the magnificent efforts of the county's under twenty-one footballers, who, with any luck at all, should have won at least a Leinster title. They started off their campaign with a match against Wicklow, and it took them two matches to see off the tough Garden County challenge. They proceeded to beat Carlow in the quarter final, and then got the better of a highly rated Kildare team in the semi final. This put them into a Leinster final against Offaly. What resulted was one of the longest running sagas in GAA history, with three replays and extra time needed to separate the sides. I was at all of the games in Carlow and, like everyone else present, was enthralled by the whole experience. As the saga went on the crowds got bigger and bigger and, in my view anyway, Wexford were the better team, had much more possession, but just could not convert their superiority to the scoreboard.

The first game was a low scoring affair ending Wexford 1-5, Offaly 0-8. The second encounter finished with the scores reading Wexford 2-6, Offaly 0-12 after extra time, the third encounter finished level also after extra time: Wexford 1-12, Offaly 1-12. The fourth coming together of the teams did not need extra time as the Offaly men finally brought the saga to an end winning by 2-7 to 2-5, but Wexford could still have snatched it at the very end, had Starlights Paul Nolan been awarded a penalty after he had been clearly hauled down in the square. But referee Joe Aughney of Carlow, who did not endear himself at all to the Wexford followers in the course of the four games, did not give it. And so the wonderful odyssey had come to an end, but these lads had given Wexford football a wonderful shot in the arm. And then there was Tullamore in May!

The Wexford panel for that Under 21 Campaign was: Pat Murphy (Bunclody), Pat Doyle (Adamstown), Michael Dillon (Volunteers), Eugene Brennan (Rosslare) Paul Nolan (Starlights), Eddie O'Connor (Gusserane), Donal Caulfield (Bannow-Ballymitty),

Barry Kirwan (Glynn-Barntown), John Harrington (Sarsfields), Noel Fitzhenry (Duffry Rovers), John Roche (Gusserane), Johnny McDermott (Taghmon-Camross), Noel Stafford (Clongeen), Michael Mahon (Bunclody), Eamonn Sinnott (Buffers Alley), John Cooper (Adamstown), Larry O'Gorman (St. Joseph's), Jay Codd (Duffry Rovers), John Joe Neville (Shelmaliers), James Quirke (St. Martin's), Paul Kavanagh (Davidstown-Courtnacuddy), Eamonn O'Leary (Sarsfields), Paddy Fitzhenry (Duffry Rovers), Michael D'Arcy (Kilanerin), Brian Moran (Kilmore), Martin Reville (Clongeen), Derek Whelan (Gusserane), Jack Redmond (Starlights), Nicky D'Arcy (Kilanerin)

Team Management: Tony Dempsey, Manager, (Davidstown-Courtnacuddy), Tom Millar (Duffry Rovers), John Lavin (Gorey), Martin Murphy (Clongeen).

Footnote: Offaly went on to win the All Ireland title afterwards, beating Kerry in the semi final, after a replay, and Cavan in the final.

Chapter 3

The Glynn-Barnstown Years, Punctuated

*"Life is about constantly making a home for ourselves
and having to leave it just as we do"*
David White

I got married to Bernadette Randall in October 1987 and moved to live in Killurin, where my wife is from. A decision now had to be made as to whether I would continue to play with Starlights or throw in my lot with the local club, Glynn-Barntown, one of the oldest in Wexford. There was another factor too. I was asked to return to play with my native club, Colmcille, in Longford having, as I stated earlier, given them (in particular the late Dr. Peter Heraty), a commitment that I would return to play for them at some stage when I left in 1982. I had only played adult football for them for three years and for one of those years I missed the championship because of injury, so I felt I had given them very little service really. However, I decided against it for two reasons: firstly I had just got married, and secondly I wanted to continue to play for Wexford which would not have been possible if I was playing club football in Longford.

But would it be Starlights or Glynn-Barntown in 1988? It was primarily due the persuasive powers of my inter-county colleagues Cormac Jevens and Barry Kirwan and visits from the local club secretary, the late Eugene Solan, that I decided to play with the team where I was now living. Of course, I was also aware that Glynn-Barntown had real potential having been beaten in a few intermediate finals in previous years. It seemed only a matter of time before they attained senior status, and I wanted to help them achieve that objective, rather than jumping on the bandwagon after they had attained it.

My first championship game in the *'blue and green'* colours was against Kilanerin at Bellefield, when we were fortunate enough to come away with a draw (0-7 each). However after such an inauspicious start, we improved considerably to defeat St. Anne's by 1-7 to 0- 3 and Bannow-Ballymitty by 1-14 to 1-5. In the knockout stages we really clicked into top gear, comprehensively beating Gorey in the quarter final (3-8 to 0-4), while doing likewise to St. James, Ramsgrange, in the semi-final (1-14 to 0-4). (We also had a good win over the latter in the Division II League final.) Naturally, it had taken me a while to get to know my new team-mates but I really got motoring after we reached the knock-out stages.

And so we had reached our fourth Intermediate Final since 1983, and hopes were high that this time a breakthrough would be made to senior level. Our opponents in the decider were to be hurling super power Buffers Alley, who had just won the county senior hurling title. So they were going for the double and would be hard to beat. But thankfully it all came right for us on the day when we put years of disappointment behind us by beating the men from Monamolin on a scoreline of 3-9 to 0-6. It was a day of mixed emotions for me personally as I was sent off after 28 minutes by Enniscorthy referee Paddy Shiggins, a former Starlights player. I had scored 1-1 from play at that stage and I thought myself it was a decision that was hard to justify in the overall context of the game. The *'Echo'* report of the game seemed to agree when it stated: *'they lost midfielder Jim McGovern, sent off in the twenty-eighth minute, and this looked like a tragic blow for it was the tall gangling midfielder who did most to settle his side with a superb sixth minute goal. This sending off acted as a tonic for Glynn-Barntown. A rather harsh decision in the circumstances, for far more dangerous incidents both before and after went unpunished.'* Things, then, did not look all that promising at half time when we only held a slender three point lead, but our lads opened up in the last quarter to record a decisive victory.

One pleasant memory I have of that day is, after being sent off, coming face to face with the great Tony Doran for the first time and shaking hands with him.

The teams, in that Intermediate Final, played at Wexford Park in late October 1988, were as follows:

Glynn-Barntown: Shane O'Brien, Johnny McDonald, Simon Laffan, Paul Brazil, Eddie Mahon (0-2 frees), Barry Kirwan, Nigel Morrissey, Jim McGovern (1-1), John Barron, James White (0-2), Cormac Jevens (0-1), James Morrisssey, Iain Wickham (0-1), Michael Walsh (1-0), Barry Doyle (1-2). Subs: Derek Kent for James Morrissey, Denis Doyle for Barry Doyle.

Buffers Alley: Ben Martin, Colin Whelan (0-1), Barry Murphy, Harry Lee, Paul Gahan, Pat Kenny, Michael Murphy, Paddy Donohoe, Matty Foley, Tom Dempsey (0-4), Sean Whelan, Eamonn Sinnott (0-1), Fintan O'Leary, Matt Furlong, Fintan Farrell. Sub: Pat Lacey for Lee.

Glynn-Barntown was now in senior football for the first time in its history, having attained that distinction in hurling the previous year, and a supreme effort would be made to, at the very least, maintain that position in 1989.

My old club, Starlights, obviously got their act together that year too as they reached the senior final for the first time since the winning year of '83. They only lost out to Duffry Rovers in a very tempestuous final by a couple of points.

Footnote: In that Intermediate final of 1988 I witnessed what was probably the finest point from play I've seen in Wexford. It was hit with the outside of the right foot into the town end, and seemed to be heading for the Bishop's Palace at one stage until, possibly divine intervention, or more likely how skilfully it was struck, made it veer in towards the goals and over the bar. It was a point of the highest quality and I can still see it in my mind's eye. And who scored it, I hear you ask? None other than hurling legend Tom Dempsey, who was a very useful footballer and well up to inter county standard.

On a personal level, I was extremely determined to do well with Glynn-Barntown in 1989. As I stated earlier, I opted out of the county senior football panel in January of that year, as I got the distinct impression from new team manager Brian Teague, that I was not part of his plans. I now embarked on a weight-training programme for the first time in my life, in the early months of that year, and certainly felt the better for it later on. The evenings I wouldn't be *'pumping iron'* I would be down in the local GAA pitch with a few footballs working on my skills. Of course I had always done this, but now I pursued it with a new vigour. My goals for '89 were very simple: to be the very best I could be, and be instrumental in helping Glynn-Barntown win its first senior football title. Larry Byrne, formerly of St. Anne's, was our manager and I was his secretary, arranging all the challenge and tournament games, and taking training sessions when Larry would be unavailable. The selectors were Paddy Kehoe, James Laffan and Tony Berney.

The championship continued to be played on a league basis, and our first game was against our rivals from Wexford town, namely the Sarsfields. The county champions of 1984 would have been favourites for this game, and they looked on target to justify that label, when leading 1-4 to 0-5 at half time. However, we gained a firm grip on proceedings after the interval, eventually running out winners by 0-14 to 1-8. The *'Echo'* report stated that: *"the Sarsfields, on their first half display, looked quite comfortable, at the end of which they led by 1-4 to 0-5 ... However, on the resumption they completely faded from the game, with Jim McGovern gaining complete control of the midfield exchanges, and with Eddie Mahon curbing the threat of the dangerous Billy Dodd. Glynn gradually got on top with James Morrissey and Iain Wickham picking off some delightful points".* Our scorers were: Eddie Mahon (0-2 frees), Jim McGovern (0-1), James Morrissey (0-5), James White (0-1), Barry Doyle (0-1), Michael Walsh (0-2) and Iain Wickham (0-2).

Our next encounter was against another traditional power, Gusserane. This turned out to be a tough but well contested match, which we won by 2-3 to 0-5. *'People'* reporter Fergus Sheil wrote: *"Glynn-Barntown's Derek Kent, Jim McGovern and Barry Doyle all had fine games for a team which took the knocks and went on to a deserved victory."* Those who notched the scores for us were; Barry Doyle(1-1), Mick Walsh(1-0), Jim McGovern(0-1), Cormac Jevens(0-1).

We were now into the knockout stages of the championship where our opponents would be my old club, Starlights! However, we had to wait five weeks for the game to take place, and in the meantime we kept on the boil with challenge and tournament games outside the county. As I mentioned earlier I organised all these games, because I felt it was vital to our development as a team that we did not confine ourselves to playing opposition from within the county but also experienced different playing styles in other counties. I had no doubt it would raise the standard of our game. In particular, we had an excellent workout against Eire Óg of Carlow and we felt we were every bit as good as them. The Carlow Town club went on to have tremendous success, winning several Leinster club titles and getting to an All Ireland club final which they were extremely unlucky to lose. It made us think what we might have achieved had we made the breakthrough in Wexford then.

It was during one of those games that our flying wing forward, James Morrisssey, picked up a knee ligament injury that threatened to keep him out of the Starlights game. This was of great concern to me personally, as I wanted us to be at full strength against my former club. Selector, Dublin based Paddy Kehoe, told me of a masseur he went to regularly, Eddie Downey, could get James right. Eddie was based at the Montrose Hotel, and was one of the masseurs Mohammed Ali used when he fought Al *'Blue'* Lewis in Dublin in 1972. It seemed worth trying, so I drove James up to Dublin to see Eddie, who was very friendly and welcoming. It did the trick, and James to my great relief, after further treatment, pronounced himself fit for the game and he made a vital contribution to our victory (1-11 to 1-7).

Alan Aherne reported in the *'People'* that: *"the victors used a match winning ploy of playing the ball to speedy wingers, James Morrissey and James White when in possession. In addition Jim McGovern had one of his better days in the Glynn-Barntown colours, and his high fielding when under pressure was of immense impor-tance, not to mention his brace of high angled points, which really broke Starlights hearts. Elsewhere, Paul Brazil and Barry Kirwan held the defence together firmly, while Cormac Jevens acted as an effec-tive play maker, particularly in the first half".* He concluded that *"it is a fantastic feat to qualify for the senior semi-final in their first year in the grade, and with the scalps of Sarsfields, Gusserane and Starlights emphatically under their belts, Glynn-Barntown can look forward to their next outing with a deserved degree of confidence."*

That next outing would be against Clongeen who were also reach-ing the semi-final for the first time. They had shocked a fancied Bunclody team who, amazingly, were competing in their thirteenth successive senior quarter final, on a scoreline of 2-4 to 0-9.

Our semi final against the New Ross district side made the nation-al newspapers but, unfortunately, for all the wrong reasons. The match had descended into quite a *'physical'* encounter, particularly after Clongeen's Seamus O'Sullivan (their ace marksman) was, in my opinion at least, rather harshly sent off for two bookable offences after twenty one minutes of the first half. However, we had lost our inspirational centre back, Barry Kirwan, due to injury after only ten minutes, so things were probably balanced out in that regard. *'The People'* report of the game, with its headline *'Glynn-Barntown stay cool and make history'*, stated that: *"Glynn-Barntown endeavoured to open up the game at every opportunity, despite the loss of centre back Barry Kirwan through injury as early as the tenth minute. It also reflects creditably on the composure and commitment of the Barntown squad that they demonstrated abundant resilience and tenacity to hold out in the face of fierce provocation to qualify for their first ever senior final"*.

We had led by 1-4 to 1-2 at half time and had increased our lead to five points, ten minutes into the second half. But Clongeen would not throw in the towel, and battled back bravely to come within a point of us with five minutes to go (1-8 to 1-7). Thankfully we didn't panic, and Iain Wickham was coolness personified as he kicked the clinching point just on the stroke of full-time.

'The People' report went on to say that: *"Paul Brazil, Eddie Mahon and Jodie Moloney were outstanding in the winners' defence, with Mahon's experience and skill seen to full value when Barntown were pinned under pressure in the closing quarter. Jim McGovern had a magnificent game at midfield, his high fielding, even when helping out in defence, being first class. In attack, Cormac Jevens, despite shipping some heavy punishment, James White and Barry Doyle, were excellent all through and showed some clever touches when in possession."*

The teams were:

Glynn-Barntown: Shane O'Brien, John McDonald, Simon Laffan, Paul Brazil, Nigel Morrissey, Barry Kirwan, Eddie Mahon, Jim McGovern (0-1), John Barron, James White (0-1), Cormac Jevens (1-2), James Morrissey, Iain Wickham (0-3, 0-2 frees), Mick Walsh, Barry Doyle (0-2). Subs: Jody Moloney for Kirwan, (inj.), Kirwan for Walsh.

Clongeen: Tom Purcell, Paddy Reville, Sean Murphy, David O'Sullivan (0-4, 0-2 frees, 0-1, 45'), Paul Rooney, Seamus Murphy, Frank Whelan, Joe White, Michael Stafford, Fintan O'Sullivan, Jim

Stafford (0-1), Seamus O'Sullivan (0-1 free), Denis Rochford, Noel Stafford (1-1), Declan Murphy. Subs: Seamus Bennett for F. O'Sullivan, Martin Reville for Declan Murphy.

Referee: Jack O'Brien

It was an absolutely wonderful feeling to be in the final, made all the more special by the fact that Glynn Parish was celebrating the bicentenary of the foundation of its parish church, it being the oldest in the diocese. The football panel was honoured by the local parish committee at a special reception, on reaching our first senior final. We received special commemorative tankards which we greatly appreciated.

There were now three weeks to prepare for the final, in which our opponents would be Duffry Rovers, who were now chasing four in a row. There was a great air of excitement and expectancy in the parish as we set about our preparations. The Duffry had hammered Taghmon-Camross in the other semi-final and looked a very good side. They were powered by the Fitzhenry brothers, and Louis Rafter, whose superb, long range dead ball kicking, was to break our hearts on many occasions. But overall Duffry had a good all round team with plenty of strength in depth, and they had an excellent trainer in Englishman Bob Brakewell, who had them superbly fit.

The final was played on the last Sunday in August before a very big crowd at Wexford Park, and it will go down as one of the most memorable finals played in the county in the last century. Apart from being a very good game of football, it will be chiefly remembered for the fact that, wind assisted, we built up a ten point lead by half time, while playing into the Clonard end, and our opponents fought back to gain a draw in the end. Eddie Mahon put us on our way with a fine long range free in the second minute, and two well worked goals finished by Cormac Jevens meant we had built up a lead of 2-5 to 0-1 by the interval. Duffry's sole first half score came from wing back and captain John Casey, who sallied forth from his position to record a fine point four minutes before half time. I felt at the time that this score was important psychologically for Duffry Rovers, as it meant that they would not be going in at half time with no score at all; it gave them a glimmer of hope and confidence for the second period.

Nevertheless, our lead seemed unassailable as we retired to the dressing rooms, leaving the field to the 1964 Ballyhogue Jubilee Team who were to be honoured, having won the senior title twenty-five years previously. I cannot remember exactly what was said in our dressing room, but I do recall thinking to myself, we have a great opportunity here if we keep our heads, continue our pattern of play and attack our lead rather than sitting back on it; there was a breeze and we would be playing against it in the second half, but it was certainly not of gale-force proportions. Within three minutes of the resumption, Duffry had cut our lead to seven points; we then sprang U.S. based Jody Moloney from the substitutes bench, but the Duffry continued to attack in waves, and had cut the lead to six points (2-6 to 0-6), with fifteen minutes to go. Our sole point of the second half had been scored by Iain Wickham in the 8th minute.

It was still very much there for us, but now our goalkeeper Shane O'Brien was instructed to keep his kick outs away from the centre of the field, but unfortunately for us, they started going over the sideline and were capitalised on by the opposition in several instances. With seven minutes to go Seamus Fitzhenry reduced the arrears to two points, and I was beginning to wonder would we survive? The Duffry were attacking incessantly, and it was becoming increasingly difficult to hold them out. Noel Fitzhenry scored an amazing sideline kick from forty yards out to reduce the margin to just a point, straight after we had just missed an easy chance of a point at the other end.

Incredibly, with two minutes left Martin Fitzhenry levelled up the game from a free. We did have one last chance to snatch a win when a high ball dropped twenty-one yards out from the Duffry goal. I went for it but just as I was sure I was about to field it, centre back John Fitzhenry came from behind, got a firm punch on the ball and drove it out over the sideline on the stand side. Eddie Mahon came up to take it but it was a very difficult kick for a right footed player; it was a pretty decent effort but the ball just sailed wide of the left post. Of course there was also incredible pressure on Eddie, as he was informed it was the last kick of the game. The final whistle did go on the kick-out, and an amazing game had finished level. It was an incredible comeback by the champions, and when you consider they pulled back a ten point lead without scoring a goal, it has to be rated one of the finest final comebacks in the history of Wexford GAA.

70

With regard to our performance, the *'Echo'* reported that: *'all their defenders were great in that first half – the strong men of the full back line, John McDonald, Simon Laffan and Paul Brazil – and the tireless half backs, Nigel Morrissey, Barry Kirwan and Eddie Mahon. Jim McGovern was a tower of strength at midfield, substitute Jody Moloney was absolutely brilliant from the time he came on the field, while the leadership qualities of Mick Walsh and Cormac Jevens in attack would be the envy of any senior football team.'*

The teams on that fateful day were:

Glynn-Barntown: Shane O'Brien, Johnny McDonald, Simon Laffan, Paul Brazil, Nigel Morrissey, Barry Kirwan, Eddie Mahon (0-2 frees), John Barron, Jim McGovern, James Morrissey, Cormac Jevens (2-0), James White (0-1), Barry Doyle, Michael Walsh, Iain Wickham (0-3 frees). Subs: Jody Moloney for Barry Doyle; Brian Cantwell for James White.

Duffry Rovers: Nicky Murphy, Ger O'Connor, Jay Mernagh, Pat Ryan, John Casey (0-2), John Fitzhenry, Paddy Fitzhenry, Noel Fitzhenry (0-2), Louis Rafter (0-4 frees), Pat O'Leary, Seamus Fitzhenry (0-2), Fran Fitzhenry, Ger Fitzhenry (0-1), Jay Codd, Matt O'Leary. Sub: Martin Fitzhenry (0-1free) for Ger O'Connor.

Reflecting on the game fifteen years on, and knowing that it is easy to be wise in hindsight, I still feel a number of points need to be made. It was our first senior championship final while Duffry Rovers were appearing in their fourth in a row. We probably lacked experience and *'know-how'*, particularly when the heat really came on in the second half. Although Jody Moloney was only recently home from America I would have started him in the final, particularly since he had come on in the semi-final and played well. Jody had been playing regularly in America, was on the exiles panel for the N.F.L. in May and was at peak fitness. He had played for Wexford at underage level before emigrating and was a very good footballer. We could ill afford to start without him against a team of Duffry Rovers' calibre.

The late Dr. Bob Bowe (after whom the current Wexford senior hurling championship cup is named), who was my doctor when I came to Enniscorthy first and who was also an avid Duffry Rovers fan, told me once, that when your team is in trouble play your best player in the middle of the field, as that is where the ball is going to be most often. This is in fact what the Duffry did with the switch of Seamus Fitzhenry to midfield from centre forward. Along with Louis Rafter, he proceeded to dominate that area for most of the second half, expertly picking up the breaks from Louis who had decided on a policy of breaking down the high ball. Jody Moloney joined me there early in the second half, and while he did win a lot of the ball and played really well, what was needed on Fitzhenry was a man marker, and centre back Barry Kirwan would have fitted the bill perfectly, with Moloney slotting in well into the pivotal position.

There are those who say I should have done better on Louis Rafter in that second half, and in subsequent finals, but I think a few points have to be borne in mind. Louis was at the height of his powers in 1989; he was one of the mainstays of the county senior team, and had been very influential in helping Wexford win the Division III title outright earlier in the year. He was easily one of the best midfielders in the country and his long range dead ball kicking had few if any equals. In addition to that he had a few years on me (he was 28 and I was 33), and that was bound to tell eventually, in a very demanding position like midfield. Some say I should have gone in harder on him, 'harder' being a euphemism for something else I suppose, but the reality was I had great respect for Louis.

Apart from playing together with Wexford for several years, Louis and I also played with McBride's in Chicago for several weeks during the summer of 1986. Arriving a week or so after Louis, and not having my accommodation fixed up yet, Louis insisted I take his bed in the apartment he lived in while he slept on the floor, saying he had a bad back anyway! It was something I never forgot. I found him to be a gentleman in all those games, keeping his mouth shut and never resorting to personal comments or acts of gamesmanship. Chairperson of the Duffry Rovers Club at the time, my teaching colleague, Josie Foley, told me that Louis had a great calming effect on the Duffry players in the dressing room at half time in that '89 final, and before they left he stopped them all at the door and warned them not to panic, to take their points and not to concentrate on going for goals. And they obviously followed his advice!

I have no doubt in my mind that we left our dressing room too early after the break, as when we came out onto the field the Ballyhogue team were still being presented with their mementos of 1964. With due deference to that great team, this may have broken the concentration of our team as we were hanging around for quite a while, and when the game recommenced the Duffry fired over three very quick points.

To this very day goalkeeper Shane O'Brien has been *'slagged'* about the amount of balls he drove over the sideline in that second half. Well, I would like to exonerate Shane from at least some of the blame because, as I stated earlier, he was instructed to keep the ball away from the middle of the field where Duffry had got the upper hand. Now I think that was an error. Shane never had a great kick out but, to his credit, worked on it repeatedly, particularly in preparation for the final. On numerous evenings after training, and on non-training nights, he and I would work on that aspect of his game – he kicking the ball out, and I fielding it in the middle of the field. With constant practice and an improvement in his technique, he had gained an extra ten to twelve yards distance wise. Over time he gained a real confidence in his ability to drive the ball a long distance. However when he was told to keep his kick outs to the side, against a contrary wind, he just could not do it and his confidence collapsed, with several balls going out over the sideline, and Duffry Rovers were good enough to capitalise on their good fortune.

With Duffry dominating in the vital midfield area, it was understandable that he be told to do this but I felt the real problem was the breaking ball which we simply were not getting. It would have been different if we were being clearly out-fielded, but such was not the case. All we needed was to win a few balls and get a few scores to add to our lead, but while we had a few chances, we were basically operating off crumbs. In addition to this, our full forward line had come too far out the field looking for possession, with the result that we lost our shape, and indeed it was galling to see a couple of balls hop aimlessly into the arms of goalkeeper Nicky Murphy with no Glynn forward within an asses roar of him.

The final chance we had of winning the game, albeit a very difficult one, has given me more than a few nightmares since. As I stated earlier, we got a sideline kick which suited a left footed kicker and it crossed my mind that I should take it, as I had pointed from almost an identical position twice in the same game for my club in Longford many years previously. But that was when I was a student and I had plenty of time to practise. I wasn't practising frees now, so I left it to Eddie Mahon who made a valiant, but unsuccessful attempt with his right foot. Incidentally, we had a left footed free taker, Barry Doyle, but he had been substituted earlier in the match.

In the aftermath of the game many of our supporters (and indeed neutrals), were critical of referee John Denton's handling of the second half in particular, feeling that he gave us *'nothing'*. This view was lent further credence in the 'County Final Comment' on the game in the *'Echo'* a few days later. In the course of a detailed assessment of the match the writer stated: *"Full marks to Duffry Rovers! Another team would have wilted. To wipe out a ten points lead in thirty minutes without the aid of a strong wind is no mean achievement. But in truth they had a little assistance. Referee John Denton provided aid practically every time Glynn-Barntown got into an attacking position in the second half. Happenings, tackles, over-carrying of the ball, which were ignored at an earlier stage, were all played strictly to the book as the challengers strove to keep ahead. The referee had little sympathy for the Glynn half forwards!"*

Be that as it may, we were now faced with a replay, but at least we had a month to prepare for it. Obviously the advantage had very much swung to the Duffry, now that the element of surprise had all but evaporated. The major thing we had to work on now was our minds, to try and remain positive and convince ourselves that we had not missed the boat.

We definitely needed the services of a sports psychologist then to help us refocus our minds and accentuate the positive but, in those days, they were virtually taboo and such a move would have been unthinkable, given that they were hardly even being used at inter county level, and if they were it was being kept very much a secret. That did not stop me however from putting up some positive and motivational things on our dressing room notice board as we set out to prepare for the replay! One plus for us was that Jody Moloney would be much more acclimatised for the replay and hopefully would start. He was due to return to the States after the game as his work awaited him, but kindly decided to hold on for the replay.

Alas, we lost the replay by four points. I don't think anybody was surprised at the outcome. The vast majority felt we had 'missed the bus' the first day. And deep down, in spite of what we told ourselves to the contrary, many of us may have feared that too.

So the dream had ended, we had not won the championship and we would not be playing in the Leinster Club Championship, at least not that particular year. The intense disappointment at losing such a big lead lingered for a long time, but time is a great healer and we decided to redouble our efforts to win the championship in 1990.

Of course I was going to be very busy having been appointed county minor football manager the previous November and my selectors and I had already done a lot of preparatory work before 1990 had even begun. There were also calls for me to be brought back into the county senior football panel after I had performed well in the '89 championship, including one that appeared in the *Wexford People* on Thursday, March 29th 1990 which stated: *"Quite a few knowledgeable followers are surprised that Jim McGovern (Glynn-Barntown) is not currently on the county senior panel. He was one of the best players operating in the county championship last year and in the past gave many memorable performances for the county senior team, against the best in Ireland."* However, had I got a recall I would have had to consider it very carefully as I had so many commitments with club, school (debating and public speaking in particular) and of course the county minors. But, ultimately, I would have to say I would probably have accepted, as I would never have let Wexford down.

Glynn-Barntown had changes on the managerial front in 1990. Larry Byrne stood down and was replaced by former Wexford senior football manager Tony Dempsey. His selectors were: Tommy Kirwan, Jim Corcoran and Paddy Kehoe.

Tony had us flying fit in 1990 and we started off our campaign with an excellent 2-14 to 0-8 win over Gusserane on the 29th April at New Ross. We followed that up with a similarly comprehensive victory over St. Martins (1-16 to 1-5), on the 23rd of June, while on the 28th of July we beat a gallant Clongeen team in the quarter final at New Ross, on a scoreline of 1-9 to 1-4. I played arguably my greatest ever game of football in this particular match. Certainly I don't recall winning so much possession either before or since and I also scored our goal, which was vital to the outcome of the match. Football connoisseur P.J. Daly (Ballyhogue) seemed to concur with this in an article he wrote on the 1990 Championship in the Wexford GAA yearbook later that year, saying it was one of the greatest second half performances he had ever seen at the venue.

After what had happened the previous year in the semi final, I think the prophets of doom were predicting a bloodbath on this occasion; however they were proved wrong as the game passed off without incident. There was however an unusual happening before the match even began! Both teams left their dressing rooms at the same time to go out onto the pitch and, as they did so, our team manager Tony Dempsey was being subjected to quite an amount of verbal abuse. I ignored it at first, as I was very focussed on the impending game. As it continued however, I turned around while still running, to see who was shouting, and ran straight into a Clongeen player who had slowed down approaching a narrow gateway. It was totally accidental, but in the hyped-up situation of a match, could have been misinterpreted.

We followed that victory up with an equally hard earned win over Sarsfields in the semi-final at Wexford Park on the 26th of August, the scores on this occasion reading: Glynn-Barntown 2-8, Sarsfields 1-6. One particular memory from this game is of a brilliant solo goal from our wing forward James Morrissey. James was a really exciting player to watch and was more than good enough to play for Wexford had he been interested. I was also very happy with my own game having much the better of my duel with John Harrington.

We were now in our second final in a row and very eager to make amends for the previous year. Our final opponents would again be Duffry Rovers who had actually lost the first match of their campaign to Starlights by 1-8 to 0-6, but got back on track with a win over Buffers Alley (1-11 to 2-4), and followed that up with a comprehensive 4-9 to 1-6 disposal of Bunclody in the quarter final, before easily accounting for Gusserane in the semi-final, on a scoreline of 1-14 to 0-2. They were now going for five in a row, and would again be very formidable opposition.

And so it proved, although we were well in the game at half time when we only trailed by six points to five, having missed a penalty. We were reasonably confident as we headed out for the second half, but Seamus Fitzhenry was proving difficult to contain and he scored three excellent points in a five-minute period to give us a real mountain to climb. In fairness, we never gave up, and it would have to be said that our opponents never succeeded in putting the game totally out of our reach with a killer goal. I was pleased enough with my own performance (scoring two points from play from midfield) but that didn't help with the disappointment of losing, and to have that feeling for the second year in a row was more than a little sickening. We had injuries going into the game; I had a groin strain, and James Morrissey, Eddie Mahon and John Barron, all carried knocks, and we just did not have the strength in depth to match the Duffry, who were equalling the record set by the wonderful Volunteers side of the 1939-'43 period by also winning five in a row.

On that September day in 1990 the teams lined out as follows:

Glynn-Barntown: Shane O'Brien, John McDonald, Dermot Whelan, Paul Brazil, Nigel Morrissey, Barry Kirwan (captain), Liam Kehoe, John Barron, Jim McGovern (0-2), James Morrissey, Cormac Jevens, Anthony Whelan, James White, Iain Wickham (0-5 frees), Eddie Mahon (0-1 free). Subs: Simon Laffan for Kehoe, Barry Doyle for A. Whelan.

Duffry Rovers: Nicky Murphy, Ger O'Connor, Jay Mernagh, Kevin Frayne, John Casey (captain), Paddy Fitzhenry, Pat O'Leary (0-1), Noel Fitzhenry (0-1 free), Louis Rafter (0-3 frees), Martin Fitzhenry, Fran Fitzhenry, Seamus Fitzhenry (0-5), Ger Fitzhenry, Jay Codd (0-3), Matty O'Leary (0-1). Sub: John Fitzhenry for Ger Fitzhenry.

1990 had been a very busy year for me, as I had put a major effort into preparing the county minors, and even had to miss some club training sessions in the process, which I believe didn't go down too well with everybody in the club. However, I had given a commitment to train the minors, and while I tried not to have clashes between club and county training, inevitably on some occasions it was unavoidable. But with Wexford sadly going out of the championship in the first round in May, I was then able to concentrate all my attentions on the club.

After our defeat to Duffry Rovers in the 1990 Final, it was the view of many that we would never make the breakthrough, at least not as long as our bogey team was around, but as I saw it, failure was only postponed success provided we learnt from our mistakes, and I personally resolved to make a huge effort again in '91. I started in early

January doing a lot of roadwork, and would also train on my own after I had coached the county minors whom I agreed to take for another year. I also persuaded my teaching colleague John Kilgannon to join the club. John had played under twenty one football for Galway and would prove an asset to us for the 1991 championship but thereafter his interest waned.

Glynn-Barntown reached the final for the third year in succession in 1991, but we did it the hard way, having to play seven games in all to get there, and we were not too impressive along the way. We lost our first game to Taghmon-Camross at Bellefield on April 21st with the scoreline reading 11 points to 7. The next round of the championship was not played until July 13th, when we got back to winning ways with an 8 points to 5 victory over Bunclody at New Ross. However we lost to the same opposition in a play-off game at Bellefield two weeks later, by 11 points to 6. We now had to beat Taghmon-Camross to stay in the championship and qualify for the quarter- finals, which we duly did on August 25 at Wexford Park on a 2-8 to 1-4 scoreline.

Its funny how you sometimes play well in a game when you know your preparation leading up to it, is not what it would normally be. This happened to me in the quarterfinal against Castletown. The game was played on Saturday August 31st 1991 at Bellefield, with an evening throw-in. That was fortunate for me, as I had spent the whole day up in Carlow managing the Wexford team at the Leinster Under Sixteen Football Blitz. I felt mentally drained as I drove back from Carlow for the Castletown game, but found new reserves of energy from somewhere to play one of my better games for the club, and that was after bursting my boot ten minutes into the game, and being kindly lent a replacement by one of our substitutes. This was a tough, hard match but we managed to pull through on an eleven points to nine scoreline. We were now through to the semi-final where we met Clongeen on September 22nd at Bellefield. The result was a draw: us scoring 0-10, to 2-4 for Clongeen, and we were lucky enough to survive as the New Ross District side grabbed the lead with a goal with just two minutes to go. Luckily, we got the equalising point courtesy of Brian Cantwell with virtually the last action of the game, and we lived to fight another day.

The replay was a poor advertisement for football; we won it in the end by 7 points to 4, but were distinctly unimpressive in doing so. I picked up a nasty ankle injury, which necessitated six stitches, and the only good thing about the game was that the positive result put us through to our third final in a row. But our confidence levels were low, as we all knew we had played very poorly.

The final was fixed for a week later and our opponents were, you know who, Duffry Rovers! I could not train at all in the days leading up to the game, as I still had the stitches in my ankle, and then despite my best precautions the ankle became infected. I went on antibiotics and was able to play in the final, but my confidence was at rock bottom, and I asked the selectors to start me at full forward even though I was very worried about the state of my ankle. I was moved to midfield half way through the first half, as the Duffry were dominating and had raced into a big lead; I seemed to forget about the ankle injury afterwards, and turned in a reasonable performance particularly in the second half. But it was all to no avail as Duffry were much too good for us on the day, winning a very poor match by 2-6 to 0-5. However it should be pointed out, that apart from an admirable scoring burst in the first quarter, which yielded them 1-4, they weren't particularly impressive either. In fact they failed to score for an eighteen minute period in the second half and, had we taken our chances, (including two penalties which we missed) we might just have pulled off a result. But it was not to be, and Duffry cantered into the history books by winning the title for a record breaking sixth successive year.

The teams on that October Sunday in 1991 were:

Glynn-Barntown: Shane O'Brien, Nigel Morrissey, Dermot Whelan, Paul Brazil (capt.0-1), Eddie Mahon, Cormac Jevens, John Kilgannon, Brian Cantwell, Jody Moloney, Liam Kehoe, Barry Kirwan, James White, Barry Doyle (0-1), Jim McGovern (0-1), Iain Wickham (0-2 frees). Subs: John Barron for Kehoe, Mick Walsh for Mahon, Ciaran Roche for Cantwell.

Duffry Rovers: Nicky Murphy, Kevin Frayne, Jay Mernagh, Ger O'Connor, John Casey (capt.), John Fitzhenry, Pat O'Leary, Louis Rafter (0-1), Paddy Fitzhenry, Noel Fitzhenry (0-1), Aidan Jordan (0-1), Fran Fitzhenry (0-1), Ger Fitzhenry (2-0), Seamus Fitzhenry (0-1), Matty O'Leary (0-1).

Incidentally, New Ross district side Rathgarogue-Cushinstown, also created their own piece of history in the curtain raiser to the senior football decider, by beating Marshalstown in the Intermediate hurling final replay. They had beaten Fethard in the football equivalent the previous week, thereby pulling off a unique double. In fact, they became the first club in the history of Wexford GAA to win both the Intermediate hurling and football championships in the same year.

We now seemed to be as far away as ever from winning our first senior title, and Alan Aherne, reporting on the game in the *'People'* said as much: *"Glynn-Barntown simply never clicked, and their chances of winning a senior title now seem far more remote than when they contested their first final in '89!"* The post match gloom was exacerbated for me personally when, at the after match dinner, my ankle became badly inflamed and I had to be rushed to hospital. I was put on very strong antibiotics and crutches and was out of work for a full week. It was a depressing end to a depressing year.

> *"But I have promises to keep,*
> *And miles to go before I sleep,*
> *And miles to go before I sleep."*
> Robert Frost

As 1992 beckoned I reflected on four years with Glynn-Barntown. We had won an intermediate championship and had appeared in four senior football finals including a replay, but hadn't won any (in fact our record in county finals at all levels is most disappointing). Nevertheless, I felt I had given my heart and soul to the club during that period of time and would continue to do so. I was as dedicated as I possibly could be, looking after myself and keeping myself very fit by training almost daily. During the summer months I would some-times train twice a day, out early in the morning and then again in the evening. On numerous occasions I trained in the afternoon, especial-ly when our corner back Nigel Morrissey needed assistance. Nigel worked nights and had no option but to train during the day. Knowing that when you want to win something in a team game, you cannot do it on your own, you have to rely on others, I was always willing to do a bit extra with anyone who felt they needed it, even if at times I felt tired myself, or that I'd had enough. Larry Byrne and Tony Dempsey had us in great shape for those finals, but for various reasons there were always one or two who were not at the required level of fitness, and that may well have been a key factor when you consider that Bob Brakewell had the Duffry players in peak physical condition

But 1992 was another year and despite all the disappointments, it couldn't come quickly enough for me. And then *"out of the blue"* in February a phone call came from Eugene McGee in Longford, wanting to know would I consider transferring to my native Colmcille who Eugene was managing at that time. My initial reaction was to say *'no way'*, that I had too many other commitments and, at any rate, I was now too old being in my thirty sixth year. But I had made a promise to Colmcille when I left in 1982 that I would return for at least a year some day, and this was Eugene McGee calling, a man from my own parish for whom I had a lot of respect, because of his achievements in the game, and who had built up a massive reputation as trainer to that great UCD of the 1970s, and followed that up by training Offaly to beat the mighty Kerry team in that never to be forgotten All Ireland final of 1982. I had never trained under Eugene, and this was a marvellous opportunity to do so while fulfilling my promise to Colmcille.

But I had a lot of things to consider, not least the prospect of a regular round journey of almost three hundred miles! There were other factors too such as the prospect of leaving Glynn-Barntown having played in four county finals with them, sharing the hope, the expectation and ultimately the disillusionment and the sadness. I was also in my second year as secretary to the Club Development Committee where we had ambitious plans to purchase land and develop a second pitch. I was in my third year as county minor football manager, and was determined to make a greater effort than ever before to make a breakthrough. I was training school football teams, and I was also putting a major effort into public speaking and debating in my school, which entailed endless hours of practice with students after school, bringing them to competitions in places as far away as Dublin, and, in many instances, delivering them to their homes afterwards, often not getting home until 1am in the morning. In addition to that I was involved in a major fundraising initiative to help raise money to improve our outdated facilities at the school. It involved a lot of hard work, which included writing to schools around Ireland, and CBS schools throughout the world looking for financial contributions.

But, overriding all those reasons was the fact that our first child, Claire, was born the previous year and that was obviously my first and foremost responsibility. And yet, in spite of that and all the other commitments, and the realisation that I was undertaking a massive task that would stretch me to my limits and probably beyond, I decided to join Colmcille.

Apart from the McGee factor, there was something else that influenced my decision. Colmcille had lost a number of key players in controversial circumstances at the end of 1991 and I felt I should help them out in their hour of need. I was also conscious of the fact that I had only played for the club for three years at adult level, and still had ambitions of winning a senior championship with them.

And now a little information about my native parish. Colmcille is located in North Longford near the border with Cavan. It gets its name from St. Colmcille who, according to tradition, ministered in the area on the local Inch Island (about half a mile from my home) many hundreds of years ago. The club won the very first Longford senior football championship in 1890 and my grandfather; Hughie Mc Govern, was on that team. He, among others over the years, has been credited, with scoring the winning goal. He was adamant himself that he did. Apparently the goal was the result of a goalmouth schmozzle with the ball being bulldozed over the line! Nevertheless it remains the most famous goal in Longford club football history. It was a remarkable final in that Colmcille got only one score, that goal, while their opponents, Honest John Martin's from Rathcline in South Longford scored four points, but given that, in those days, a goal was worth any amount of points, Colmcille were declared the winners. The Roscommon Herald reported on the final and stated that: *'to describe the furious joy with which this victory was received by followers of the Saints (as Colmcille were known) would be impossible. They leaped about like children – old men hugged one another like young lovers and the rejoicings of a Waterloo victory was not to be compared to their frantic joy'*. At a subsequent County Board meeting the Rathcline team objected to the result, mainly on the basis that the Colmcille goal was illegally secured, but the result stood with the losers receiving silver medals as runners up.

My grandfather on my mother's side, James Brady, also played for the club and in 1913, was on the Colmcille team that won the very prestigious Foresters Cup, reputed to be the most beautiful and most expensive cup ever to be presented in Longford. His sons, my uncles

James and Michael Brady, also contributed a lot to the club, the latter winning senior championship medals in 1949 and 1952. My own
father was also very much involved; though he played very little he did
put in a lot of work as an administrator, serving as chairman of the
club when the senior championship was secured in 1949, and also
as secretary for a time.

I myself played for Colmcille up until about fifteen years of age.
Then, feeling that the club was neglecting my part of the parish, I
transferred my allegiance to St. Columba's, Mullinalaghta, our next-
door neighbours, with whom my brother Hughie was playing. St.
Columba's is a famous club in Longford, and is steeped in the finest
GAA traditions. It is in fact a half parish, the other half being Gowna
in Co. Cavan. It therefore draws on a very small population base and,
during the middle of the last century, basically depended on less than
half a dozen families to field a team. In spite of this, during the 1940s
and early '50s they were one of the strongest senior clubs in the
county. Although only managing to win the senior championship in
1948 and 1950, they won the hotly contested Leader Cup (the
Longford senior league) a magnificent seven years running, from
1945 to1951 and were a much feared proposition at that time. As
time went by they gradually slipped into the doldrums and did not
experience success again until 1977 when they triumphed in the
Junior Championship. My brother Hugh and I were members of that
team and it is a cherished memory.

Hugh and I werc asked to rejoin Colmcille in 1980, which we agreed
to do, joining our younger brother Gerry, but never won anything with
them until I left for Wexford in 1982. Now, ten years later, I was back
with Colmcille and looking forward to the challenge. We went okay in
the all county league, and one game I can clearly remember was
against Sean Connolly's from Ballinalee (the birthplace of General
Sean Mac Eoin, of War of Independence fame) We had the Derry
minor footballers down in Wexford that particular weekend as part of
our preparations for the Leinster Championship, and it was really a
time I needed to be with the minor footballers. We had a challenge
game against the Oak Leaf lads in Wexford Park on the Sunday morning, while the club game was due to be played up in Longford at 3pm
that afternoon. I had been hoping against hope that the match in
Longford would be called off as the weather had been very inclement
up there and the pitch was in a poor state in the days leading up to

the game. However, conditions improved in the twenty-four hours or so before the game, and I got a call from Eugene McGee just before I left for Wexford Park, telling me the game was on and to travel up. So I went in and spoke to the Wexford players, passed over control to one of my selectors, and headed for Longford. Thankfully my wife Bernadette was able to drive me leaving our one-year-old Claire in the very capable hands of Bernadette's Godmother, Mrs. Hamilton. You may wonder why I didn't skip that league game, given that I had the Derry minors to attend to? Well, had it been any other club we were playing I would certainly have stayed at home but, as I stated earlier, three of our former players and key players at that, had transferred to the Ballinalee club and there was apparently quite a bit of ill feeling about it so it was a very important game for us to win, from a morale point of view particularly.

To make things worse for me personally, I had a stomach bug through Friday and Saturday and was often in better form. In spite of everything I felt I had to travel, as I did not want to let Colmcille or Eugene McGee down. And it did not have a happy ending either, as Sean Connolly's beat us before a big crowd on our home ground. I didn't play badly but it was certainly not one of my better games.

Of course it was not the normal way I would have prepared, as I nearly always went up the night before a match to ensure I was well rested for a game. I later learned that some people involved in the Wexford minor set up were annoyed by my hasty exit but I don't think they fully understood my predicament. I must say it was the only time my commitment to the club in Longford clashed with my duties as Wexford minor football manager.

Colmcille had a reasonably good league campaign, only losing two games, and we looked forward with enthusiasm to the championship where we were drawn against our old adversaries Rathcline in the quarter- final. This game was on the same day (Sunday, July 26th1992) as the minor semi-final replay against Meath, but thankfully it was fixed for 7o'clock in the evening so I had time to make my way from Croke Park to Pearse Park in Longford. I was under orders from Eugene McGee to leave immediately after the minor game, and not stay to see the Leinster senior final clash between Kildare and Dublin. I had asked former county and club colleague Eddie Mahon to drive my car up, as I travelled with the Wexford team on the bus. The

*Iain Wickham who captained Glynn-Barntown to its first
Senior Football Championship title in 1996
is pictured with the Liam McCarthy Cup in Paris, February 1998*

minor game of course went to extra time, where we lost by a margin of three points. Bitterly disappointed, I spoke to the players, thanked them for their herculean efforts and then headed for Longford. I was glad I took Eugene McGee's advice to leave early, as I got hopelessly lost in my attempts to negotiate the recently opened M50. When I was a student in Maynooth in the1970s and early 80s,the road to Longford from Dublin via Maynooth was pretty straightforward, but now I hadn't a clue where I was, never having been on the M50 before. It certainly did not help my mood, which was already gloomy to say the least.

In fact, I was severely tempted to turn around and head back for Wexford but eventually, having gone round in circles for what seemed like an eternity, I finally got on the road for Longford and arrived for the game in reasonably good time. Rathcline had beaten us in our first league game, so we knew we had a tough task ahead of us. I felt very deflated and found it extremely difficult to motivate myself for the game. Really, my mind was still in Croke Park and what might have been, but I soon realised that I was about to play in a county senior quarter final, and if I did not get myself focussed quickly it would soon pass me by. I started sluggishly, and found it difficult to get into the game, particularly in the unusual position of left corner forward, but later I got going and while not scoring myself, was fouled for three converted frees and a penalty, which was also converted, and had a crucial bearing on the outcome of the game which we won by a couple of points. It's amazing what a win can do, it really puts you on a bit of a high and I, along with the other Colmcille players, was in great form after the game. We were now in a county semi-final, and I decided, given that the Wexford minors were now sadly out of the championship, to move up to Longford for a couple of weeks to prepare for it. I thought the move was essential given that I had done no collective training all year. I just could not bring myself to train with Glynn-Barntown, so I trained on my own, usually after taking school and county minor training sessions. Now I did train hard, but it is no substitute for training with your teammates, hence my decision to spend some time in Colmcille. I knew that this could be my last chance of playing in a Longford senior final and winning a senior medal, and I gave the training everything I had.

Then on the Tuesday week before the game disaster struck; I was running out to collect a ball at training, and suddenly my right leg seemed to go from under me. Luckily, we had a doctor on the team and he diagnosed torn knee ligaments. He gave me some cream to rub on the knee, but to no avail. I even went back to Wexford to a consultant I knew, and he was initially very hopeful that the knee would be okay in time, but alas it was not to be. I put on a heavy knee bandage an hour before the game but couldn't even run properly, let alone think of kicking a ball. I was out of the semi final and it was one of the greatest disappointments I've ever had. To make things worse we lost the game by a single point (1-6 to 0-8), although we had enough chances to win or at least get a draw. To rub salt into the wounds, our opponents were Sean Connolly's, and their vital goal was scored by one of the players who had left our club at the end of the previous year.

There was devastation in the dressing room afterwards, and I took the defeat particularly badly as I reckoned that given my age and the amount of travel involved, it was the last chance I would ever have of following in my grandfather's and uncle's footsteps and winning a senior medal with my native parish. I really felt like giving up completely, but time, as they say is a great healer, and I returned to play a few league games after the knee got better, though I took the precaution of wearing a knee bandage. In one if those games we finally got the better of Connolly's at their venue, but subsequently lost to them by a single point after extra time (3-7 to 1-12), in an All County League Division I Play-Off. As I saw it at the time, it was my last game for the club and it went well for me, scoring three points from play and setting up the goal.

That game was played in late October 1992, and I spent the next four months in the gym doing weights to strengthen my knee. I'd never had a knee injury like that before, and I put it down to my age, and the wear and tear of travelling up and down to Longford all year. I look back on 1992 as my *'Annus Horribilis'!* In many ways I don't know how I survived it, given the huge amount of commitments I had, and the immense pressure I put myself under. As I said earlier I was heavily involved in my school's fund-raising campaign, having linked the school up with Éire Óg GAA Club in Carlow, in their fund raising draw. As secretary of the Development Committee in Glynn-Barnstown in 1990, I had proposed getting involved in the Éire Óg draw as a means of raising money. This was agreed, and the Board of Management of CBS Enniscorthy also took the idea on board in 1992.

By playing in Longford in 1992, I also felt I missed out on an All Ireland Junior Football medal with Wexford, as I would probably have been on the panel at least, having been on the team in '90 and '91. I also played midfield for the team in 1993. Wexford does not win much of note in football, and I would have to say that it is a big disappointment to me not to have been part of that victorious squad that beat Cork in the final at Dungarvan. The late and legendary Wexford District Secretary, Pat Ffrench, who was a selector on that team, also expressed his regret to me personally that I was not involved.

Incidentally I was lucky enough to be at that game and witness the model county lads win a thrilling encounter on a scoreline of 1-9 to 0-11.

The victorious Wexford team and substitutes were as follows: John Cooper, Sean O'Neill, Tom O'Gorman, Mick Caulfield, John Casey (capt.), John Dunne, Padge Courtney, Padge Walsh, Brendan Kavanagh (0-1), Jim Byrne (0-3, 2 frees), Niall Guinan (0-1), Nicky D'Arcy (1-2), Sean Dunne, Michael Furlong (0-1), Garry Byrne (0-1). Subs: Michael D'Arcy for S. Dunne, Mick Mahon for M. D'Arcy, also Paul Merrigan, Eoin O'Gorman, R.J. Blake, Michael Berry, Willie White, M.J. Kehoe, Noel Stafford, Noel Swords, Darragh Kissane.

Cork fielded: John O'Brien, Alan Devoy, Paul Coleman, Marc Farr, Seamus Coughlan, Niall Murphy, Mark O'Connor, Declan Devoy, Ciaran O'Sullivan, Ronan Sheehan (0-1), Ger Manley (0-1), Diarmuid Lynch, Niall O'Connor (capt., 0-2, 1 free), Eoin O'Mahony (0-5, 2 frees), Mick Lewis (0-2). Subs: Greg Cooney for Lynch, Aidan Berry for Sheehan.

Referee: Sean McHale (Mayo).

In January 1993 I made up my mind that I could not risk my knee travelling up and down to Longford for another year. I wanted to give Colmcille more, but realistically I knew it just was not on. If I'd been ten or fifteen years younger it would have been a different story altogether, but the travelling was just too much and I also had a wife and baby to think about. Our second daughter Susie was born later in the year. Eugene McGee did ring in February asking me to commit for another year but my mind was made up. I would be returning to Glynn-Barntown. The players wanted me back as player manager. And so it came to pass.

However, 1993 would also prove to be a very busy year for me, as after three years managing the minor footballers, I moved up to become county under 21 football manager. It was very difficult juggling the two roles for a while, but with our unlucky exit to Meath in the Leinster semi-final I was then able to give my full attention to the club team.

Being a player-manager is a very challenging responsibility. You train the team and yet you have to ensure that you are fit yourself. You devise the tactics and the game plans, and yet when you're in the middle of the action and trying to concentrate on your own game, it can sometimes be difficult to determine whether your game plan or tactics are working or not. If you are not playing well yourself you are loath to give instructions to other players, or make changes and sub-stitutions. I think the whole thing can be a very draining experience, and all the distractions can easily affect your own game.

My first competitive game back in the Glynn-Barntown colours was against Gusserane in the Championship. The New Ross District side have a great football tradition and would be very strong opponents, although we'd had the upper hand on them recently. I felt I had the team prepared well for the encounter and, basically, I prepared myself separately, doing a lot of work on my own. It was very important for me to return with a good performance. We won the game, which was played at Wexford Park on a points scoreline of 0-8 to 0-6, perhaps not in a totally convincing fashion, but it was important to get off to a winning start. *'The People'* in its report of the game stated that: 'Glynn-Barntown dominated the opening half, and should have been out of sight having kicked eight wides, Cormac Jevens and Paul Brazil proving too strong in defence … and they dominated midfield with the returned in form Jim McGovern'.

Despite having an enormous amount of possession we lost our next outing to Kilanerin on a scoreline of 2-7 to 0-9, but bounced back with a fairly flattering 3-6 to 0-7 win over Rathgarogue-Cushinstown. *'The People'* reported: *"it looked as if the Ross District contenders were going to cause an upset when they led by 0-7 to 0-5 entering the last quarter after dominating the play in many sectors. However, Glynn-Barntown never looked back after big Jim McGovern brilliantly put away the first goal after a pinpoint pass from substitute Barry Doyle".*

We had now reached the quarter- finals of the championship and I decided to bring in a coach, as I wanted to concentrate fully on my own game. As usual I entered the club in the Éire Óg Tournament in Carlow where we played Civil Service of Dublin. Coaching the Dublin side was former Derry footballer Philip McElwee. I had first come into contact with Philip when he was coach of Rosmini Gaels in Dublin where my brother Gerry played. He had wonderful success with this team, leading them to a Dublin Junior Championship and winning several other competitions as well. What struck me most about him was his coaching prowess; he could improve players' games immensely, which is really the *'raison d'etre'* of a coach. My own brother Gerry was a case in point. He gives credit to Philip for improving his game to such an extent that he was good enough to play midfield for Longford in the Leinster Championship against Louth in Drogheda in 1986.

Philip's training sessions were really enjoyable with the emphasis very much on ball work. We were drawn to play our district town rivals, Sarsfields, in the quarterfinal and I've no doubt we were very well prepared; well, as prepared as you can be within a dual club scenario. At our last training session, having consulted with Philip and my selectors Paddy Kehoe and Aidan Roche, I gave each player specific written instructions as to his role in the team. I did this for two reasons: firstly because when people are told something verbally they may forget exactly what they were told particularly in the pressure of a match situation, whereas with written information there is a constant reminder at least before the game starts! Secondly, I wanted to be able to focus entirely on my own performance, and not be worrying about how everyone else was playing.

To our great disappointment we lost by 0-14 to 1-10, but it was a game we could have won. I started full forward and set up a goal for James Morrissey which brought us right back into the game, but John Harrington dominated the third quarter for Sars. (as he had done for most of the first half), and things were looking bleak enough. I moved to midfield with fifteen minutes to go and did curb the rampant Harrington. But it wasn't enough, as Sars. got three vital points in the last ten minutes to clinch it. Billy Dodd who was being marked by Eddie Mahon got two of those scores, as unfortunately Eddie was now severely curtailed by a hamstring injury, having held Billy very well up to that point. It's easy to be wise with the benefit of hindsight, but, as many people said to me after the game I should have gone to midfield much earlier or maybe even have started the game there. I suppose I'd hoped to get in for a decisive goal but found Sarsfields goalie Ciaran O'Leary in brilliant form. And so the Wexford town team prevailed and we were out.

We were also out of the senior hurling championship six days later when, having had little time to prepare, and carrying injuries from the football game, we received a hammering from Rapparees from Enniscorthy. This sct me thinking further about the fixtures structure then in place and how it could be improved. It was certainly no help to a serious dual club like ours. I was convinced then that having a hurling season and a football season was the way to go. It would certainly have avoided the situation we faced in 1993.

With an excellent coach in Philip McElwee (probably the best we have ever had), I have no doubt that had we negotiated the Sarsfields hurdle and then being free to concentrate on football, we could very well have gone on to win the championship. As it was Sarsfields went straight to the final where they lost to Kilanerin, but only after a replay. In fact, with John Harrington again dominating at midfield, they owned the ball for long periods, and had only themselves to blame for losing the replay on a scoreline of 1-5 to 1-3.

Our season was not quite over yet as we scored a comfortable victory (1-10 to 0-6), over county champions Kilanerin in the league semi-final in November, only to lose yet again to old nemesis Duffry Rovers in the final.

I felt we'd had a reasonably successful year, and I again took charge in 1994, ditto with the county under 21 football team. It was going to be another very demanding year but we were hoping to build on the success of the previous one. We started our campaign with an excellent 7 points to 6 win over Kilanerin at Bellefield. This win was all the more pleasing given that even our own supporters gave us no chance, and considering that we had got an unmerciful hammering in the U21 championship from the same opposition a week earlier. Australian Rules player David Griffin (who had never played a competitive game of Gaelic football in his life), made an appearance in this game, and his endless running and boundless enthusiasm caused panic and confusion in the Kilanerin ranks. Afterwards everyone was asking *'who was that guy?'* and therein lies a tale.

Given our very depleted panel that year, I was very anxious to pick up any player I could find to strengthen it. It was former club chairman, Bobby Goff, who alerted me to David who was working in Cork at the time. I arranged for David to be picked up from the bus station in Waterford and brought to a challenge game in Marshalstown where we were playing a Bank of Ireland selection from Dublin, and he certainly made a grand entrance! The players were togging out when David arrived and the place erupted in laughter as he dumped his huge rucksack in the middle of the dressing room floor saying: *"G'day mates. I'm David Griffin and I'm here to play for you"*.

That win over the county champions gave us a major boost, and we looked forward to our next game against Taghmon with renewed confidence. I had tried the tactic of a third midfielder against Kilanerin, and it seemed to work very well but, for the match against our neighbours Taghmon I was even more radical, taking out our two corner forwards to midfield, and getting our two wing forwards to drop deep into that area also, when we were attacking, so effectively we were playing with only two forwards – full forward Cormac Jevens and centre forward Ciaran Roche, both intercounty players. The game plan was based around the need to score goals, and the strategy involved our two wing forwards luring their two wing backs into midfield when we were working the ball out of defence, and then hitting sole full forward Cormac Jevens with long accurate balls, who in turn would feed the inrushing Ciaran Roche, who hopefully would goal. Roche was never to be any further out than the forty yard mark and a variation on the plan was to feed him with balls put in front of him, where he could use his blistering pace to good effect. We practised it in training a few times and it worked reasonably well. But could it work in a competitive match?

Beyond our wildest dreams! *'The People'* report on the game contained the following: *"The tactic of playing Cormac Jevens as the sole occupant of the full forward line worked a treat as inter-county player Ciaran Roche availed of the open spaces to race through almost at will and crack home three fine goals"*. Roche scored a total of 3-2, but Jevens was not far behind him on 2-2. The remainder of the scores came from Corkman, Jim Ryan (1-1) and Willy Carley (0-1). We won on a scoreline of 6-6 to 2-7, and a very useful Taghmon-Camross side were absolutely shell shocked and did not know what had hit them. Sure, our points tally was quite low, but then, we were looking for goals! It was a very radical game plan, and one could really only dream of it working. The fact that it worked out so well in reality gave one a tremendous sense of satisfaction.

Of course you could not possibly use the same tactic in every game, as the opposition would eventually come up with measures to counteract it. So, for our next game against Fethard we reverted back to an orthodox game plan. Our hand was forced to a certain extent as we were without four key players: the injured trio of Iain Wickham, Barry Doyle and Jim Ryan, and Cormac Jevens, who was getting married. Our team therefore was badly disrupted, and we were well beaten by a good Fethard team on a scoreline of 14 points to 7.

Up to this point I had not played myself, because I wanted to see how the team would operate without me, and in addition to that Colmcille came calling again, and, out of courtesy, I did give it some consideration before deciding against it. In conjunction with my selectors, Jim Farrell and Tony Furlong, I decided to come on in the second half when we were in serious trouble, but could make no real impact on the game as Fethard were firmly in the driving seat.

We played the sea-siders at the end of May but did not contest our next game against Bunclody until the end of August. We were very depleted again for this game as, for various reasons, we were without Barry Kirwan, Ciaran Roche, Iain Wickham, Jim Ryan, and John Kilgannon. In addition to that the Junior'B' team was going well so we were loath to use any of their players. In the circumstances we put up a very good show with senior debutant Brendan Swan doing very well at centre forward on inter-county player, the highly experienced John Dunne. My most abiding memory of the game however, is of receiving a thumb injury half way through the first half, an injury that grew increasingly more painful as the game wore on. Since this game was not a knockout one, and not wishing to call on any of our Junior Bs, who had reached the District Final, I stayed on to the end. We only lost the game by 9 points to 5 and it subsequently transpired that I had a broken thumb, which was to keep me out of the game for the next six weeks. It meant I missed our next match against St. Anne's, which we lost by 0-10 to 2-2. I was back however for our next assignment, a play off against a team who had beaten us in a previous round, Fethard. We had to win the game to stay in the championship, which we duly did at Grantstown on a scoreline of 2-8 to 1-7.

This result put us into the quarter- finals of the championship, and we were drawn to meet our old bogey team Duffry Rovers. Of all the games we had played Duffry in since 1989, this was certainly one game we could and should have won. In fact it was a match that very much got away from us. Using basically the same tactic as we had used against Taghmon, we created a number of goal chances but on this occasion did not take them. Players totally unmarked in front of the goal should have got the ball but didn't, with one individual going for glory the whole time; in spite of this we led by a point at half time having played against the wind. Our backs were superb and Duffry did not score at all from play in the opening period. Not for the first time, however, Louis Rafter broke our hearts with his brilliant long range free taking. As reporter David Medcalf stated in his report on the game in *'The People'*: *"With Rafter capable of sending over frees from 55 yards into the wind, Duffry were not greatly disadvantaged by the elements"*. With 8 minutes to go the sides were level for the fifth time but Duffry won it in the last 5 minutes with punched points from former Offaly player, Pat Spollen and Jay Codd. So, despite being given little chance before the game we had given the Duffry a major fright; they were very vulnerable in fact, and we missed a great opportunity of beating them. The teams were:

Glynn-Barntown: Shane O'Brien, Dermot Whelan, Eugene Furlong, Paul Brazil, Willy Carley, Barry Kirwan, Conor Wickham, Iain Wickham, Jim McGovern (0-1), Ciaran Roche (0-3 frees), Cormac Jevens (0-2), Barry Doyle, James White (0-1), Shane Carley, James Morrissey (0-1).

Duffry Rovers: Paul Coleman, Martin Fitzhenry, Jay Mernagh, Ger O'Connor, John Casey, Paddy Fitzhenry, Pat O'Leary, Noel Fitzhenry (0-1 free), Louis Rafter (0-6, 5 frees), Damien Fitzhenry, Fran Fitzhenry (0-1), Thomas Kavanagh, Pat Spollen (0-1), Jay Codd (0-1), Matt O'Leary.

The Junior *'B'* football team went on to win the championship that year with a very comfortable win over Fethard in the final. However, we could have done with the services of several players from that team as we had a very small panel ourselves, being further depleted when our Australian Rules player, David Griffin, who had been improving rapidly, picked up an injury and had to return home to Australia. Had we had those players, I've no doubt we would have had a great chance of winning the championship, as, after beating us the Duffry went on to win their eighth title in nine years – an amazing record. After all, a junior *'B'* championship was poor compensation for Glynn-Barntown in 1994 when a senior one was well within our grasp.

I stepped down as player-manager at the end of 1994, as I wanted to try and reduce my commitments somewhat. In fact, I found player management draining me of the energy I needed for playing. There were just too many distractions to be able to focus entirely on getting the best out of myself on the field of play. I could empathise entirely with Sports Psychologist Niamh Fitzpatrick who worked with the Irish athletes at the Athens Olympic Games in 2004, and who performed the same role for Wexford senior hurlers in 1996. In an interview in the *Sunday Tribune* she told reporter Kieran Shannon that: *"She shows athletes a full glass of water. Then she starts tipping some water out. That glass is the athletes' energy. Every time they think of something not related to the task in hand, they're draining out more water, more energy"*. I found myself seriously distracted in 1994, and my game suffered as a result.

The club now decided that it would seek team managers from outside for its senior hurling and football teams and I was instrumental in having John Burke of Gorey whom I worked with at county minor level, appointed as senior football manager, while I also recommended that newly arrived colleague in the CBS, Adrian Walsh of Monageer, get the nod as coach to the senior hurling team and club trainer. Adrian went on to be very successful trainer and coach with us, guiding the club to senior hurling championship finals in '95 and '97 and, of course, as club trainer he would have had a role to play in the club's football success in 1996.

1995 of course marked the introduction of the All County Leagues and Knockout Championships and one had to be very well prepared for the first round, as there was now no second chance. I was made captain for the year but given the contacts I had built up over the years, John Burke asked me to continue to organise challenge and tournament matches outside the county. We were drawn against Duffry Rovers in the first round, and given how close we had run them the previous year, we reckoned, that with the right approach, we could take them on this occasion.

On Sunday 16th of July at Wexford Park we eventually lay the Duffry bogey to rest by winning on a scoreline of 1-8 to 0-7. The match winning goal was scored five minutes into the second half by Seanie Kinsella, (how we could have done with his services the previous year), who was making his senior championship debut. Seanie had an excellent game scoring four points from frees as well. Sadly, our victory was completely overshadowed by the tragic death of our club secretary Eugene Solan, who collapsed and died minutes after the game had concluded. The sudden death of the genial giant, Eugene, cast a black cloud over an historic day for us and truly put football into its proper perspective.

If we were going to win the championship in '95, it would have to be done the hard way, as we were drawn against '93 champions Kilanerin in the quarterfinal. We would also have to do it without our high fielding midfielder Iain Wickham, who had his leg broken in the Duffry game as he went down bravely to block a ball. The quiet man of the team was going to be a huge loss particularly in terms of winning aerial ball possession in the vital midfield area. At almost forty years of age, I just could not hope to do that any more on a regular basis, but I was, I felt, making a useful contribution from the centre forward position.

The match was fixed for Gorey and it was part of a double header, with Starlights and Castletown playing before us. Neither the Enniscorthy side nor ourselves were one bit happy about having to travel to north Wexford, to a venue that was effectively a home one for our respective opponents. Because of the curtain raiser and being cognisant of the fact that Gorey town had a festival on that weekend, which usually lead to severe traffic congestion, we travelled up early and did our warm up at the nearby Garden City grounds. I could see team manager John Burke's thinking on this matter, and I agreed with him entirely. With the Castletown-Starlights game going on we would simply have had no room to do a proper warm up, (which is vital in the modern game), at Páirc Uí Síocháin.

We had a specific game plan for the match, which amounted to the same one we had tried the year before (i.e. taking our two corner forwards out and playing with one full forward). We had tried it out in a challenge game against top Wicklow side, Rathnew, about ten days before the game, and it worked a treat with us scoring three or four well-taken goals, if memory serves me right.

But when our match against Kilanerin began, their corner backs remained firmly in position and would not follow our corner forwards out the field, in fact they easily mopped up a number of balls that were played into the full forward line. Our team management, which also included Willie Carley and Tommy Kirwan, had to quickly change our tactics to a more orthodox formation. It subsequently transpired that the Kilanerin team manager, Gerry Farrell had been present at our game against Rathnew, (he must have been in disguise as none of us recognised him), and took careful note of our tactics. Gerry is a Wicklow man, and obviously found out about our challenge match with Rathnew, and you could say it was naive of us to play up there under the circumstances, but it was a last resort as we simply could not get a quality game anywhere else outside the county that particular weekend. I had spent several hours as was my wont, ringing a host of top clubs in Leinster and Munster, looking for a game, but no club was available to play us bar Rathnew.

In spite of everything we only lost the game by two points (1-9 to 1-7), and it was one we could and should have won as, apart from the massive absence of Iain Wickham we missed a host of scoreable frees, Seanie Kinsella's scoring boots deserting him on this occasion. In fairness to Seanie, he collected footballs from me on an almost daily basis in the lead up to the game in order to practise his free taking, and it was a pity it did not pay off for him on the day.

There was certain criticism of the warm up we did before the game, some citing it as a factor in our defeat as it was supposed to have tired us out, but that was far wide of the mark, as we finished much the stronger team and, had the game lasted five minutes longer, we could well have been triumphant. Kilanerin went on to win the championship and once again we could only ponder on what might have been. Would we ever get to the Holy Grail? Would the hard work ever pay off? We had been there or thereabouts in '93, '94 and '95, could we finally do it in '96? Time would tell.

Glynn-Barntown has a long and proud tradition of hurling dating back long before the foundation of the GAA itself. This is clearly evident from a poem describing a hurling match, written by Robert Devereux of Carrigmannon in 1779. An excerpt from this marathon poem runs as follows:

"Mind how they struggle, see them how they stride,
Till from the crowd one slily takes the ball,
And on a well-poised hurl prevents its fall,

And tips it often as he scours the plain,
While his antagonists pursue in vain,
Till quite at liberty, this happy soul
Drives it directly o'er the adverse goal."

It is also a little known fact that the great Nicky Rackard won his first championship medal with the Glynn minors in 1939. The reason for this was that, in those days, rural parishes could field isolated players.

In 1995 the club reached its first ever senior hurling championship final only to lose to Oulart-The Ballagh on a 2-15 to 2-9 scoreline. New coach Adrian Walsh had made an immediate impression and was unlucky in that key players were suffering from injuries in the lead up to the final which disrupted preparations. Of course we also had to plan without Iain Wickham and, while obviously much more noted as a footballer, he could also be a very effective hurler; his overhead pulling on the ball being a particular feature of his game and something that would have come in handy against Oulart! Defeat was a big disappointment for our lads but in general it was a very young team so the future looked bright. In their historic first senior final Glynn-Barntown lined out as follows: James Morrissey, Cormac Jevens, Michael Laffan, Darragh Byrne, William Carley, Shane Carley, Barry Kirwan, Tommy Kehoe (0-7, 6 frees, 1 '65), Gavin Ryan, Ciaran Roche, Eugene Furlong (0-1), P.J. Carley (0-1), John Barron (capt.) Shane Stafford (1-0) Garry Laffan (1-0). Subs: Paul Laffan for Byrne, inj.; Anthony Whelan for Ryan.

Footnote: While 1995 was a sad year for the club in that we lost our esteemed secretary Eugene Solan RIP, it was also tinged with deep sadness for us as a family with the death of my wife's godmother, Margaret Hamilton RIP. Mrs. Hamilton's husband Andy who passed away in 1983 had been prominent in the club for many years and in fact helped to revive it in 1930 along with Micheál Kehoe (later to become president of the GAA) and Dick Wadding. The club actually won it's first ever county title (the county junior hurling championship) in that year and won the intermediate title the following year.

1996 will never be forgotten by Wexford people and rightly so. It lifted the self esteem of the entire county, and I have fond memories of bringing my two girls, Claire and Susan, to Wexford and New Ross to see the victorious Wexford team parade the McCarthy Cup. It was a really memorable time and it brought great joy to Wexford people and even the blow ins were thrilled!

I will remember that year for other reasons too, not least of which was the birth of our third daughter Eimear. I did not play in Wexford in 1996 returning to play yet again for Colmcille in Longford. But it was very different from 1992; this time I made it clear to Colmcille manager Matt Murtagh that I would act only as a substitute, and that it could not conflict with my duties as a recently appointed Wexford senior football selector. I also made it clear to Matt that I would not be available for every game. I know it seemed like a mad thing to do at the time, but I did feel I owed Matt Murtagh a favour as in 1994 he had convinced me that Colmcille had a great chance of winning the Longford Senior Football Championship (they got to the final), and I had even gone so far as to sign a transfer form so long as it did not conflict with my duties as Glynn-Barntown senior football manager. If you recall, I did not play in Glynn-Barntown's first two championship games that year, and, apart from seeing how the team would operate without me, the Colmcille factor was another reason. However, the uncertainty over my position was causing unease in the club and, also taking into account our depleted squad due to the Junior 'B' situation, I decided to withdraw the transfer much to the great disappointment of the Colmcille manager; so I really felt I should give him some form of commitment in1996 before he stepped down as manager. I was realistic enough to know that at forty years of age I was probably well beyond my best, but if I could make any form of contribution, even as a substitute, I would be happy to do so and Matt himself seemed to be O.K. with that. You may wonder what drives people to do things like that, but doesn't the savage love his native shore? And in my case it was particularly apt as Lough Gowna's lovely shores are only about half a mile from my home.

Inevitably, I missed some games due to my involvement with the Wexford senior team, but drove up when I was available, acting as substitute. By the summer, however, and with Wexford's sad exit from the championship, I was suddenly a free agent, well not totally free in that I still had an obligation to attend club matches in Wexford to spot talent, which I did quite religiously. However, as the summer began to unfold I found myself making my place at full forward on the Collmcille team. I was supervising Leaving Cert. Exams in Dublin and travelling down to Longford with fellow Colmcille players based in Dublin, for training. Things were going well and I was looking forward to the first round of the championship against Kenagh, the club of GAA Director General, Liam Mulvihill.

And then disaster was yet again visited upon me; I was struck down by a severe virus about nine days before our opening championship game. It necessitated a six-day stay in Wexford General Hospital, and for five of those days I was on a drip and feeling distinctly unwell. Slowly but surely however, I regained my strength and got out of hospital on the Thursday evening before the Sunday we played Kenagh in the championship. I was getting better all the time but still hadn't regained my full strength. In spite of my wife's protestations, I decided to drive up to see Colmcille in action. As I drove out the gate, purely as an afterthought, I stopped the car, jumped out and headed back into the house to get my gear. My wife of course thought I was stark mad, and couldn't see how I could even think of playing in such a weakened state. Just in case they're stuck, I'll bring my gear anyway, I told her.

I arrived at Pearse Park 145 miles later and the Colmcille team management asked me to consider togging out, which I eventually agreed to do, though hoping I wouldn't be needed. But with about 17 minutes to go we were a few points down and playing badly. I was called into the fray, and I think I did okay. The Longford Leader reported that I turned things around in helping Colmcille to fight back for a draw, and that gave my self esteem and confidence an enormous boost. Unfortunately, even though I prepared meticulously for the replay, and was picked at full forward, things just did not work out, and I didn't come out for the second half. We won the game however and advanced to meet Rathcline in the quarter- final.

It was on the same day as the Leinster Senior Hurling Final. I came on with about fifteen minutes to go, got a point almost immediately and felt I had made a difference, but it was too little too late, and we lost by a couple of points.

In the dressing rooms afterwards when I enquired how Wexford were doing, I was told they were ahead but that it was a real ding-dong battle. I made a fast track for my sister Dolores' house just outside Longford town, and was just in time to see Tom Dempsey's goal and the almost immediate reply from Michael Duignan. I stayed standing as I just could not sit down, wondering if Offaly were going to thwart my adopted county yet again, but no, things were different this time, Liam Griffin had imbued the team with tremendous self-belief and will to win. They were not going to be caught this time and they outscored the Faithful County by 0-7 to 0-2 in the final ten minutes, to record a spellbinding victory. I was absolutely delighted; not just for the county but for the many players on the panel that I had got to know well through their involvement with the Wexford minor and under 21 football teams, and of course I had played county football with George O'Connor and Billy Byrne. For those two men in particular it was success at last after so many heartbreaks, and I was so pleased for them.

But what of Glynn-Barntown in 1996? Having reached the senior hurling final in '95 there was apparently a big emphasis on the small ball the following year, and it was only after the narrow defeat of the hurlers by Oulart -The Ballagh in the quarter-final, that any real attention was paid to football. Of course all games were put on hold until the All Ireland was over, and the Championships took on the form of a blitz (i.e. a match every weekend), with the football final not being played until November. Glynn-Barntown finally won the championship in '96, beating Bunclody and Fethard on the way to the decider, where they got the better of county champions Kilanerin, winning by 2-3 to 0-7. I was with the Wexford team in Galway that day for a National League game but returned as fast as I could after the game to congratulate all concerned on their great achievement. Although not in the club, I had at their request organised two challenge games in the lead up to the final, one against Éire Óg in Carlow, and another against the Wexford Under 21 team. Naturally, I was delighted the lads had emerged victorious at long last having come so close to winning in previous years, and obviously I was terribly disappointed not to have been part of it, but such is life!

But again, it's an ill wind that blows no good as in 1996 I was forty years of age and so eligible to play with the Longford Masters football team. We got to an All Ireland semi final where we lost to local rivals Cavan after extra time, but we went on to win the Shield final beating Dublin. I went mad that day, scoring six points from play. We were later presented with genuine All Ireland medals for that achievement.

I returned to play with Glynn-Barntown in 1997, but we were knocked out in the first round of the championship by district rivals Sarsfields. We had much better luck in the hurling, reaching our second senior final in three years where we had again to give best to Oulart-The Ballagh on a 2-11 to 0-14 scoreline. However, the game was in the balance right up to the end; in fact with two minutes to go there was only two points in it (1-11 to 0-12) but then Oulart got a goal direct from a mis-hit free, a free that should never have been allowed in the first place, as it appeared to me that Anthony Whelan had perfectly timed his shoulder on Martin Storey as he galloped through the middle. *'People'* reporter Alan Aherne writing on the game seemed to concur with my, and many other people's sentiments when he wrote: *"From my vantage point it looked like an extremely harsh decision"*.

The Glynn-Barntown team was: Paul Carley, Donie Doyle, Eugene Furlong, Darragh Byrne, Willie Carley, Shane Carley, Eamonn Moore, Tommy Kehoe (capt., 0-6, 5 frees), Barry Kirwan (0-1), P.J. Carley (0-3), Iain Wickham, Anthony Whelan (0-1), Ciaran Roche (0-2), Gavin Ryan (0-1), Cormac Jevens. **Subs:** Francis Morrissey for Byrne, inj., John Barron for Jevens, also Paul Roche, Emmet Whelan, Garry Laffan, Eunan Doyle, John Doyle, John McCormack, John Colloton, Mark Carley, Tony Butler, Mick Lanigan.

Also in 1997 in the absence of any Wexford Masters team, I was persuaded to return and play a few games with the Longford Masters. We again got to an All Ireland semi final, where this time we were beaten by Monaghan, Nudie Hughes and all! Longford eventually won the competition a few years later with the help of a few players from Westmeath, but 1997 was my last year with the team. However, I do wish Wexford County Board would get a Masters team going again, as I find it tough going, running after eighteen and nineteen year olds in the All County Leagues! After all the GAA has, in my opinion, a responsibility to facilitate and encourage its older players to maintain and use the fitness levels built up in years of service to the association, especially as it still needs these people to participate in passing on their expertise to the next generation of players. So many people feel the need to turn to other sports e.g. golf, to continue in sport and this is a major drain of human resources from the GAA.

Since then I have continued to play with Glynn-Barntown at senior and more recently junior level. I managed the senior team in 2000 and the senior and junior teams in 2002. We got to the semi final in the Millennium year after beating traditional powers Gusserane and Kilanerin, the latter a thrilling 1-9 to 1-7 victory at Monamolin, which is memorable for a brilliantly decisive goal scored by sixteen year old substitute Derek Leonard. We lost to St. Anne's in the semi final when the concession of some needless frees, and non-adherence to the game plan allowed the opposition to score a vital goal a few minutes before half time to give them a 7-point lead. It was a crucial score and we never recovered from it. Of course, St. Anne's beat us in the hurling that year too as they went on to win a marvellous double.

We had a remarkable situation in 2004 when our two junior 'B' football teams met in the District Championship semi final at Killurin. It drew a very big crowd with the first team beating the second team by 0-11 to 1-3. I played with the second team, and but for the fact that we were missing three first choice forwards in Jim Sutton, Aidan Denton and Barry Doyle we could well have caused a surprise. Our first team went on to contest the county final where they lost to Bannow-Ballymitty after a replay. However, they were limited in their choice of players, as they had to name twenty-four players at the start of the championship. Contrast that with Bannow-Ballymitty who were permitted to use players who had played in a senior relegation tie only weeks earlier. We were not allowed to call on any of our players from the second junior 'B' team after the latter's exit from the championship; had that been possible I'm sure it would have made all the difference, particularly as the final went to extra time and we were down to seventeen or eighteen fit players.

I never thought I'd see the day when I would have to give up playing football, but I know that day is coming fast and I'm resisting it with all my might! I suppose I am, in the words of the poet Dylan Thomas, *'raging, raging against the dying of the light'!*

Chapter 4

Gaelic Games in CBS Enniscorthy

There has been a long and proud tradition of Gaelic games in CBS Enniscorthy both at primary, (now amalgamated with St. Aidan's) and secondary level. This may very well date back to 1864, when the founder of the GAA, Michael Cusack, taught at the old model school. A plaque to commemorate this was unveiled at the present CBS Secondary School, by then GAA President Paddy Buggy during the Centenary celebrations of the GAA in 1984.

Although we won several U14 and U16 Leinster Hurling 'B' Championships in the '80's and early '90's,I want to focus on the period 1995 to 2000 inclusive, which was a particularly fruitful one for the school, culminating in an historic All Ireland Senior Hurling 'B' title in 1999, and an equally historic Leinster U16 'A' Hurling title in 2000, beating famed St. Kieran's College, Kilkenny along the way.

When we won the Leinster Colleges Senior Football 'B' title for the first time in March 1995, it was a wonderful feeling to have achieved something at long last, and special also as we would be generally seen as being a hurling school, given that we draw mainly from hurling areas. It was a long, hard campaign which involved seven matches, starting with a victory against F.C.J., Bunclody, in Bunclody and culminating in a thrilling triumph against St. Joseph's De La Salle, Kildare in the Leinster Final at Dr. Cullen Park, Carlow.

There were some memorable games along the way, and one that stands out in particular was a victory against Lucan Community School, at the Lucan Sarsfields GAA grounds In Dublin, on a scoreline of 2-5 to 0-8. It was a thrilling game from start to finish and we had to dig very deep to forge a famous victory. One special memory from the game was the truly outstanding goalkeeping of Shamrocks John

O'Connor. A specific incident I will never forget came just before half time when we were leading 2-2 to 0-3. The referee awarded a dubious penalty to Lucan just after our goalkeeper had made a brilliant save, securing in the process a nasty cut under the eye. After medical treatment the Shamrocks man took his place in the goal and proceeded to bring off a magnificent save from the ensuing penalty. This was undoubtedly the game's turning point and really inspired the team, and even though Lucan put us under some sustained pressure in the second half, we held out to secure a memorable victory.

That win put us into a Leinster quarter final against a school from my own county, Moyne Community School. The latter is located in north Longford on the border with Cavan, and their panel contained some players from that county, and also players from my own native parish, Colmcille. My abiding memory from this game is that we were out on the field at Portarlington, ready to play at the appointed time, a considerable length of time before the Longford school even arrived at the venue! We were informed that we were well within our rights to claim the game, but much preferred to win it on the field of play which we did deservedly by a one point margin (2-7 to 1-9).

That victory put us into a Provincial semi final where we met St. Joseph's CBS from Drogheda, a team that contained a mixture of Meath and Louth players. As a reward for reaching this stage of the competition and to strengthen the self-belief and confidence of the players, I worked really hard to ensure that the team would have new jerseys, togs and socks for the match. I succeeded and the general feeling was that the team looked resplendent in their new gear. The game was played at Ashford in Co. Wicklow, and we began our preparations by stopping off at the Arklow Bay Hotel where we had tea and sandwiches, followed by a team meeting. We also togged out there so that we would be 'raring to go' when we got to the venue. And we did start the game in devastating fashion, being 2-5 to 0-2 up after about twenty minutes. Then a remarkable thing happened: there was an absolute downpour of hailstones, the referee stopped the game and we all retired to the dressing rooms. The game resumed after several minutes, and I was worried that the whole episode had broken our momentum, but thankfully that was not the case, and we went in at half time leading by 2-8 to 0-3, having played with a strong wind. We eventually ended up winning by 3-9 to 0-11.

We were now through to the Leinster Final, where our opponents would be St. Josephs De La Salle of Kildare, a school that had been beaten in the previous year's final, but who were reputed to have up to nine of that year's team and were hell bent on taking the title on this occasion. I had driven to Athy to see their semi final against Knockbeg of Carlow and was certainly impressed by them, although I did consider them beatable. Subsequently, I heard that the game had been videoed by Knockbeg, and with their kind permission I drove to their school to collect the video. Along with fellow trainer, Brendan O' Sullivan, a considerable amount of time was spent studying it, noting the Kildare dangermen and laying plans accordingly.

'*Mary's Courage Duly Rewarded*' ran the headline in the now defunct Irish Press, the day after the final. And under the headline was the scoreline: St. Mary's CBS, Enniscorthy 0-10; St. Joseph's De La Salle, Kildare 1-6. It went on to state that: "*St. Mary's CBS showed great courage and commitment to lift the Coca Cola Leinster Colleges SFC 'B' title for the first time, at Dr. Cullen Park, Carlow, yesterday. Mary's conceded a second minute goal, and their half time advantage of 0-7 to 1-2 looked entirely inadequate. However, the Wexford side hit a high gear, made light of the elements, and outplayed Kildare for the remainder of the game*".

It was a truly historic and unforgettable victory, made all the more memorable by the fact that it was won against the odds. As the newspaper report said, we were rocked back on our heels by a St. Joseph's goal after just two minutes. Given that we were playing with a very strong wind such a score appeared to be a serious setback. But our lads fought back bravely, and were level by the 9th minute. We went in at half time leading by 0-7 to 1-2, but such a lead seemed totally inadequate given that we had to face the elements. This was further reinforced when the Kildare school shot two quick points to level the game shortly after the resumption. The writing was now really on the wall for our lads, but they responded magnificently, roared on by their great drum beating band of supporters, and showing in the process, that the spirit of '98 was still very much alive and well in Enniscorthy. The lads in the green and gold jerseys really took the game to the navy clad Kildare representatives, and with 9 minutes to go had raced into a three point lead with scores from Davidstown's Anton Stafford (2 frees), and a classy point from play from Oylegate substitute Neil Garry. We could have put the game completely out of reach at this stage, but over anxiousness in front of goal cost us some scores. The Kildare side came at us with a vengeance in the last five minutes, but our defence held out clearing their lines in magnificent style, and limiting their opponents to just two further points. The referee played almost four minutes of injury time and I thought he would never blow his whistle, but when he did, it was joy unconfined. The Dr. Stuart Cup was presented to captain Johnny Murphy from Crossabeg-Ballymurn amid scenes of wild jubilation; we had waited so long for this, and it was really a moment to savour. For Corkman, Brendan O'Sullivan, who trained the team with me, it was a great start to his career as a teacher in the CBS, but for everyone associated with the school it was a very special moment indeed.

The teams lined out as follows:

CBS: John O'Connor (Shamrocks), Paul Whelan (Shamrocks), John Millar (Shamrocks), Thomas Byrne (Ballyhogue), Conor O'Neill, (Shamrocks), George Jacob (Shamrocks), Seamus Doran, (Davidstown-Courtnacuddy), Anton Stafford (Davidstown-Courtnacuddy - 0-4, 2 frees, 1 line ball), Jack Bolger (Marshalstown), Jason O'Brien (Davidstown-Courtnacuddy 0-3), Adrian Maher, (Shamrocks) Laurence Kehoe, (Davidstown-Courtnacuddy) Michael Walsh (Starlights 0-1), Johnny Murphy (Crossabeg-Ballymurn Capt.), Daithi O'Brien (Starlights 0-1)

Subs: Damien McGrath (Shamrocks) for Laurence Kehoe, Neil Garry (Oylegate-Glenbrien 0-1) for Adrian Maher. Also, Cyril Delaney (Davidstown-Courtnacuddy), Padraig Doyle (Starlights), Michael Franklin (Starlights), Michael Hall (Starlights), Eric Flynn (Starlights), Colm McGee (Shamrocks), Michael Donnelly (Shamrocks), Wesley O'Connor (Shamrocks), Liam O'Brien (Shamrocks), Colm Moriarty (Ballyhogue), Peadar Leacy (Monageer-Boolavogue)

St Joseph's: David Houlihan, Mark McLoughlin, John Dempsey, Keith Doyle, Tom Behan, Eoin Byrne, Eoin Hipwell, Patrick Behan, Barry Quinn, Aidan Leonard (0-2), Liam Ryan (0-1), Peter McLoughlin, Bernard Behan (1-0), Robert O'Neill (0-3), Aidan Conlon,

Subs: Jason Delaney for Peter McLoughlin, John Morrissey for Aidan Conlon.

I had been very single minded in pursuit of success in that school year of 94/95, and was very driven; no doubt not getting the county under-21 football job had a lot to do with it (please see next chapter). I probably stepped on some toes as well but then that's almost inevitable when you have an utterly single minded pursuit of success. I went out and sought sponsorship for the school teams that year, and managed to raise over £3,400, a considerable sum at the time, and I would like to put on record my deep appreciation to those sponsors, in particular David and Niall Wall, Murphy Floods Hotel, Jim Byrne, The Bookshop, and Garry McCauley, Sport and Style, who made the team look so resplendent by sponsoring jerseys, togs and socks respectively. Michael Doyle, Duffry Stores, and Sam McCauley, Chemist, also contributed very generously to team expenses. Thanks also to the Arklow Bay Hotel for meal vouchers.

Inspired no doubt by this thrilling success, the hurlers, containing seven members of the victorious football team, went on to claim the Leinster Colleges Senior Hurling 'B' title (our first Leinster Senior Hurling title in over 30 years), with a 1-10 to 1-7 success over Cistercian College, Roscrea at Dr. Cullen Park, thus completing a magnificent double success for the school.

The victorious team was: Michael Hall (Rapparees), Brian Shiggins (Crossabeg-Ballymurn), Eric Flynn (Rapparees), James Walsh (Oylegate-Glenbrien), Enda Cahill (Rathnure), George Jacob (Shamrocks 0-2, 1 65) Seamus Doran (Davidstown-Courtnacuddy Capt.) Jack Bolger (Marshalstown), Kenneth Farrell (Shamrocks 0-1) Trevor Hogan (Rathnure), Conor O'Neill (Shamrocks), Johnny Murphy (Crossabeg-Ballymurn 0-3), Wesley O'Connor (Shamrocks 1-0) Anton Stafford (Davidstown-Courtnacuddy 0-1) Michael Walsh (Rapparees 0-3)

Sub: Peter Daly (Monageer-Boolavogue), for Hogan

They played Doon CBS from Limerick, in the All Ireland semi final, and this was a proud moment for Limerick man, Donal O'Brien, team mentor (along with Michael Carty and Adrian Walsh), and Chairman of the School's Sports Committee. Donal, you see, who had put a great amount into hurling since his arrival at the school in 1982, (the same year as myself), was a past pupil of Doon CBS! However his local knowledge was all to no avail, as his alma mater proved too good for us on the day, on a scoreline of 3-8 to 1-5. Well-known Tipperary hurler, Eugene O'Neill, was very influential for the Limerick school, scoring two goals in the last five minutes to clinch victory.

But, back to the football. We were drawn to meet Dingle CBS in the All Ireland semi final, a school right in the heart of Kerry footballing tradition, an awesome task indeed. Our preparations for the game were far from ideal, given that many of the players had to switch codes to concentrate on winning a Leinster Hurling title. On the day (the match was played in Fermoy), we were simply no match for the Kerry school, who were powered from midfield by 2004 Footballer of the Year, Tomas Ó Sé. We ended up losing heavily even though we only trailed by three points at half time. Nevertheless, we had a great year pulling off a wonderful double in hurling and football, and what made it extra special for me was the fact that I also coached Emmet Moorehouse to win the All Ireland Individual Debating title in April of that year, the final taking place at Trinity College.

For the school year 1995-96 we decided to compete at 'A' level in senior football. There were a number of reasons for this. Primary among them was the belief that if the players could only hold their own at that level, they would learn an awful lot more than from playing at the lower level. They, and the clubs they came from, would gain more in the long term. Once they could hold their own, being exposed to a higher level of competition could only do them good, and would mean an awful lot more to them than continually winning 'B' competitions. Even though we had lost a lot of the players from the previous year, we still put a useful team together and on our inaugural entrance to the South Leinster Senior Football 'A' League we did really well, beating St. Peter's College and Naas CBS, and drawing with Ballyfin College.

So hopes were high as we approached the championship. We made our debut in the senior 'A' championship against St. Saran's of Ferbane, a place made famous by the great Tony McTague, and a school right in the heartland of Offaly football. Our debut in the competition was marked by a gift: a set of shorts presented by Wexford Farmers Co-op.

Even though we had home venue, we would certainly not have been favourites going into the game but put up an excellent performance before losing narrowly after extra time on a scoreline of 1-12 to 0-13.

Centre forward Jason O'Brien turned in a five star performance scoring eleven points in all, eight from frees. I had high hopes of Jason eventually making the grade at senior inter county level but his career to date has been blighted by a persistent back problem.

The CBS team on that historic late January day in 1996 was as follows: John O' Connor (Shamrocks), Barry Whelan (Shamrocks), James Walsh (Oylegate-Glenbrien), Brian Shiggins (Oylegate-Glenbrien), Colm Moriarty (Ballyhogue), Thomas Byrne (Ballyhogue), Colm McGee (Shamrocks), John Millar (Shamrocks), Padraig Doyle (Starlights 0-1), Joseph O'Connor (Starlights), Jason O'Brien (Davidstown-Courtnacuddy 0-11, 8 frees), Neil Garry (Oylegate-Glenbrien), Michael Donnelly (Shamrocks 0-1), Jim Carberry (Ballyhogue), Mark Quigley (Starlights)

Subs: Laurence Kehoe (Davidstown-Courtnacuddy) for McGee, Brian Howe (Shamrocks) for John O'Connor, Mick Jacob (Oulart-The Ballagh) for Donnelly. **Extra time:** Barry Millar (Monageer-Boolavogue) for Shiggins, John Hudson (Starlights) for Carberry, Noel Winters (Monageeer-Boolavogue) for Garry

Sadly, we were without the services of last years inspirational captain, Johnny Murphy, who missed the game due to illness. Kenneth Farrell of Shamrocks was another notable absentee due to injury.

However, it's an ill wind that blows no good, and our exit from the football championship meant that we could now put all our energies into the hurling. A young team, expertly coached by Adrian Walsh, and assisted by mentor Eddie Nangle, brought the school to its first ever All Ireland senior final, only to suffer defeat to a strong, forceful but quite accomplished hurling school, namely De La Salle from Hospital in Co. Limerick. We had beaten FCJ Bunclody, Gorey Community School, Cistercian Roscrea, Castlecomer Community School, Portlaoise CBS and St. Mac Nissi's, Cushendall, Co. Antrim, en route to the final. Our only previous experience of an All Ireland final was at under 16 level in 1988, when a team that included Wexford senior star Adrian Fenlon, lost to Presentation, Athenry, in St. Brendan's Park, Birr.

In this, our latest final, played at Carrick-on Suir, (not a very suitable venue) in late April 1996, we suffered the misfortune of losing a man ten minutes before half time, when Kenneth Farrell was dismissed for a second bookable offence. A harsh enough decision in the circumstances, it made our task a mountainous one, especially when we went in at half time two points in arrears, having played with a strong wind. And so it proved in the second period, with De La Salle using the wind and the extra man to maximum effect, to run out easy winners in the end, by 1-13 to 0-4. But, it would have to be said that our lads never gave up, and battled what was essentially a lost cause, to the very end.

We lined out as follows: Trevor Kelly (Monageer-Boolavogue), Brian Shiggins (Oylegate-Glenbrien), James Walsh (Oylegate-Glenbrien), John O'Loughlin (Monageer-Boolavogue), Barry Millar, (Monageer-Boolavogue), Peter Daly (Monageer-Boolavogue 0-1), Peadar Leacy (Monageer-Boolavogue), Laurence Kehoe (Davidstown-Courtnacuddy), Jason O'Brien (Davidstown-Courtnacuddy), Noel Winters (Monageeer-Boolavogue), Kenneth Farrell (Shamrocks), John Millar (Shamrocks), Mick Jacob (Oulart-The Ballagh), Richie Murphy (Crossabeg-Ballymurn) (0-2), Trevor Hogan (Rathnure 0-1)

Subs: Jim Jacob (Shamrocks) for O'Brien, Tony Boland (Rapparees), Colm McGee (Shamrocks), Pat Bolger (Marshalstown), James Buckley (Rapparees), Michael Donnelly (Shamrocks), Sean Kehoe (Davidstown-Courtnacuddy)

Footnote: I made my debut as a hurling reporter that day when I was asked by South East Radio to report on the game!

Of course 1996 was a wonderful year for Wexford hurling, and the school was delighted to have had a number of past pupils on the panel of players that brought the Liam McCarthy Cup back to the county. On the team itself was captain, Martin Storey and Adrian Fenlon, while in the substitutes were Declan Ruth, Sean Flood and Michael Jordan. Sean was ruled out of the final through injury. The lads came around to all the classes with the Cup, and their achievement was a great source of pride to everyone in the school, but especially to those teachers who would have coached the lads on school teams over the years.

The '96/'97 school year dawned with a determination on my part that we would maintain our status in the 'A' football championship, and go one better than the previous year and win our very first match in that grade. It was a realistic goal and even though we had lost a lot of very good players from the previous year's team, I did not think it was beyond us. We continued to compete in the South Leinster Colleges 'A' Football League, and had a very good campaign, culminating in an excellent semi final victory over highly rated Patrician College, Newbridge, at Grange, Co. Carlow, (1-12 to 0-7), and a merited draw with reigning Leinster champions Good Counsel, (at their venue) in the league final (Good Counsel 1-9, Enniscorthy 2-6).

So it all augured well for the championship, where we were drawn against a traditional stronghold of the game, St. Joseph's, Fairview of Dublin. This school had produced many outstanding Dublin footballers down through the years, and even though they would not have been as strong as previously, it was still a daunting task for us, particularly as we had to travel to play them in their own backyard, (St. Vincent's GAA Grounds in Marino).

On Friday 24th of January 1997 we made our own little bit of history when we defeated the Dublin school by a one point margin, (0-7 to 1-3), to register our first ever victory in the Leinster Colleges 'A' Football Championship. St. Joseph's got a goal in the closing stages and we then had to survive some anxious moments before emerging victorious. Perhaps the significance of the occasion lay a little too heavily on our lads, as we should have been out of sight long before the opposition scored their goal, having missed a host of easy scoring chances. Nevertheless, we got through and that was the all-important thing.

The history making team lined out as follows: John O' Connor (Shamrocks), James Doyle (Starlights), Peadar Leacy, (Monageer-Boolavogue), Tom Wall (Starlights), Colin Ruth (Shamrocks), Thomas Byrne (Ballyhogue 0-1), Sean Crotty (Starlights), Padraig Doyle (Starlights 0-5 frees), Laurence Kehoe (Davidstown-Courtnacuddy), Mark Quigley (Starlights 0-1), Joseph O'Connor (Starlights) Mick Jacob (Oulart-The Ballagh), James Buckley (Starlights), Jim Jacob (Shamrocks), Sean Kenny (Davidstown-Courtnacuddy)

Subs: Michael Kehoe, (Marshalstown), for Quigley, Alan Lyons (Starlights) for J. Jacob, David Kelly (Oylegate-Glenbrien), for Kenny.
We were now through to the quarterfinals of the Leinster

Championship, and who were our opponents to be? Who else but my old alma mater, St. Mel's College, Longford! As I stated at the outset, I was a student in that hallowed academy from 1968 to 1973 and football was an absolute religion then; in fact if you didn't play ball you had a pretty miserable existence, especially if you were a boarder, which I was. We had three pitches at the College, namely Prep field which first years and second years played on, Junior field where third years and some fifth years exhibited their skills, and Senior Field where those who made the senior panel, plied their trade. I suppose the ambition of any serious Gaelic footballer at the college was to get to Senior field and make the senior team. But you had a hard apprenticeship before you reached that point. Prep field during the winter was in very poor condition, and often waterlogged, but we still had to play on it several days a week, and if you were unlucky enough to fall into one of the many pools of water, you were in big trouble, as in those days you generally had the same set of gear until your mother washed it at the weekend. So, if you did have a mishap, you would have to put on stinking wet gear for your next training session or match, and naturally enough your boots would be completely sodden. It was a harsh regime but one just about survived to tell the tale!

I started off well in St. Mel's myself, by making the first year team at corner forward, and I can well recall us playing and losing narrowly to St. Finian's College, Mullingar at their venue. However, I did not go on to make the senior team, and therein lies a tale! As I said earlier, it was everyone's ambition to play on senior field as that meant that you had a chance of making the senior team. If you cried off a match or training on the hallowed surface you had to get someone to replace you. I should emphasise that this was a very rare occurrence, and would seldom be tolerated. I think I was in third year when my opportunity came. A fellow called Gerry Farrell had to cry off and he asked me to replace him. Of course, I immediately jumped at the chance. However, I had a slight difficulty as I had only just given a loan of my gear to a lad from my own year, Stephen Smyth (who had also been called up to senior field), and was reluctant to ask for it back as he was using it at that stage. No greater love can a man have than giving up his gear for his friend!

I was determined to get gear from somebody else and scoured the school looking for same, but to my utter disbelief and even despair I couldn't get any, as anybody I asked seemed to be involved in some activity or other. I was totally forlorn at the turn of events, and felt I'd missed a great chance to impress. The situation was made worse for me when the priest in charge of senior field, the senior team trainer, informed me later in front of a number of other students, that there would be a *'blue moon'* before I ever got another chance, or words to that effect. I was actually afraid to approach him to tell him I couldn't play, because I couldn't find any gear. I don't think he had any idea of the lengths I had gone to, to try and appear on senior field that day. Well, he knows now! In fact I never did get another opportunity, to make the senior team in Mel's and I felt that incident had a lot to do with it.

But I digress; our quarterfinal was fixed for Mountmellick in Laois, and Brendan O'Sullivan and myself were under no illusions about the massive task facing us. We were about to take on the kingpins of Leinster Colleges football, a school that had won twenty-nine Leinster senior titles up to that point. They had the pick of several counties with future senior stars like Westmeath's Dessie Dolan, and Roscommon's Stephen Lohan in their ranks. By contrast, we would have been seen as primarily a hurling school with a limited pick of players.

And yet for close on forty minutes we had them genuinely worried. It was 1-7 to 1-3 at half time in Mel's favour. It should have been closer but we had had missed a penalty half way through the first half. We reduced the deficit to three points two minutes after the resumption. Two minutes later we inexplicably missed an easy twenty one yards free, to reduce the margin still further, and I felt this had a detrimental effect on the team, especially when Mel's added two quick points to leave five points between the sides, (1-9 to 1-4). And then all hell broke loose! I will let Alan Aherne, reporting on the game for the *Wexford People,* describe what happened next: *"...the game exploded with fifteen minutes left when up to twenty players got involved in an unseemly row which was quickly brought under control. The disagreement arose when Enniscorthy CBS forward, Sean Kenny, was forcibly 'blocked' by his marker, Tomas O' Rourke, as he made an attempt to move in and tackle another St. Mel's player who was in possession ... Enniscorthy CBS were trailing 1-9 to 1-4 at the time of the row, and they fell apart completely when play resumed. The Slaneysiders lost their shape all over the field, and Mel's capitalised to the full, by adding 1-4 without reply before the final whistle".*

Now I can vouch for Alan's account of the row, as I was standing on the sideline straight in front of the incident as it happened. I did not like what I saw and, while I have always found third man tackling to be irritating in the extreme, our player should not have retaliated in spite of the provocation. I can categorically state that none of our players were instructed to act in an unsporting fashion, either before the game or at half time, and I would have to say with the utmost sincerity that it (the row) was the very last thing I wanted to see happen, particularly against my old school. In fact, I was acutely embarrassed by the whole thing, almost wanting the ground to open up and swallow me. When some of our subs, who were directly behind me, tried to get involved, I ordered them back into the dugout immediately.

The report in the Wexford People was the most balanced I read, with some reports in other newspapers very one sided and unfair. Under no circumstances will I defend rough or dirty play, though I would point out that some of our players subsequently told me that they found some of the St. Mel's players to be a bit cocky, though I suppose there would be a temptation to act in that manner when you had 29 Leinster titles and 4 All Irelands to your credit. I had no quibbles with the result, as Mel's had simply far too many big guns for us, and overwhelmed us in the end. We had done very well to stay with such illustrious company for so long.

I had a serious rethink after the St. Mel's game about my workload, and found that I just had too many commitments. I was also feeling very drained and on doctors advice cut back on my sporting workload. I opted out as a county senior football selector, and from September 1997 dropped my involvement with school GAA squads, deciding instead to totally focus my attentions on our debating and public speaking teams who have been quite successful down through the years.

The school reached its third Leinster Senior Hurling 'B' final in four years in 1998, only to lose gallantly to Portlaoise CBS. Meanwhile the Senior 'A' footballers lost out to St. Michaels of Trim, having earlier achieved a fine first round victory away to St. Saran's of Ferbane, thereby avenging the 1996 defeat.

1999 was a wonderful year for the school on the playing fields as we won our first ever All Ireland Senior Hurling *'B'* title, with a convincing win over St. Caimin's College, Shannon in the final, on a scoreline of 4-11 to 0-17. Three members of the 2004 Wexford Leinster Senior Hurling winning side played a notable role in the success, namely John O'Connor from Rathnure and Michael and Rory Jacob from Oulart-The Ballagh. Goals in the first ten minutes from Marshalstown's Michael Kehoe and the aforementioned Rory Jacob, paved the way for a tremendous first half display by the CBS team, which resulted in a 3-5 to 0-7 lead at the interval. And while St. Caimins were first to score on the restart, a goal from Monageer's Stephen Murphy really put our lads in the driving seat. However, in fairness to the Clare school, they never lost hope and kept picking off their points until they had reduced the deficit to a mere three points with three minutes to go. However, our lads did not panic and finished strongly with points from Michael Jacob (2) and John O'Connor. The final whistle blew soon afterwards and amid scenes of great rejoicing the Cup was presented to captain Michael Jacob by then president of the GAA, Joe McDonagh. It was appropriate that Michael was captain as he was the only surviving member of the team that lost to De La Salle, Hospital of Limerick in the 1996 All Ireland final. He was not to be denied this time, and it was a well deserved victory over a very good St. Caimins team, (containing as it did a son of the great Ger Loughnane) who beat four strong Tipperary schools on their way to the Munster title. This was a talented and dedicated CBS team; an example of their commitment was the fact that they came in to train four times during their Easter holidays in the weeks before the final. Of course great credit for the team's success must go to their trainer Adrian Walsh, assisted by Eddie Nangle and Michael Carty, a fitting reward for the latter two, in particular, having given almost a lifetime of service to the GAA in the school.

Later in the afternoon, to complete a really memorable day for Wexford schools, Good Counsel of New Ross went on to win the All Ireland Colleges Senior *'A'* Football title with a thrilling victory over king pins of the code St. Jarlath's of Tuam. It was an outstanding team effort, but Eric Bradley's brilliantly taken goal will live long in the memory. Trainers Aidan O'Brien and Kevin Kehoe deserve great credit for this immense achievement.

The achievement of the CBS in winning the All Ireland *'B'* hurling title was fittingly recognised by Enniscorthy Urban Council at a Civic

**PICTURED OUTSIDE THE IRISH AMBASSADOR'S RESIDENCE IN THE HAGUE,
AFTER THE ST. PATRICK'S DAY RECEPTION IN MARCH 2000**
Left to Right: Tom Rossiter (Senior Hurling Team Manager),
John Swift (Irish Ambassador) and Myself

MY FAMILY
Back Row: My Daughter Susan and wife Bernadette
Front Row: Daughers Claire Eimear and Myself.

THE INAUGURAL PURPLE AND GOLD STARS FOOTBALL SELECTION

Back Row, Left to Right: Kevin Kehoe (Joint Manager), Fran Fitzhenry, Brendan Doyle, Diarmuid Kinsella, Philip Wallace, Sean Whitty, Matty Forde, Willie Carley (Capt.), David Murphy, John Hudson, Tom Wall, John Cooper, Aidan O'Brien (Joint Manager)

Front Row, Left to Right: Philip McGovern, Patrick Naughter, Derek Leonard, John Hegarty, John Mernagh, Colm Morris, Jason Russell, Leigh O'Brien, J.J. Doyle

Missing: Ken Furlong.

THE INAUGURAL PURPLE AND GOLD STARS HURLING SELECTION

Back Row Left to Right: Damien Fitzhenry, Declan Ruth, Dave Guiney, Keith Rossiter, Joe Mooney, Barry Goff, Jim Doyle, Martin Kehoe, Miceál Jordan, Brian Ivers.

Front Row Left to Right: Tom Dempsey, Fergus Heffernan, Paul Codd, Tomás Furlong, Paul Carley, Frank Boggan Michael Redmond

Missing: Colm Kehoe, David O'Connor, Michael O'Leary and Rod Guiney.

HISTORY MAKERS
THE ENNISCORTY C.B.S. SENIOR FOOTBALL PANEL
WHO WON THE LEINSTER SENIOR FOOTBALL "B" COLLEGES TITLE 1995
Back Row, Left to Right: M. Donnelly, P. Hall, J. Millar, C. Moriarty,
J. O'Brien, M. Walsh
Third Row, Left to Right: P. Leacy, C. McGee, N. Garry, C. Delaney,
A. Stafford, L. O'Brien, P. Whelan, L. Kehoe.
Second Row, Left to Right: P. Doyle, T. Byrne, J. Bolger, E. Flynn,
D. McGrath, M. Franklin, W. O'Connor
Front Row, Left to Right: G. Jacob, C. O'Neill, J. O'Connor,
J. Murphy (Capt). S. Doran, A. Maher
Missing from phtotograph: D. O'Brien.
Pictured with panel are team trainers Brendan O'Sullivan (R) and myself.

HISTORY MAKERS
THE ENNISCORTY C.B.S. SENIOR HURLING PANEL
WHO WON THE ALL-IRELAND SENIOR HURLING "B" COLLEGES TITLE 1999
Back Row, Left to Right: D. Fitzpatrick, S. Redmond, M. Reddy, C. Daly,
B. Doyle, G. Doyle, L. Leacy, D. Nolan
Middle Row, Left to Right: J. Millar, M. Hughes, M. Gahan, S. Deegan,
M. Kehoe, R. Jacob, L. Boland, J. Ormonde, J. Carley.
Front Row, Left to Right: W. Hudson, N. Doyle, J. O'Connor, T. Wall,
M. Jacob (Capt.), E. Furlong, P. O'Connor, A. Flynn, A. Russell, S. Murphy.

LAUNCH OF COMMUNITY DEVELOPMENT PROJECT, FEBRUARY 2001

Back Row, Left to Right: Fr. Pat Stafford, Oliver Raftery, Mai Doyle, Shane Carley, Christy Goggin, Ambrose Madde"s.
Front Row, Left to Right: Cathy Atkinson, John Barron (Chairman Development Committee), John Doyle (Club Sponsor),
Jim McGovern (Club Chairperson) and Liam Griffin, who launched the project

PARIS TOUR 1998
Roisin Dockery, Manageress of the Irish College in Paris,
making a presentation to me on the occasion of the club's visit to the Library.

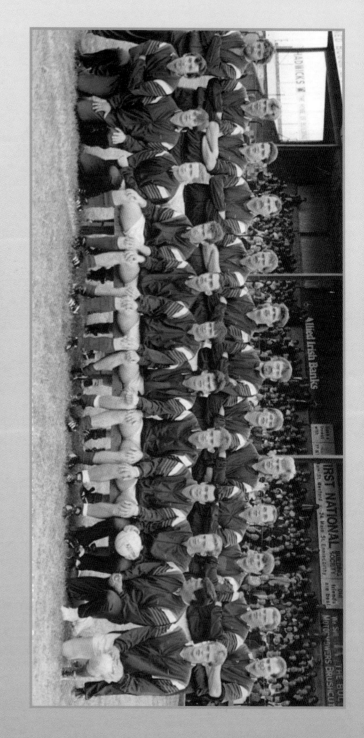

THE GLYNN-BARNTOWN SENIOR FOOTBALL PANEL
BEFORE THEIR HISTORIC FIRST SENIOR FINAL IN AUGUST 1989
Back Row, Left to Right: Jim Laffan, Jody Moloney, Brian, Cantwell, Mick Walsh, Lorcan Doyle, Paul Brazil, Jim McGovern,
Barry Kirwan, Iain Wickham, John McDonald, Simon Laffan, Nigel Morrissey, Dermot Whelan.
Front Row, Left to Right: John O'Rourke, Derek Kent, Mick Casey, Barry Doyle, James White, John Barron, James Morrissey,
Cormac Jevens Eddie Mahon, Karl Sexton, Larry Byrne (Trainer) and Shane O'Brien.

Reception in the '98 Centre on Friday 7th May 1999. It was a gesture much appreciated by the panel of players and the team management who were present on the occasion. And so for the first time since 1968 two Wexford teams came to Croke Park and carried away two cups. The words of Julius Caesar came to mind: veni, vidi, vici, I came, I saw, I conquered!

The CBS history making team was: Eamonn Furlong (Rapparees), Liam Boland (Rapparees), Chris Daly (Monageer-Boolavogue), Michael Reddy (Oulart-The Ballagh), Paddy O'Connor (Rathnure), Jamie Millar (Monageer-Boolavogue), Nicky Doyle (Rapparees), Tom Wall (Rapparees), Shay Deegan (Rapparees 1-0) John O'Connor (Rathnure 0-2) Michael Jacob (Oulart-The Ballagh, Capt., 0-2, 1 free, 1 65) Michael Kehoe (Marshalstown, 1-1) Adrian Flynn (Monageer-Boolavogue 1-1), Stephen Murphy (Monageer-Boolavogue), Rory Jacob (Oulart-The Ballagh, 1-1).

Subs: Joe Carley, Anthony Russell, Mark Gahan, Willy Hudson, Graham Doyle, Barry Doyle (all Rapparees), Michael Hughes, John Ormonde, Diarmuid Fitzpatrick (all Marshalstown), Lorcan Leacy, Darren Nolan (both Oulart-The Ballagh), Stephen Redmond (Crossabeg-Ballymurn).

Not to be outdone, our Under Fourteen footballers also created their own little bit of history early in February 1999 by winning the Leinster U14 'B' championship for the first time. They won a thrilling final after extra time on a scoreline of 5-5 to 4-7. Their opponents were Maynooth Post Primary School. Monageer-Boolavogue's Marty Kelly was the hero of the hour, coolly slotting away a penalty in the last minute of extra time to grab victory from the jaws of defeat. But it was a victory that our lads deserved as they simply never gave up.

The victorious team was as follows: Billy Millar (Starlights), Joe Cooper (Starlights), James Carty (Davidstown-Courtnacuddy), Joe Millar (Starlights), James McCauley (Starlights), Noel Flynn (Monageer-Boolavogue), Michael Heffernan (Olyegate-Glenbrien), Vincent O'Brien (Davidstown-Courtnacuddy Capt.), John ·Darcy (Monageer-Boolavogue, 1-0), David Tyrell (Starlights), Pat Mernagh (Starlights 1-2), Marty Kelly (Monageer-Boolavogue 1-2), Eddie Weafer (Shamrocks), David Breen (Ballyhogue 2-0), Liam O'Loughlin (Monageer-Boolavogue 0-1)

Subs: William Whelan (Oulart-The Ballagh), Bill Rigley (Starlights), Pat Kinsella (Marshalstown), Laurence Prendergast (Oulart-TheBallagh), Patrick O'Reilly (Shamrocks), Shane Kirwan (Ballyhogue), Tony Crosbie (Starlights), Stephen McDonald (Starlights), Ronan Wallace (Shamrocks), John Thorpe (Shamrocks), Michael Kavanagh (Cloughbawn), Ger Martin (Davidstown-Courtnacuddy),

In winning the Leinster Colleges Under 16 *'A'* hurling title in November 2000, our school bridged a gap of well over thirty years since the last *'A'* title was won. And it was achieved in some style too, beating three Kilkenny schools en route: St, Kieran's in the quarter final, Castlecomer Community School in the semi final, before getting the better of Kilkenny CBS in the decider on a scoreline of 3-7 to 1-8. Probably the crucial score of this game, which was played at O'Moore Park, Portlaoise, came after thirteen minutes of the second half when centre half back Michael Heffernan floated in a ball from long range, which was misjudged by the Kilkenny goalkeeper and ended up in the back of the net. That score brought the sides level and our lads added a goal and two points without reply before the final whistle, to emerge victorious. However, they had to survive an anxious last ten minutes, as Kilkenny threw everything into attack in an attempt to rescue the game. But our defence stood firm with goalkeeper Mark Dempsey and the aforementioned Michael Heffernan, being particularly outstanding.

Playing for CBS that day were: Mark Dempsey (Crossabeg-Ballymurn), Bill Rigley (Rapparees), Ger Flood (Cloughbawn), Shane Dunbar (Rapparees), Bob Jacob (Oulart-The Ballagh 0-3, 2 frees, 1 65), Michael Heffernan (Oylegate-Glenbrien 1-0), Noel Flynn (Monageer-Boolavogue), Vincent O'Brien (Davidstown-Courtnacuddy), John Thorpe (Shamrocks), William Whelan (Oulart-The Ballagh 0-1), David Tyrell (Rapparees 1-1), Anthony Byrne (Crossabeg-Ballymurn 0-1), Marty Kelly (Monageer-Boolavogue), Alan Carton (Cloughbawn Capt.), Harry Goff (Shamrocks 1-0).

Subs: Dwaine Kelly (Shamrocks), John Darcy (Monageer-Boolavogue), Pat Kinsella (Marshalstown), Barry Murphy (Crossabeg-Ballymurn), Davy Morrissey (Rapparees), Ted O'Connor (Rathnure), Eoin Doyle (Cloughbawn), James Doyle (Monageer-Boolavogue), Joe Millar (Rapparees).

Mentors, Justin Waldron and Brendan O'Sullivan, did a marvellous job with the team, with the former helping to plot the downfall of three teams from his native county.

Undoubtedly, the period 1995 to 2000 inclusive was a golden one in the school's GAA history, and while it may be equalled, I doubt if it will ever be surpassed. Apart from teachers previously mentioned, many others have also contributed to the well-being of the GAA in the school with two ladies, Mrs. Foley (nee Murphy) and Mrs. Gartland playing a pivotal role in keeping the games alive and well, particularly during the 1970s. But really all teachers have played their part, particularly when it comes to covering classes for teachers who are away at matches.

Chapter 5

Putting Something Back

I felt I had been privileged and honoured to play with Wexford, and for me therefore, it was important to put something back into the game as recognition of this. Of course I had trained school teams in Enniscorthy CBS since 1982, but in 1987 I became involved with the county minor footballers as part of a five-man selection team, which included Michael Caulfield (Gusserane), Rory Kinsella (Bunclody), Paddy O'Reilly (Taghmon-Camross) and Eddie Mahon (Glynn-Barntown). We were all teachers, so the discipline in the team was bound to be good! We put in a major effort from February onwards but were just not at the races when we played Kildare in the Leinster Championship on Sunday 24th May. We were hammered by 3-12 to 0-3 at Newbridge. It was a bad day all round for Wexford because, as I stated earlier, we also lost the senior game to the same opposition.

We had decided not to utilise dual players and so the team was per-haps not as strong as it could have been, but even if we had, it is doubtful if we would have matched a very talented Kildare team.

The team was as follows: John Cooper (Adamstown), Ritchie O'Connell (Volunteers), Norman Fitzharris (Gusserane), Paul Harrington (Sarsfields), Cathal White (St. Anne's), Liam O'Neill (Bunclody), Sean Flynn (Starlights), Enda Murphy (Bunclody), Paul O'Neill (Starlights), Donal Power (Shelmaliers), Brendan Howlin (Bannow-Ballymitty), John Buckley (Davidstown-Courtnacuddy), Robbie O'Callaghan (Taghmon-Camross), Seamus Byrne (Starlights), Brendan Walsh (St. James'). Subs: Seamus Berry (St. Anne's), Peter Collins (Starlights), Eamonn Jones (St. Anne's), Brian Ivers (Starlights), Eddie Kelly (Davidstown-Courtnacuddy), Michael Furlong (Adamstown).

It is interesting to note that only two players from that minor squad went on to play senior championship football with Wexford, namely Paul Harrington and John Cooper, the latter of course is still excelling in goals.

Not surprisingly, I suppose, we were not retained for the following season, and my next involvement came with the county minors of 1990. I was appointed manager of this team and my selectors were John Burke (Gorey), Sean Nolan (Starlights), Jim Ferguson (Bannow-Ballymitty), and Seamus Seery (Volunteers). We put in an incredible amount of hard work from the first time we met until our exit from the championship at the hands of, – you've guessed it, – Kildare, in May 1990. We had a meeting with the overall panel of players in mid December 1989, and we then proceeded to hold a series of trials after Christmas and in early January.

A remarkable forty-seven players turned up for a trial on Saturday 27-12-'89 at St. Patrick's Park Enniscorthy. They were as follows:

Gorey: Conor Kinsella, Pat Butler, John Byrne, Seamus Kavanagh, John Ryan, Greg Whelan, Mattie Butler, John Lambert, David Byrne, Ivan Byrne, Seamus Byrne, Michael McGovern, Seamus Hughes, Seamus Kavanagh,

New Ross: Declan McWilliams, Michael Moran, N. Whelan, Andrew Reville, Shay White, Paud O'Dwyer, Andrew Culleton, Philip White, Michael Foley, Alan O'Shea, P.J. Cullen, Joe English, Nicholas Harpur, M. Breen, P. Barron,

Enniscorthy: Sean O'Neill, Robert Hassey, Des Stafford, Martin Kehoe, Colm Kehoe, Niall Guinan, Tomas Kavanagh, Tom Atkinson,

Wexford: Wayne Murphy, John McNicholas, Eamonn Cullen, Fintan McClean, Anthony Corish, Owen McCarthy, Diarmuid Berry, Seamus Fitzgerald, Tony Lahoff, Anthony Whelan.

After a further series of trials, we whittled the panel down to thirty-five players and began serious preparations for the Leinster Championship on Saturday 20th January 1990. A week earlier we had had a meeting with the boys' parents at which we outlined our plans for the forthcoming campaign and emphasised our concern for the boys general welfare, what with the Leaving Cert coming up etc. County Board Chairman, Joe Shaughnessy was present at the get-together, and it should be mentioned that the County Board was extremely helpful in every respect. An example of this was the fact that they provided transport for every training session; in contrast to this we found when the panel visited Monaghan with the senior footballers for a challenge against the Monaghan minors, that the latter had to provide their own transport to training!

Other challenge games we played were Tipperary (home and away), Cork and Monaghan (a return game at Gorey). I felt that a weekend away would help the players to get to know each other well so we spent a marvellous weekend up in Derry, playing the Derry minors twice. Derry had won the All Ireland title the previous year with one Anthony Tohill making a major contribution to their success. This was indeed a great bonding weekend, and we were treated royally by our hosts, who took us to see the Giant's Causeway among many other attractions. The visit up north was also an eye opener for our lads, in that it showed them what could be achieved in the face of adversity. One could not but be impressed by the magnificent clubhouses we visited (some having been burnt down and rebuilt) and the great resilience, not to mention stoicism of the GAA people we met.

Back home we also played in the South East League beating Carlow and Kilkenny and overcoming Waterford in the final.

The team then was, I believe, very well prepared for the clash with Kildare in the championship on Sunday 20th May, but things went badly wrong on the day and the Lilywhites beat us by 2-13 to 1-7. This was a terrible disappointment after all the hard work that had gone in, but we could never get a look in at midfield, where the brilliant Niall Buckley and Glen Ryan ran the show. We certainly had the forwards to win the game but they just didn't see enough of the ball.

The Wexford team and substitutes for that game was: John O'Connor (St. Joseph's), Pat Hunt (Horeswood), Sean O'Neill (Starlights), Adrian Culleton (Gusserane), Anthony Whelan (Glynn-Barntown), Paud O'Dwyer (Rathgarogue-Cushinstown), Colm Kehoe (Bunclody), John Lambert (St. Pat's Ballyoughter), Fergal Foley (Glynn-Barntown), Michael Foley (Horeswood), Niall Guinan (Bunclody), Eamonn Scallan (Castletown, 0-5, 0-3frees), Paul Berry (St. Anne's), Seamus Hughes (Kilanerin), Larry Murphy (Cloughbawn, 1-1).

Subs.: Wayne Murphy (Volunteers) for Lambert, Seamus Kavanagh (Castletown) for Kehoe, Joe English (Gusserane, 0-1) for M. Foley. Also: P.J. Gethings (Kilanerin, sub. goalkeeper), Des Stafford (Davidstown-Courtnacuddy), Eamonn Dodd (Sarsfields), Seamus Byrne (Ballygarrett), Robert Hassey (Davidstown-Courtnacuddy), David Byrne (Kilrush), Fintan Mc Cleane (Sarsfields), Eamon Cullen (Crossabeg-Ballymurn), Pat Butler (Kilrush),

Kildare lined out as follows: C. Byrne, N. Campbell, L. Saxe, C. O'Brien, K. Dixon, J. Loughlin, M. Lawless, G. Ryan (0-2), N. Buckley (0-4, 3 frees), B. Foley (1-1), R. Quinn (1-1), A. O'Sullivan, K. Horgan (0-3 frees), C. Conlon (0-1), T. Sullivan (0-1).

We had a lot of dual players that year and, as a result, did not have the full panel together as often as one would have liked, particularly as the championship approached. But that is something you have to live with in a dual county I suppose.

Many of the 1990 team went on to make the grade at adult county level. Sean O'Neill of Starlights won an All Ireland Junior medal with the county in 1992, and also played some senior games. Adrian Culleton of Gusserane played in a Leinster semi-final with Wexford U21s. Paud O'Dwyer of Rathgarogue-Cushinstown did likewise and also played senior for Carlow. Niall Guinan of Bunclody played U21 and senior for the county, as indeed did Eamonn Scallan of Castletown, Larry Murphy of Cloughbawn, Seamus Hughes of Kilanerin, Colm Kehoe of Bunclody, Seamus Kavanagh of Castletown, and Des Stafford and Robert Hassey of Davidstown-Courtnacuddy. Pat Butler played junior for a number of years while Paul Berry of St. Anne's emigrated to University in America after his Leaving Cert, but returned many years later and played a number of senior games for the county. Paul was a gifted forward and, while his years out of top-level competition didn't help him, his brilliant individual goal against Kilanerin in the county final of 2001 will be talked about for many years to come.

Looking back on that 1990 minor campaign, I thought at the time and still think, that it was absolutely ludicrous that after such thorough preparation and expense incurred we should be out of the championship after just one game. Thankfully nowadays, teams do get a second chance through the round robin competition, but I am not in full agreement with that either as it interferes far too much with the club scene. I would prefer our minor teams just to get a second chance as in the All Ireland senior football championship.

Having put in a major effort with the 1990 minors, and to be out of the championship after just one game, one had to take serious stock of the situation. However, time is a great healer and by late in the year I had got enthusiastic about giving it another go. I had new selectors in Seamus Kennelly (Ballygarrett), George Rankins (Bunclody), Pat Bates (Kilmore) and John O'Heihir (Fethard). We had only four of last years panel, P.J. Gethings (Kilanerin), Colm Kehoe (Bunclody), Paud O'Dwyer (Cushinstown) and Niall Guinan (Bunclody), but after an exhaustive series of trials, league games in the South East League, and a series of challenge games against Wicklow, Dublin, Laois and Kerry we felt we had put a very useful team together, and so it proved when we trounced Carlow in the first round of the championship, winning by 5-11 to 0-6. Although the opposition was weak we played very well with some moves worked on in training coming off very well. As the report in *'The People'* stated: *'it was a game which Wexford had prepared very well for and they took the game to Carlow, thus putting them on the defensive. They also interchanged positions quite a lot making Carlow's defensive game even more difficult'.*

Wexford lined out as follows: Francis Byrne (Sarsfields), David O'Dwyer (Rathgarogue-Cushinstown), P.J.Gethings (Kilanerin), Trevor Hayes (Horeswood), Colm Kehoe (Bunclody), Paud O'Dwyer (Rathgarogue-Cushinstown), Phelim McGillycuddy (Shemaliers), Niall Guinan (Bunclody), Philip White (Bannow-Ballymitty), Scott Doran 0-7 (Kilmore), Jim Byrne 0-1 (Fethard), Derek Wall 1-0(Clongeen), Tommy Farrell 1-0 (Bunclody), Derek O'Reilly 2-3 (Horeswood), Eddie O'Neill 1-0 (Bunclody). Subs: Greg Whelan (Realt na Mara) for Guinan, Ciaran Roche (Glynn-Barntown) for Wall, Ivan Byrne (Kilrush) for O'Reilly. Also on the panel for the game were: Keith Sheehan (Starlights, sub goalkeeper), Eamonn Dodd (Sarsfields), and Walter Kelly (St. Fintan's).

We could afford to give a number of substitutes a run and they certainly gave us food for thought as we turned our attentions towards a quarterfinal clash with Offaly. We suffered a heart breaking defeat in this game, with two fatal defensive errors in the last five minutes being the cause of our downfall. Ahead by two points with five minutes to go, two lapses in concentration allowed the Faithful County in for two killer goals, which we simply could not recover from. The final score was 3-10 to 2-9 but, as *'The People'* report stated: *'despite losing, Wexford can be proud of what was one of their best performances in some time. They worked hard as a team throughout the game, and they made an Offaly side who were favourites, work very hard for a victory'.*

It was all so disappointing, but at least we were making progress, having gone a step further than the previous year. I was keen to push on to see could we make the breakthrough in 1992. Having been a selector with the under sixteen football team in 1990 under Jim McGillycuddy, I was now prevailed upon to also manage the under sixteens in 1991, with selectors Pat Dunphy (Adamstown), Denny Grannell (St. Joseph's), John Curtis (Ballyhogue) and Mick Byrne Kilrush). Although I could have done without the extra commitment, it gave me the opportunity to run the rule over prospective minors for 1992.

1991 was not without its brighter moments however. As county minor football manager I was asked to select some players to participate in trials for the Leinster *'International Rules'* Under 17 team against the visiting Australian Rules team. It was not easy getting the players I wanted and transport was also a major difficulty. I ended up bringing the players to all the trials, training sessions and games myself. The situation was exacerbated by the fact that I had just purchased a brand new car, yet it was cutting out frequently on me, at traffic lights, stop and yield signs etc. And given the fact that I was transporting players on roads that I had hardly ever been on before, it was a challenge in more ways than one. I brought the following players to trials in Gormanstown College, Co. Meath: Michael Redmond, Bunclody Vocational College, Shane Carley, Wexford CBS, David O'Dwyer, Good Counsel College, Colin Clancy Wexford Vocational College and Enda Roche, Bunclody Vocational College. After further trials which included a challenge game against Connacht in Tullamore, three of the lads made the panel for the game against Australia, namely Michael Redmond, Shane Carley and David O'Dwyer. Louth's Paddy Clarke was manager of the team and I was assistant coach along with Declan Rowley of St. Mel's College Longford.

Getting the players familiar with the new compromise rules, in particular releasing the ball when tackled, was the biggest task we faced, but the players were very keen to learn and adapted well. We played the Australians in Pairc Tailteann, Navan, on Monday evening, 15th April 1991. Although we put up what I felt was an excellent performance, the superior fitness of the young men from 'down under' told in the end, and they won on a scoreline of 66 points to 44. However we did best of all the provinces with Ulster going down by 70 to17 in Scotstown, Munster losing by 74 to 34 at Killarney while for their final provincial game the Aussies travelled to Galway, and in spite of resting some of their top stars, they still beat Connacht by 54 to 24. I honestly felt we were at a disadvantage playing them first, and could have run them very close had we more time to prepare.

Apart from their tremendous fitness, what struck me most about the young Aussies was their wonderful physique, their superb teamwork and their quickly learned ability to handle and kick the round ball.

For the record the panels were:

Leinster Schools:

1. Brendan Murphy, Trim CBS
2. John Brady, St. Patrick's Classical, Navan
3. Damian Burke, St. Mary's CBS, Mullingar
4. Niall Carew, St. Faran's, Prosperous
5. Kenneth Claffey, Ferbane Vocational School
6. Roberty Coffey (Capt.), St. Faran's, Prosperous
7. Ciaran Donohoe, Ard Scoil Rís, Marino
8. Declan Flynn, St. Mary's CBS, Mullingar
9. Kieran Harten, St. Patrick's Classical, Navan
10. Jim Holland, Bush Post Primary
11. Ken Lyons, St. Mary's CBS Mullingar
12. David Martin, Ard Scoil Rís, Marino
13. Denis McCormack, Naas CBS
14. Colm McDonald, Tullow Community School
15. Kieran McEvoy, St. Joseph's CBS Portarlington
16. Gary McGillicuddy, Colaiste Eoin, Booterstown
17. Damien McMahon, Scoil Chonglais, Baltinglass
18. Fintan O'Donnell, Knockbeg College, Carlow
19. David O'Dwyer, Good Counsel, New Ross
20. David O'Hanlon, Colaiste Dhulaigh, Coolock
21. Derek Quirke, Scoil Chonglais, Baltinglass

22. Michael Redmond, Bunclody Vocational School
23. Shane Ryan, Ferbane Vocational School
24. Peter Sullivan, Gormanstown College
25. Michael Whelan, Tullow Community School
26. Anthony Coyne, Killucan Vocational School
27. Shane Carley, Wexford CBS

Australia:
1. R. Maironani, Victoria
2. S. West, Victoria
3. S. Wood, Victoria
4. T. Cook, South Australia
5. B. Copeland, Northern Territory
6. B. Hehir, Victoria
7. M. Mercuri, Victoria
8. M. Scarfone, Western Australia
9. M. Edwards, Queensland
10. J. Georgiou, Victoria
11. A. Hamer, South Australia
12. B. Hart, South Australia
13. B. Sanderson, South Australia
14. P. Sharkey, Victoria
15. S. Watson, Victoria
16. D Southern, Western Australia
17. R. Neill, ACT
18. J. Misiti, Victoria
19. S. Burgmann, Victoria
20. J. Cook, Tasmania
21. S. Drennan, New South Wales
22. N. Neitz, Victoria

Manager: Grant Dorrington

Coach: Rod Austin

We had a lovely meal afterwards with the Australians, and overall it was a very good occasion. The team management received Leinster tracksuits, and I still wear mine now and again, thirteen years later. I thoroughly enjoyed the whole experience in spite of all the travel involved.

With regard to the county minors of 1992, we had five survivors from the '91 panel: Feidhlim McGillycuddy (Shelmaliers), David O'Dwyer (Rathgarogue-Cushinstown), Franny Byrne (Sarsfields), Scott Doran (Kilmore) and Ciaran Roche (Glynn-Barntown). Along with selectors Paddy Hughes (Kilanerin), Jim O'Connor (Geraldine O'Hanrahans), Pat Bates (Kilmore) and George Rankins (Bunclody), I was determined to leave no stone unturned as we sought that elusive breakthrough. Again we held a series of trials and challenge games, and participated for the first time in the North Leinster League, where we played teams such as Dublin, Kildare and Westmeath. I felt we needed this higher level of competition to improve our game, although we had to field depleted teams, due principally to the success of St. Peter'College and FCJ Bunclody in the provincial Colleges championship.

The victory of St. Peter's College in the Leinster Colleges Final gave us a great boost, and we decided to bring in their trainer Mick Caulfield, to assist with the coaching of the team. We hosted the Derry minors for a weekend in late April, and then we had All Ireland winning coach with Offaly, Eugene McGee, down for a full days coaching session at Blackwater. Our final workout before we played Dublin in the first round of the championship was against Cork at Youghal.

So it was a well-prepared and confident Wexford team that headed for Wexford Park on Saturday 23rd May to take on the Dubs, a side that contained future senior stars in Enda Sheehy and Senan Connell. The Dubs hit hard from the start and had a player sent off in the 23rd minute of the first half, but our lads kept their composure and went on to play some excellent football, recording a very decisive 1-8 to 0-3 victory. Paul Hughes became the extra man and executed the role to perfection, but really everybody played their part in a thrilling victory that was a huge boost for underage football in the county. What made the victory even more notable was the fact that we had to field without four key players: Darragh Ryan, Ciaran Roche, Scott Doran and Damien Fitzhenry.

We were now into a provincial semi-final where we would meet Meath who had earlier disposed of Louth and Laois. To warm up for the game we played Armagh in a challenge at Gorey on the Saturday week before the game. It was a very highly rated Armagh team containing future senior stars such as Paul McGrane and Diarmuid

Marsden, and who had only recently hammered Tyrone on a 3-12 to 1-8 scoreline in the Ulster semi-final. We had now tremendous competition for places, and this game provided an opportunity for players to stake a claim for a place on the team against Meath. We turned in a tremendous performance, running the Orchard county lads ragged, and winning the game easily on a scoreline of 3-16 to 0-7. Remember, this was the same Armagh team that subsequently went on to the All Ireland Final, where they were desperately unlucky to lose to our eventual conquerors, Meath.

The performance in that game gave us plenty of food for thought and we made four changes in personnel for the game against the royal county. Into the team came the four players who were not available against Dublin: Darragh Ryan, Ciaran Roche, Scott Doran and Damien Fitzhenry. The unlucky players to lose out were: Darragh Byrne, Ger O'Brien (both quite restricted by injuries in the lead up to the game), Enda Newport and John Foley. Now, the conventional wisdom is that you do not change a winning side but we felt that the changes made were going to considerably strengthen the team.

'Scott's left foot saves the day!' ran *'The People'* headline the week after the game, and the Kilmore lad was definitely our saviour as he converted a last minute *'45'*, which was shown on the RTE News that night, to give us a second bite at the cherry. We had not played well, with a number of the team appearing to be over awed by the occasion. Nevertheless, we hung in there to get a deserved draw on a scoreline of Wexford 0-11, Meath 1-8.

The replay was set for two weeks later, Sunday 26th July, as a curtain raiser to the Senior Football Final between Dublin and Kildare, so we had plenty of breathing space to reassess the situation and look at our options. After long and prolonged discussions, we decided to revamp the team and play a more direct game. We felt that our over reliance on the short passing game was playing into the hands of the tough tackling Meath lads, so we moved Darren Browne from midfield to full forward to act as a target man, but this was not our sole tactic, as basically we wanted a combination of the short passing game, and the judiciously used long ball. Other changes involved Darragh Ryan going to full back in place of the injured Michael Higgins with David O'Dwyer taking his place at corner back and Ciaran Roche coming back from left corner forward to right wing back and Kenneth

Leacy coming in at midfield; the Monageer man had completely blotted out Portarlington danger man, Hughie Emerson, in the recently played Leinster Colleges Final and we rated him highly.

The team in full read: Barry Hughes, David O'Dwyer, Darragh Ryan, Rory McCarthy, Ciaran Roche, Feidhlim McGillycuddy, Paul Hughes (capt.), Kenneth Leacy, Franny Byrne, Damien Fitzhenry, Tomas Kavanagh, Michael Redmond, Scott Doran, Darren Browne, Enda Newport.

We started very brightly and, wind assisted, looked like we would overrun Meath, but despite an enormous amount of possession, scores were slow in coming and we only led by four points at the interval (0-4 to 0-0). It did not look to be sufficient, given that we had to face the wind in the second period. However our lads showed great character on the resumption, and now, playing the possession game, had maintained their lead and were six points up with eight minutes to go (1-6 to 0-3), the goal being really well taken by Volunteers, Ger O'Brien, after good approach work by Michael Redmond, Scott Doran and Tomas Kavanagh.

Things were looking good but then disaster struck. Darragh Ryan, who had been soundness personified at fullback, particularly under the high ball, was dragged outfield by his opposite number, Caimin Hall. Obviously the intention was to create space in front of goal and it worked to devastating effect; the next high ball that came in caused panic stations in our defence, and as the ball broke, the talented Peter O'Sullivan (I'm surprised he didn't make the grade with Meath at senior level), pounced to drill a low shot to the net. Meath were right back in it now, got a point almost immediately and then O'Sullivan scored two close in frees to bring the game to extra time. We had had the game won, but typically Meath, no doubt inspired by the exploits of their seniors the year before, just would not accept defeat. We were immediately aware that Darragh Ryan was being lured from the square, but we didn't want to leave them with an extra man out the field; its easy to be wise after the event but it was a mistake to let Darragh go, one I have always regretted.

We could still win it of course and the words Alf Ramsay said to his players just before they started extra time in the 1966 World Cup Final immediately sprang to mind: *'you've won it once, now go out and win it all over again'.* And in fairness to the players they did really dig deep and were on equal terms with Meath (2-8 each), after the first period of extra time, despite having played against the wind. But the Royal County seemed to dig that little deeper in the second period and ended up winning by 3-10 to 2-10.

In front of a packed Croke Park, this was a hugely disappointing defeat and I was absolutely gutted, as were the players and everyone else associated with the team. And twelve years later the disappointment still lingers, as this was definitely a team that could have won an All Ireland. Meath went on to do exactly that, beating Armagh in the final, a team, as I said previously, we had comprehensively beaten earlier on in the campaign in a challenge game.

That minor panel of 1992 was the best I was involved with, and I would just like to make a brief comment on each of the twenty-seven players in the squad.

Barry Hughes, Kilanerln: Barry was our first choice goalkeeper and has gone on to enjoy great success with his club.

David O'Dwyer, Rathgarogue-Cushinstown: David was a very dedicated player who showed great promise. In 1991 I had brought him to trials for the Leinster Under 16 Compromise Rules team and he played his part in the test against the Australians. Unfortunately injury and illness curbed a very promising career.

Darragh Ryan, St. Anne's: Darragh went on to play senior football for Wexford, but persistent knee injuries have meant that he has concentrated on hurling alone in recent years, and very successfully too.

Rory McCarthy, St. Martin's: Rory was a classy footballer and a fine reader of the game. He too has concentrated on hurling and I was delighted for him when he won an All Ireland Senior hurling medal in 1996.

Ciaran Roche, Glynn-Barntown: Ciaran was a very versatile footballer and you could play him almost anywhere. Played some senior football for the county but never really fulfilled his great potential.

Feidhlim McGillycuddy, Shelmaliers: Showed great promise but did not fulfil his potential for a variety of reasons. In the 1992 All Ireland Colleges semi-final, Feidhlim was centre back on the St. Peter's team; his counterpart on the St. Brendan's College Killarney team was Seamus Monynihan. Both shone on the day, but the latter has gone on to be one of the giants of Gaelic football.

Paul Hughes, Kilanerin: Played the extra man role superbly against Dublin and goaled against Meath. Paul was a good, hard working captain and could tackle his opponent without fouling. He has enjoyed great success with his club.

Kenneth Leacy, Monageer: I had Kenneth on CBS Enniscorthy teams for three years before he went to St. Peter's to do his Leaving Cert. In the Leinster Colleges Final of 1992 he completely nullified the threat of future Laois star Hughie Emerson. His outstanding display was vital to his team's victory. He started the replay against Meath.

Franny Byrne, Sarsfields: Franny was a marvellous fielder of the ball and was also well able to score. Caught some fantastic balls in the replay against Meath. He played in the 1993 County Senior Football Final. Drifted away for a while but is now back with his club.

Damien Fitzhenry, Duffry Rovers: Had a great ability to kick points from long range, was very strong and forceful on the ball and definitely a player who could have gone on to play senior football for Wexford. Damien's legendary exploits in hurling have thrilled the county on many a heart stopping occasion.

Tomas Kavanagh, Duffry Rovers: Had an uncanny ability to score goals which he showed to great effect in St. Peter's run to the All Ireland semi-final. Tomas seemed a bit tired during the '92 campaign and I don't think we saw the best of him. He played senior football for Wexford for a while.

Michael Redmond, HWH Bunclody: I rated Michael very highly and he was another player I brought to the Compromise Rules trials. He was a very incisive forward with great pace and ability to score, but could have been more consistent. I expected him to go on to play senior for Wexford and it was a great pity that didn't happen.

Scott Doran, Kilmore: Had tremendous ability and with his superb score taking prowess would have been on any team in the country. Scott had a long career on the Wexford senior team and played right up to 2004.

Darren Browne, Sarsfields: we moved Darren to full forward for the replay against Meath to add variation to our game and to act as a target man. It didn't really work out and we had to replace him, but he returned in extra time. A good fielder of the ball with a knack of getting goals, which he showed at full forward in the Leinster U 16 blitz of 1991. He played in the 1993 County Senior Football Final but soon after lost a lot of his interest in the game, but is now back playing with Wexford.

Enda Newport, St. Fintan's: played a major role in St. Peter's Leinster Final win in '92 and was a great opportunist. However, we did not see Enda at his best in the '92 minor campaign; has gone on to play junior football with Wexford.

David Furlong, Kilmore: David was the sub goalkeeper and there was very little difference between Barry Hughes and himself in terms of ability but Barry shaded it because of his height. David continued to play with his club and was rewarded for his dedication when Kilmore won the junior championship in 2003.

Michael Higgins, Kilanerin: Michael was sure and steady and very hard to get by; an excellent tackler but a little one footed. Has enjoyed great success with his club and made brief appearances for Wexford seniors.

John Hassey, Davidstown-Courtnacuddy: Distributed the ball well at centre forward and worked tirelessly. I felt that John could have achieved more in the game but tended to drift away from it.

Ger O'Brien, Volunteers: Had a very good game against Dublin although slightly troubled by injury. He was unlucky to lose out in the subsequent reshuffle for the Meath game, but came on in the second half. Ger was a really sticky player and would do exactly as he was told. I thought very highly of him. He continues to play with his club.

John Foley, Sarsfields: John was a stylish player and a very good free taker. He could distribute the ball well and was quite versatile; his lack of size and strength came against him. .

John Hegarty, Kilanerin: Went on to make a major impression with the Wexford senior team. John came really good towards the end of our campaign and was perhaps unlucky not to make the team for the replay against Meath. He was a minor again in '93, and has been very influential in his club's successful run.

Philip Dowdall, Sarsfields: Philip was a lovely footballer and midfield was his natural position. A tall player he did not always use his height to full effect. Has returned to play with his club.

Darragh Byrne, Glynn-Barntown: Darragh played well against Dublin but was unlucky to lose out (although carrying a slight injury), for the Meath game. He was an intelligent footballer who always tried to use the ball well, being particularly adept at working it out of defence. Played senior for his club, but work commitments took him away from home.

Enda Roche, Marshalstown: Enda had plenty of ability but seemed to lack confidence in himself. He was a very useful utility player. Enda emigrated during the 1990s.

Michael Mahon, Bunclody: Michael was a very dedicated wholehearted player who always and gave his all in training; he continues to play.

Michael Pitt, St. Martin's: Michael was a very hard working player, who played an important role in St Peter's College's run to the Leinster Final; a good utility player.

Tomas Kane, Horeswood: played well in some challenge games but seemed to lack belief in his own ability.

When I reflect on my involvement with the county minors of '90, '91 and '92 a number of things come to mind: it was a pleasure to work with all those lads as they entered adulthood. I know we did not win anything, but is it all about that? As a teacher, I knew the pressures those lads were under and I certainly did not want to add to it. I was looking as much to the long as the short term and, at the end of the day, I was only helping them to grow and develop as human beings. I wanted them to develop good habits with regard to fitness and spent many hours taping fitness tapes for each of the players for their own private use. Each training session was meticulously planned in advance and there were regular fitness assessments done. Obviously there was a physical element to the sessions but a lot of it was also done using the ball. The players were fit, probably as fit as they had ever been. It was nice to hear Colm Kehoe state in an interview in the *'Road to Glory'*, a Wexford People publication on the eve of the All Ireland Hurling Final in 1996, that: *"the demands of Jim McGovern when I was in the Wexford Minor Football Panel (Colm was a minor in '90 and '91) were as severe as anything required by Griffin and Co."*! It was certainly pleasing to get feedback like that. I also became a member of the British National Coaching Institute so that I would be thoroughly *'au fait'* with the most up to date methods in physical and mental fitness and the principles of coaching. I obtained several videos on these areas, which I analysed in great depth. I took a particular interest in the whole area of sports psychology and I particularly emphasised to the players the following mental skills:

1. Goal setting
2. Confidence building
3. Concentration
4. Mental visualisation
5. Emotional control
6. Interpersonal relations

They all got handouts concerning these skills, and I was at pains to point out that goal setting was probably the most important of them all. The setting of realistic, attainable goals in a personal sense (in terms of self improvement) and in a team sense were, I stressed, essential to the future prospects of a team and its success. I stressed to the lads that you had to practise these skills, particularly mental visualisation, on a daily basis if you were to improve at them. In fact the experts claimed that you had to work on these mental skills just as often as you practised the physical skills, if you were to become really proficient in them. The English Rugby team was using mental training tapes around that time and coach Geoff Cooke was quoted as saying that they were an important element in their improving fortunes. Subsequently, I purchased these tapes myself and found them to be an invaluable help in team preparation.

At the post match reception to the inaugural Purple and Gold Stars in December 2002, I had a long chat with Larry Murphy concerning the preparation of the 1990 Wexford minor footballers (Larry was a member of that team), and he felt that an introduction to sports psychology at that time heralded a whole new approach and that such a venture, was well ahead of its time.

I read voraciously on the whole area of team preparation paying particular attention to what they were doing in other sports, hoping to pick up something that I might use in my own preparation. I was very much into video analysis and had a lot of our games videoed. I would spend hours analysing these videos and would take notes on what happened each minute of the game. I was well aware that you can overdo this area and there was always the danger that it could lead to 'paralysis by analysis', so usually when showing videos to the players I had them edited to illustrate particularly constructive points, but I always accentuated the positive when doing so, being very careful to sandwich constructive criticism between pieces of praise.

I don't want the following to be a criticism of any of the selectors I worked with over my three years as Wexford Minor Football manager, and it is certainly not intended to be so, as they were all decent, honourable men who gave their all for Wexford. But the fact remains that I thought that the system then in vogue, of the county board picking a selector from each district to work with an appointed manager, was, and is outdated and archaic. I believe that a manager should pick his own men, (which in fairness is generally the case today), and the management team should not number more than three in total. In fact, I would go further and state that I think a manager should just have an assistant, as pertains in the English Premiership. It goes without saying that in such a scenario there would have to be proper back up support, and that would include a person up in the stand, away from the action, taking a detached view. Why only two on a management team? Well, I feel that once the proper preparatory work has been done and possible changes etc have been anticipated, (within reason), it is much easier for two people to consult and make changes than it is for three or five. Indecision or procrastination on the sideline can lead to a team losing a match, and so any delay in making a substitution or a positional switch can be fatal to a team's chances.

I stepped down as minor football manager after the replay defeat to Meath. I felt that three years was enough and that I should hand it over to someone else with fresh new ideas. However, I was interested in taking on the county Under 21 football team and was appointed to do so by the county board. I picked my own selectors from a list supplied by the board, and they were: Mick Caulfield (Gusserane), Kevin Kehoe (Gusserane), and later, to provide continuity, as he had managed the County Under 21 team the previous year, Paud Moriarty (Ballyhogue).

It is notoriously difficult to prepare a team at this level. Most of the lads are at third level or university, and at a time when you want them most to prepare for the first round of the Leinster Championship they are deeply involved with their own colleges or universities, preparing for the Sigerson and Fitzgibbon Cups. I played Sigerson so I know the set up very well. Nevertheless, in spite of all the difficulties, we had to get on with it and I must say we were very lucky to have the services of the late and great Paddy Roche (Rosslare) as Secretary. Paddy was very efficient, paying meticulous attention to detail. He certainly made my job that bit easier, as indeed did a clubmate of Paddy's, current assistant county secretary Margaret Doyle during my time with the county minors. We were drawn against Kildare in the first round of the championship, and this provided me personally with a great opportunity to get revenge for the minor defeat of 1990. We prepared well as usual and approached the game in a positive frame of mind, even though it was at a Kildare venue (Athy).

I travelled to the game from Galway where I was attending the annual ASTI Conference. Being fiercely determined that we would win the game, I had put a lot of time into preparing a pre match speech. In fact, I'd say many of the contributions at the conference went over my head as I was so focussed on the game. We had a daunting task ahead of us. Kildare were the reigning Leinster Champions, they were playing at home and they were hot favourites. There had been terrific interest in football since Mick O'Dwyer arrived to manage their senior team, and there was bound to be a very big Kildare crowd present. We also had our injury problems, being forced to field without Colm Kehoe, Sean O'Neill and Feidhlim McGillycuddy. Jim Byrne also cried off just before the game. It was probably the best pre match speech I ever gave, for the simple reason that I had prepared it so thoroughly, and had chosen what I felt were the right words. I subsequently heard that some of those words offended a Kildare official who happened to be walking by our dressing room window at the time! Anyway the speech seemed to have the desired effect as Wexford reporter Brendan Furlong described in his report on the game. I quote an excerpt: *"Kildare were unable to meet the Wexford Challenge and with Adrian Culleton superb at fullback, Darragh Ryan outstanding at midfield, and Scott Doran on song in attack, it was evident from a very early stage that a surprise result was on the cards".*

It was four points to two at half time and although we were only two points ahead, we were dominating midfield with Darragh Ryan giving an exhibition of high fielding. We came under considerable pressure in the third quarter but with Gusserane's Adrian Culleton in regal form at full back and Franny Byrne confidence personified in goal we weathered the storm and went on to record a thrilling victory on a nine points to four scoreline. Scott Doran was excellent at point taking, scoring two from play and six from frees, from a variety of distances and angles. Our other point was kicked by Niall Guinan from play. There were wonderful scenes of rejoicing afterwards and my fellow selectors and I felt a great sense of satisfaction, but the credit belonged to the players who had dug deep to record a famous victory.

The team and substitutes were as follows: Franny Byrne (Sarsfields), Dessie Stafford (Davidstown-Courtnacuddy), Adrian Culleton (Gusserane), Brendan Redmond (Cloughbawn), Paud O'Dwyer (Rathgarogue-Cushinstown), Seamus Kavanagh (Castletown), Ciaran Roche (Glynn-Barntown), Robert Hassey

(Davidstown-Courtnacuddy), Darragh Ryan (St. Anne's), Scott Doran (Kilmore), Niall Guinan (Bunclody), Dermot Keating (Ramsgrange). Diarmuid Berry (St. Anne's), Seamus Hughes (Kilanerin), Eamonn Scallan (Castletown). Subs: Sean Whitty (Adamstown), for Keating. Also: Paul Whelan (Gusserane, sub goalkeeper), Tomas O'Rourke (Starlights), Mick Kehoe (St. Mary's Rosslare), Larry O'Connor (Bunclody), James Breen (Ballyhogue), Darragh Kenny (Gorey), Walter Kelly (St. Fintan's).

It is interesting to note that there were only five survivors from the minor team of 1990 namely, Adrian Culleton, Paud O'Dwyer, Niall Guinan, Eamonn Scallan and Seamus Hughes. However, three of the minor substitutes in 1990 made the team and they were: Seamus Kavanagh, Dessie Stafford and Robert Hassey.

We were now through to a provincial semi-final against Meath. The Royal County were favourites for Leinster having won the All Ireland minor title in 1990 and had outstanding players in Trevor Giles, Graham Geraghty and Enda McManus to name just a few. We were facing formidable opposition therefore and would be going into the game very much as underdogs. In such a situation one would seize on any motivational tools that were going. I searched for one and was delighted to get one in the *Meath Chronicle.* It read: *"Meath will be long odds on favourites in next Sunday's Leinster under 21 FC game against lowly Kilkenny at Pairc Tailteann, Kilkenny actually drew with Meath in this competition in the 1970s before losing the replay narrowly. But a repeat result is highly unlikely now and Meath may not get a decent warm up for the crucial semi-final against Kildare on April 25th".*

Against Kildare! They weren't even considering us. What greater motivation could you have? I decided I'd blow up the article and put it on the back of the dressing room door in Newbridge where the game was played. I drew the players' attention to it and soon they were all reading it. I sensed an air of quiet but fierce determination and this manifested itself throughout the first half, and we went in at the interval leading by 2-3 to 0-6. I told our lads to play as they were playing and they would win it, but then absolute disaster struck. We won the throw in, but a cross-field pass was intercepted by a Meath player who drove in a high ball towards our square. The full lines had come out and the ball appeared to be hopping harmlessly into the arms of our goalie Franny Byrne, but then as it hopped it seemed to hit a divot on the 21yard line and instead of hopping inwards, hopped outwards. An inrushing Meath forward had the relatively simple task of planting the ball in the back of the net.

I had a bird's eye view of what happened as I was behind the goal, having just spoken to our goalkeeper moments before the throw in; the incident may have cost us the game, as we were in the driving seat up to that time. We did regain the lead briefly after that with a point from Niall Guinan, but Meath took over afterwards for about fifteen minutes, and stretched well ahead. Our lads however showed great character to fight back and there were only two points in it as the game entered injury time; however Meath got the final score of the game to run out three point winners. It must be pointed out that we had four costly misses from frees in the second half, three from Scott Doran and one from Jim Byrne.

And therein lies a tale. For Scott's first miss I had no doubt whatsoever that a Meath player was not standing the required fourteen yards from the ball, in fact half that distance was more like it. This was intimidation of the freetaker, but the referee would do nothing about it. When Scott came to take his next free the same procedure applied. I went down and tried to draw the referee's attention to it but I found myself man marked by the Meath manager, who seemed to have no problem with such gamesmanship. Again, Scott missed and the very same applied for his third miss. It was very unsporting behaviour, and I was disappointed the referee did not take stern action. I haven't a clear recollection of Jim Byrne's miss from a free, as it was on the far side of the field but it's likely the same encroachment may have occurred. After beating us Meath went on to win Leinster and later the All Ireland. Enda McManus of Meath later told our Feidhlim McGillycuddy in UCG (where they were both students), that Wexford had given them the hardest game they had got all year, not much consolation I suppose.

An interesting aside from that under 21 campaign was the fact that we 'loaned out' so to speak, selector Kevin Kehoe to the county senior hurlers to act as their trainer. I was requested to do so by County Chairman Joe O' Shaughnessy and was initially taken aback by what I considered to be an unusual request. I had to think long and hard about it and of course discuss it with Kevin and the rest of the selectors. I feared that sharing Kevin with the senior hurlers would dilute his focus and have a disruptive effect on our preparations. It was only after long chats with Wexford senior hurling manager, the late Christy Kehoe and his namesake Kevin (who informed me that the county chairman was putting him under a lot of pressure to do the job), that I finally consented to the loan arrangement. I did so in the greater interests of Wexford GAA and, by all accounts, the Gusserane man was an instant success as trainer playing a prominent role in helping to get the county to a League and Leinster finals, finals Wexford were desperately unlucky to lose. We were unanimously returned for the 1994 championship at a county board meeting at the end of July '93, and soon set about sorting out a panel. Wicklow were our opponents in the championship, a game that was played at Gorey. It ended in a draw, one goal and eight points each but was completely marred by a cowardly assault from behind on Scott Doran, not long after he had scored a smashing goal; Scott unfortunately retaliated and he and his attacker were sent to the line. I was extremely angry at what happened as I knew the loss of Scott, halfway through the first half, would prove detrimental to us, and had he remained on the field we would almost certainly have won the game. The proof is in the pudding: in our two championship games the previous year we scored a total of twenty-two points (2-16) – Scott was responsible for fifteen points of that, (1-12), two thirds of the total. Enough said!

The team for that match was: Ollie Murphy (Gusserane), Declan Davitt (Rathgarogue-Cushinstown), Eugene Furlong (Glynn-Barntown), Colm Kehoe (Bunclody), Tomas Kavanagh (Duffry Rovers), David O'Dwyer (Rathgarogue-Cushinstown), Ciaran Roche (Glynn-Barntown), Franny Byrne (Sarsfields), Darragh Ryan (St. Anne's), John Hegarty 0-1 (Kilanerin), Shane Carley 0-1 (Glynn-Barntown), Jim Byrne 0-5, 4 frees (Fethard), Paul Hughes (Kilanerin), Scott Doran 0-1 (Kilmore), Niall Guinan 0-1 (Bunclody). Sub: Trevor Hayes (Horeswood), for Carley.

We were able to introduce Damien Fitzhenry for the replay in Wicklow, and while the Duffry Rovers man played well, ultimately it was to no avail as Wicklow had the better of things, winning the match by 1-6 to 0-4. We really lacked scoring power in attack and, in that regard, the absence of ace marksman Scott Doran was very sorely felt indeed.

Looking back on that campaign it was not one that had run entirely according to plan. As pertained the previous year there was a difficulty in getting players together for training sessions with a lot of them away at college and many participating in third level colleges competitions. In addition to that, two of my selectors, Mick Caulfield (St. Peter's) and Kevin Kehoe (Good Counsel) were caught up in successful runs with their schools and understandably could not give a full commitment all the time. In fact both St. Peter's College and Good Counsel were involved in the Leinster Colleges Championship the day of our first Leinster Championship match against Wicklow, and so Mick and Kevin were unavoidably absent from our game. Being a teacher myself, preparing teams, I fully understood their predicament and had no problem with it. But I now understand that not everyone felt the same. However, remaining selector Paud Moriarty and myself, assisted in no small way by secretary Paddy Roche, did work hard to ensure that the team was well prepared on the few occasions when Mick and Kevin were absent. I would have to say that I found that period rather difficult, as I was also player manager of the Glynn-Barntown senior football team. I can clearly recall one occasion when I trained the under twenty one team, and then rushed down immediately to Barntown to chair a players meeting of the Glynn-Barntown senior football panel. In addition to those commitments, I was now hard at work examining the fixtures situation in the county, but more about that in the next chapter.

With these and other commitments, particularly family (our second child Susan was born the previous year), I had to think long and hard before I let my name go forward to manage the team the following year. I shouldn't have bothered. To my great surprise and disappointment I was not given the job. At that stage I had regained my enthusiasm and was looking forward to giving it another shot, particularly as the under twenty ones of 1995 would effectively be the so unlucky minors of '92. These minors were now *'coming of age'* and I felt I could make a major breakthrough with them in '95. But alas it was not to be, and it certainly left a bad taste in the mouth. I have no doubt but that there were politics involved in the decision.

As a matter of interest, the 1995 under twenty one team containing only half a dozen of the gallant minors of '92 were almost shocked by lowly Kilkenny in the first round of the championship. The sides were level with three minutes to go and a major surprise looked on the cards before two late points won it for Wexford (1-12 to 2-7). However, it was really only postponing the inevitable as they were well beaten by Offaly at Wexford Park in their next match. Of course, its an ill wind that blows no good and my disappointing experience in being overlooked for the under twenty one job gave me the drive and the determination to succeed with my own school team, as I said earlier. We won the Leinster Colleges Senior Football 'B' title for the first time ever in March 1995 and no success has given me greater satisfaction.

I was approached to act as a county senior football selector in October 1995, and immediately accepted as I considered a great honour was being bestowed upon me, but I really should have thought about it much more as I was definitely acting on the rebound. It was a disastrous experience for me and I wanted to get out at the end of the first year. We had got an absolute hammering from Carlow in the first round of the Leinster championship and I was extremely unhappy about the unprofessional nature of some of the preparations for that game, but I had other concerns as well, and expressed them all to a senior county board official who was sympathetic to my plight, but who advised me not to desert a sinking ship. I took his advice, which I thought was fair enough at the time, and stayed on for over another year but eventually opted out on doctor's orders. In any event, it seemed to me that I had lost the respect of some of the more senior players (players whom I would have played with myself) who were obviously heaping most of the blame on my fellow selectors and myself for the way things were going. I was extremely annoyed by this, as I was every bit as disillusioned as those players were. It was the most unhappy period I ever spent in Wexford GAA

Chapter 6

Fixtures Frustration

I was first alerted to the fixtures situation in Wexford through my involvement with Starlights in 1983. We started training in February of that year but, with inordinate gaps between games, did not play the county final until November. It gave us little or no chance to prepare for the Leinster Club Championship. In fact as I've already mentioned we were lucky to play in it at all, having to do so three days after the county final.

In an article in 'The Echo' newspaper on Friday, November 18th 1983, the week after our county final victory, the writer ('I. R.') wrote: *"Lets be honest – the present league-championship system is nothing short of farcical. What kind of championship is it when the interest of clubs, players and spectators is gone out of it except for the opening round, or the semi finals or finals? The obvious answer is a knockout championship and a separate county league."* 'I.R.'s words must have been heeded by the powers that be, for in 1984 a knockout championship was introduced and was repeated in 1985. However, we reverted back to the old format in 1986. I became convinced that this system was resulting in a lowering of standards and was impacting negatively on the performances of our inter county teams. I was asked to write an article on this matter for the 1988 Wexford GAA Year Book and I now quote part of that article: *"If standards in this county are to be improved to the extent that both hurlers and footballers are challenging on a regular basis for All-Ireland honours it is essential that we return to a knockout championship, a properly organised league taken seriously by all the clubs with an attractive prize, a much greater emphasis on coaching, particularly at underage level and finally a closer liaison between the GAA (club) and the schools.*

A Knockout Championship

The present league-championship format has, in my view, failed and will continue to fail, if persisted with, with a consequent further lowering of standards. The present system benefits nobody. It does not benefit:

(A) The Players
(B) The Spectators
(C) The County Board
(D) The Clubs
(E) The County Teams

(A) The Players:
The players are the lifeblood of the GAA. Without them the organisation would cease to exist, however magnificent the pitches and clubhouses that have been opened over the years mainly through the labours of selfless and dedicated people. People nowadays expect a high level of organisation and efficiency from whatever sport(s) they pursue and GAA players are no different. Many players have become frustrated and disillusioned with the present system because: (a) There is no master fixtures plan. The league-championship can drag on indefinitely with players often not knowing when their next game is going to be played, making it difficult for them to arrange their annual holidays without fear of missing a vital game. (b) Games can be called off or rescheduled at short notice. Players working hard towards a particular fixture can be put off form if that fixture is suddenly postponed. (c) There is no proper winter league. Club players therefore turn to other sports and for many the GAA becomes only their second sport.

(B) The Spectators
We live in an age of stringent cutbacks and general tightening of belts and GAA followers are no exception. Spectators will only come to games in large numbers where value for money is guaranteed. Followers of our games don't enjoy matches that lack 'bite' where even if a team loses a couple of games it still remains in the competition or where a team may not be playing at its best because it has already qualified for the play-offs. Neither do spectators appreciate teams being given walkovers, particularly at senior championship level.

(C) The County Board
For a financially pressed Count Board a league-championship format is never likely to be a money-spinner. The earlier rounds lack publicity and are put on at different venues when some of them could be put on at the same venue, thereby maximising the attendance.

(D) The Clubs
The clubs deserve tremendous credit for the way they keep the games alive in spite of the many counter attractions available to young people nowadays. A lot of them are dual clubs, that is, they have hurling and football teams, often of equal ability and can be caught between two stools preparing both, and often end up winning in neither. In a knockout format if you were defeated in one you could then put all your energies into the other. Clubs are also frustrated by the late finish to the championships, because even if they win they may not get a chance to represent their county in the Leinster Club Championship. It has happened at least twice in recent years that the county board has had to nominate a club because the championship was not finished in time.

(E) The County Teams
The county teams are our shop window. They reflect the standard of hurling and football within the county. Above all our county teams do not benefit from a league-championship format, because it is so drawn out that the finals usually run into October (some years it has been later). October of course is the time when the National Leagues start and rarely have Wexford teams been fully prepared for the opening games. The reason for this of course is that due to pending county finals the teams have had to field much under strength, for example: the county hurlers played Clare in the league this year and had to field an under strength team due to the fact that the county hurling final was on the same day. They lost that game, albeit narrowly, but I wonder what would have happened had a full panel been available.

The 1984-85 league season saw Wexford footballers take the footballing world by storm with marvellous victories over Offaly, Dublin, Roscommon, Louth and an excellent draw with Mayo in Crossmolina. They were decidedly unlucky to lose to Monaghan in Castleblayney by one point. Monaghan went on to win the league and have been a power in the football world ever since.

The footballers then lost a play-off for Division One to Roscommon on an absolute quagmire of a pitch in Athy.

After that game there was a firm resolve to consolidate our position in Division Two for the following season. The first game of the 1985-'86 season was against Donegal and plans for that game were completely disrupted because the county final had not yet been played. Wexford lost that game, and proceeded to lose every game in the division. They were duly consigned to the obscurity of Division Three South from which they now operate.

It is a fact that most counties have certain fixed dates for their county finals and stick with them. They play their county finals during September, (usually the second week) with the result that their county teams are well prepared for the commencement of the National Leagues. Of course, counties involved in the All Ireland campaign will not be able to have their county finals in September. This is a problem that Wexford have not had in recent years, (it would certainly be a nice problem to have!) and yet the competitions are running far too late. It begs the question, what would happen if Wexford did get through to an All Ireland?

A properly organised league

It is necessary first of all to note that in All Ireland terms the National League is second only in importance to the Championship and in my view the same should be the case within the county. Most counties have very well run leagues, which are taken seriously by the clubs. Last year the St. Mary's Rosslare club proposed at convention that a proper league be established and this was passed by a very large majority, but sadly it was a bit of a flop mainly because the top clubs refused to play in it, in spite of the majority decision. These clubs are to be congratulated on their progressive approach, their pursuit of excellence and the fine ambassadors they have been for Wexford in Leinster and All Ireland competitions, but they must realise that they have obligations within the county as well. I think that serious participation in a properly run league would lead to a betterment of standards all round and benefits would certainly accrue to the county teams. We must be interested in all our players from Junior "B" right up to Senior, and we must give them all a fair deal in terms of regular competition.

The GAA is not, and was never intended to be, an elitist organisation where the strong benefit at the expense of the weak. I have no doubt but that the majority of the players would favour a properly organised League".

These were my sincerely held views, but I don't think they went down well with everybody. A number of caustic comments were thrown my way to the effect: *"Who does he think he is?"* and *"He's no veteran of the inter-county scene!"* I felt a bit frozen out in fact, but did not regret writing the article, as I was adamant that these things needed to be properly aired in a public forum. There was great dissatisfaction regarding fixtures but nobody seemed to be prepared to do anything about it and yet, as is often the case when someone does grasp the nettle they are slated for it by some individuals, who, one can only assume, must have their own agendas.

However a separate league and knockout championship was not introduced and as time went on, things got worse and worse and headlines such as the following started appearing in our local newspapers. *"Fixtures Frustration", "Slim chance of early championship finish", "Fixtures in disarray", "Fixtures problems causing concern", "Footballers crippled by domestic delays", "Fixtures foul-up is out of control", "Fixtures fiasco", "Officials move to cool Fixtures Fury", "Its time for GAA to get its act together", "Is Wexford GAA becoming a washout?".*

I could go on, but suffice to say that the league-championship format then in operation was extremely unpopular and there were repeated calls for a new system to be introduced. Players in particular were crying out for change. I was one of those players but rather than continue to moan and groan like so many others, I decided to try and do something concrete about it. I sat down for a long period of time and studied the whole fixtures set-up in minute detail, eventually coming up with a twenty page typed document which I sent to many prominent GAA people in the county for their consideration. The essence of the document was, that we needed to return to a knockout championship structure with a separate league system, and that a two season approach to playing our championships had to be seriously considered.

On the 29th December 1993, I sent a copy of the document to Alan

Aherne, Sports Reporter with The *Wexford People*, with the following cover letter:

Dear Alan,

Please find enclosed motion regarding "The Domestic GAA Scene in Wexford" (the document had now turned into a motion to be discussed by County Board). I believe that of all the counties in Ireland we are the worst afflicted with regard to the dual player/dual club, syndrome. The nettle must be grasped and it must be done now. In virtually every other county, for example, Cork, Offaly or Galway, there are generally distinct areas for hurling and football, but in Wexford almost every club plays both, and what is worse and to the detriment of both, alternates them from one week to the other. The whole thing has become extremely distracting for the dual player. He cannot really focus on one game for any sufficient length of time in order that he will be proficient in its skills. Therefore, how can he reach a really high standard in either? It's a proven fact of sports psychology that you have to practise a skill hundreds of times in training before it can be done properly under match conditions.

Why do we persist with a system that is holding us back? We are not winning at inter county level. Has it dawned on anyone that perhaps a major reason why this is the case is because of major flaws in our own domestic system, e.g. no knockout championships and no long established leagues etc.?

I have put forward the enclosed motion for many reasons:

A. With the two seasons approach, and the complete emphasis on one game, standards should improve greatly, our games would have greater quality and appeal, and more potential county players should emerge. At present the early games in the league-championship have little or no appeal or 'bite', and as a result, the county board has lost thousands of pounds in revenue over the years.

B. With knockout championships and specific dates for each game, clubs could thoroughly streamline their preparations and have players at their peak at the right time.

C. With regard to the Leagues the average club player would benefit,

148

particularly the 'fringe' player who would get more games when county players are absent.

D. *Again in relation to the proposed Leagues, there is an incentive for a Junior or Intermediate team to work its way up through the vari ous divisions to compete with the senior teams. This is bound to help them in their ultimate objective of achieving Senior Championship status.*

E. *In the present system a club promoted to senior ranks one year could be relegated immediately the following year, (e.g. Rathgarogue-Cushinstown). Is this fair? Surely a club, having fought hard for many years to achieve the top rank, deserves a two or three year period at least to establish itself in senior competition?*

My motion was discussed at the next County Board Meeting and the decision reached was to set up a special fixtures sub committee to study the motion in greater detail and come up with a new system that would stand the test of time. The committee consisted of the following people: John Denton, (Faythe Harriers), Michael Wallace, (Bannow-Ballymitty), Oliver McGrath, (Shelmaliers), Sean Quirke, (Oylegate-Glenbrien) and Denis Cadogan, (Horeswood). Bill Nolan, (Ballyhogue) and Pat Doyle, (Bunclody), were initial members of the committee but dropped out because of other commitments.

I chaired proceedings, and we set to work with great gusto in mid July 1994. One of the first tasks we set ourselves was to study the fixtures system then in use, namely the league-championship. In our opinion it had the following flaws:

1. Its irregularity and unpredictability: players would get a couple of games in April and perhaps a game in May, but then due to the progress of county teams would usually not get another game for maybe ten or eleven weeks. Its unpredictability arose from the fact that when you run a league-championship you do not know when you are going to end, with draws, play-offs etc.

2. We felt that the lack of a meaningful, properly run league was the key to the fixtures problem in Wexford.

3. Championships were running very late, (Oct.-Nov.-Dec.), and this was affecting county teams, (weakened teams for National Leagues), and Leinster Club championship, (county board having to nominate a team).

4. In the prevailing system, one time relegation candidates could later win a County Final.

5. The absolute impossibility of operating a Master Fixtures Plan.

6. Fixtures and Information Booklet a non-runner.

7. Spectators having to view semi finals and finals in dreadful weather conditions and players having to endure terrible pitch conditions thereby risking serious injury.

Having considered the above flaws in great detail, our next step was to draw up a comprehensive questionnaire and send it to every county secretary in Ireland, enquiring about how they went about implementing a games policy. It was suggested to us that we would get very few replies, but we were quite delighted when twenty-three responded, and were further pleased when many of them also sent on their fixtures booklets so that we could study their systems in detail. I managed to contact most of the remaining county secretaries by phone, so you could say we were in touch with virtually every county in Ireland.

We studied all their systems in great detail and the way a lot of counties went about their business really opened our eyes. We were very impressed by their organisation and efficiency, and were determined to take the best from their systems and apply it to the model county. But that was far from being the end of our work. We also interviewed at length our senior inter-county managers of the day namely Liam Griffin and Liam Fardy, to ascertain what was needed from an inter-county perspective; we spoke to the four districts and took their views on board; we met representatives of the referees and listened to them and I studied in great depth a 1980 report entitled *"The GAA in County Wexford – A Report on Organisational Structure"*. This was a study commissioned by the county board and carried out by two researchers from the Rural Sociology Dept. of An Foras Taluntais, and one of its main recommendations was that *"a fixtures plan should be*

*drawn up and strict rules laid down concerning what conditions justi-
fy postponements."*

We also sent out letters and questionnaires to clubs. Two hundred
players were surveyed from various clubs around the county, and we
found that 98% of them wanted change; they found the existing system intolerable and they wanted something new and workable. I could
go on and on, but suffice to say that we left no stone unturned, holding more than forty meetings in a seven month period, a couple of
them went on into the early hours of the morning. I can clearly recall
writing a final letter to the clubs until 4am, getting three and a half
hours sleep, rushing to work, having the letter typed during my break
and making a mad dash with it up to the County Board Office, then
situated in Murphy Floods Hotel, to have it sent out that afternoon, so
that the clubs would have extra time to study it before the next county board meeting.

And what did we finally come up with, you might well ask? Well, we
decided on a properly structured, meaningful league and knockout
championship. We felt that the two-season approach was too radical
for that point in time, and would not gain the support of clubs. The
overall aim of our new plan was to give the average club player games
on a regular basis, and to facilitate the preparation of county teams.
We saw the following advantages in our new system:

1. As stated, to provide regular, well structured games for all players.

2. To complete County Championships earlier in the year, so that
   County Champions can represent the county in the Leinster Club
   Championship.

3. To facilitate the county teams by: (a) giving players competitive
   games prior to the Leinster Championship. (b) having players available to county team managers, so that teams can by prepared
   properly for the National League.

4. The provision of a master fixtures plan and a detailed Fixtures and
   Information booklet for players, officials and supporters, so that all
   could plan their holidays without missing a vital match.

In due course we presented our new plan to county board, (having gone over our presentation thoroughly beforehand), in January 1995. It was very well received and got overwhelming approval at a subsequent county board meeting in February of that year. Also, at that particular meeting my committee was unanimously adopted by the delegates as a monitoring body on the new system for a three-year period (something, incidentally, we did not specifically ask for and that I, personally, was uneasy about in case it would cause offence to the Fixtures Committee). Naturally, as originators of the plan, we expected to have some serious input into its implementation, at least in its initial stages. But this did not happen. Why, I do not know, as all we were trying to do was to be helpful and lend our advice to the successful implementation of the plan. Personally, I had great respect for the Fixtures Committee and realised that they had a very difficult job to do, a job that led to a lot of meetings and phone calls and often, late hours. Under no circumstances would I, or any member of my committee, have been telling the Fixtures Committee what to do, or have been in any way dictatorial towards them. However, I did think it was vital for the first few months of the plan at least, that the two committees worked together so that any possible flaws or misunderstandings could be worked out, as obviously we were extremely *'au fait'* with all the regulations.

I was subsequently given to understand that some members of the main fixtures committee may have felt that we were out to usurp their positions, but nothing could be further from the truth, as all we were interested in was the successful implementation of the new system, something we had given a lot of our own time to. As I've said, we had a lot of regard for the fixtures committee and knew they had a very difficult job to do, but we had been given a task to do as well by county board, namely the monitoring of the new system and we wanted to do that to the best of our ability. However we found that an arduous task, since we never got any specific terms of reference despite repeated requests. In such circumstances, it was difficult to keep a committee motivated or even in being, and during the three year period from 1995 to 1997 we met only about half a dozen times, and most of those meetings were in vain, and usually ended in frustration.

Eventually two of our members, Oliver *'Hopper'* McGrath and Michael Wallace were co-opted onto the main fixtures committee and a League Secretary was appointed in Seamus Kennelly of the Ballygarrett-Realt na Mara club. Seamus had written to me in late

1997 concerning the new system and excerpts from his letter ran: *"as far as our club is concerned, the fixtures sub-committee did an excellent job in drawing up structures for Leagues and Championships for the county in 1995. The new leagues in particular were welcomed enthusiastically by most ordinary clubs as being a major step forward. Instead of having to organise meaningless practice matches, clubs were now hosting teams at their own grounds, taking in gate receipts to boost their struggle with finance and also playing against new/different clubs.*

The fixtures booklet produced by An Oifig was most impressive and many players and officials commented that at long last the GAA was matching the organisation of other sports. For the first time ever the ordinary player was getting regular games and discipline was being

WEXFORD MINOR TEAM 1992
Pictured above is the gallant Wexford Minor Team before their replay with Meath,
Sunday 26th July 1992.
Back Row, Left to Right: Ciaran Roche, David O'Dwyer, Darren Browne,
Darragh Ryan, Barry Hughes, Thomas Kavanagh, Kenneth Leacy,
Feidhlim McGillycuddy.
Front Row, Left to Right: Damien Fitzhenry, Michael Redmond, Paul Hughes (Capt).,
Scott Doran, Franny Byrne, Rory McCarthy and Enda Newport.

enforced on and off the field i.e. official starting times, pitches properly marked out, official referees etc.

As we see it the leagues ran well during 1995 and 1996, and it is interesting to note that Wexford's Senior and Under 21 successes coincided with their advent. However, as we approach the end of 1997 the leagues have diminished in the eyes of many players, mentors and supporters. The year started well with again, an excellent fixtures book being produced. Unfortunately, as the year progressed things deteriorated. Fixtures became very irregular, notice of games was poor, press coverage become almost non-existent and only one Points Table was published in the paper between March and November!! We feel it is vital to the future of Gaelic Games in Wexford that the leagues be got back on track."

I was delighted to get the above letter from Seamus and was soon asking him if he would consider doing League Secretary. He said he would think about it, and eventually agreed to do so, taking up the position in 1998 and serving for a five year period until the end of 2002. He has not been replaced to date (2004), and that is a cause for concern. It also means that the county board office, in particular county secretary Michael Kinsella, is left with a lot of extra work, which was never the original intention.

The all county leagues have now been in operation for ten years, with the second chance element being introduced into the championships in 2001, in keeping with similar developments at inter county level. And yet, ten years on from the introduction of the new system there is still a lot of dissatisfaction about, chiefly concerning championship games not being played during the summer months, although thankfully, newspaper headlines like those of the early 1990s have not reappeared. But the current situation simply can't continue, as it could be detrimental to clubs who find it difficult to keep their players interested and motivated when no championship matches are being played, particularly during the months of June and July.

I think what needs to be done is a major review of the league regulations, which are now ten years in operation and should obviously have been looked at before now. We devised them under ten main headings, and they were unanimously accepted by the clubs, who agreed to be bound by them. The headings were:

(1) Title, (2) Entry, (3) Grading, (4) Eligibility, (5) Organisation, (6) Venues, (7) Public Relations, (8) Referees, (9) Inter County Players, (10) Sportsmanship.

Let's look at each of them in detail.

(1) **The title of the leagues was the All County Hurling and Football Leagues,** (the term *'all county'*, I have to confess, being borrowed from my own native county). The emphasis was on *'all'* in that the leagues were not to be confined to the districts, (many players complained that they were sick and tired of playing 'the same old teams' in district competitions every year), but would be open to the whole county. Although some teams had to travel great distances at times, particularly during the week, the feedback we got was generally very positive in that a lot of players and officials were commenting that through the leagues they were in parts of the county they had rarely if ever been before, and also they were playing teams they had never played previously and were even shown after match hospitality by many of them, a social aspect I will return to later.

(2) **Entry** – we set an entry fee of £10 per team, and to ensure that all clubs entered we made the proviso that clubs who did not participate in the leagues would not be allowed by the county board to take part in any other competitions. It was also intended that the leagues be well sponsored, and while that was slow enough in coming initially, there is now adequate sponsorship for most if not all of the divisions. But it is really something that should be looked at further, as greater and more attractive sponsorship would further enhance the credibility of the leagues. There are huge sums of money being put into the training and preparation of our county teams, some of which I believe to be unnecessary and superfluous. Surely some of this money at least could be diverted towards our domestic system. After all, what is the main purpose of a county board? To cater for an elite to the exclusion of real promotion of the games? I for one, don't think so. Clubs seem to be subservient at the moment. The vast majority of the players in the association are club players, and county boards must bear that in mind at all times.

(3) **Grading:** There has been no real problem with grading for the various divisions as that has been efficiently done by the grading committee.

(4) **Eligibility:** Our requirement here was that each club must supply a list of its first fifteen players, its second fifteen players, and where necessary its third fifteen players, to the County Board, two weeks prior to the commencement of the League. While this has been generally well adhered to, we have had several instances where clubs have not listed all their best players in their first fifteen, players have been listed who have emigrated, have been carrying long term injuries or who have long since retired. This is most unfair on other clubs who are abiding by this regulation, and the County Board should come down heavily on the offenders. Also, some clubs seem to overreach themselves by entering too many teams, with the result that several players in a number of clubs have to play two games at the weekend. This should not be necessary, as in the vast majority of clubs there are more than enough players for two teams; it's just a question of getting them out to play. Club players in general retire far too early nowadays. In any event these players should show loyalty to their clubs by answering the call when asked.

(5) **Organisation:** League games have been played on a home and away basis, with the first named team having home venue. League draws were for a two-year cycle. As in any league there was promotion and relegation. We were very conscious of the fact that one of the major reasons why previous leagues in the county had failed was because there was no real 'fines' structure in place. With no fear of punishment, teams basically did what they liked when it came to postponements and walkovers. We were not about to make the same mistake, and put a stringent set of rules into place. They were as follows: (i) Teams failing to fulfil a league game will be fined £50. Teams failing to fulfil two league games will be fined £50 per game, and will be eliminated from the league. (ii) Teams dismissed, or who withdraw from, any division of the league will be automatically placed in a lower division for the following season. (iii) For fielding late, a team will be fined £10 for every five minutes, or part thereof to a maximum of fifteen minutes. If a team is over fif-

teen minutes late in taking the field it "shall be liable to forfei-
ture of game in which case the game shall be awarded to the
opposing team (Official Guide, Rule 105)". (iv) All teams must
wear the proper uniform dress. Failure to do so will result in a
£10 fine for a first offence, £20 for a second offence and £50
for a third and subsequent offences. Not having a pitch marked
properly would also result in the above fines. (v) Fines were to
be paid within a month (28 days) of imposition; otherwise the
fine would be doubled. These rules had a dramatic effect as is
evidenced by the following report in the *'Wexford People'* after
the first round of games: *"GAA clubs around the county were
feeling the pinch this week after the imposition of over £800
worth of fines from the first round of games in the new All
County Football League. The guidelines for dealing with late
arrivals were strictly enforced by the Fixtures Committee on
receipt of the referees' reports, with numerous clubs falling foul
of the regulations."* This was obviously a culture shock for many
clubs and may have sounded a bit draconian, but simply had to
be done, given the county's previous bad experience of leagues.
For the latter to succeed there had to be good discipline all
round and all the regulations had to be enforced with great
vigour. Strict rules were also laid down with regard to postponements, with the deferring of a match only possible on the
death of a player or official of the club or on the death of a member of the immediate family of a player or official, with no
rearrangement of games permitted after the Monday prior to
each round of the league. Unfortunately, not all clubs adhered
to this, and we have had spurious reasons for the calling off of
matches, and games being refixed without the press or general
public being told, which is simply not good enough.

(6) **Venues:** As stated, the matches were to be played on a home
and away basis. The first named team had home advantage,
and was responsible for providing a suitable venue, properly
presented. The latter referred to pitches being made as
enclosed as possible with a minimum requirement being a rope
around the pitch. The vast majority of clubs took their duties in
this area seriously, and were only too happy to show off their
hard earned facilities. They were also able to collect money at
the *'gate'*, thereby helping their fundraising, and relished the
prospect of hosting clubs from different parts of the county.

Many of course also provided hospitality to visiting teams particularly those who had to travel a long distance, and this proved to be one of the great social aspects of the leagues. With regard to deciding whether pitches were playable or not, it was the responsibility of the home club to contact a member of the Fixtures Committee and the Referee on the morning of the game, who would then inspect the pitch to ascertain whether a match could be played on it or not. Failure to contact those officials would result in loss of game for the home club.

(7) **Public Relations:** We felt that good public relations were vital to the successful running of the leagues, and that every club should have an active public relations officer, who would report on matches played at their venue. He/she had responsibility for notifying the County PRO (or the County Board Office), and the media of the match result. In addition the PRO of the home club was also asked to provide a very brief report for the local newspapers, citing the final score, who scored and who played well on each team. The two newspapers even provided a specific page for the writing of this report. While many clubs were most cooperative in this regard, others were totally negligent. As a result it was difficult if not impossible for the county PRO or the newspapers to have up to date league tables. Journalists cannot cover every game, and need to be supplied with results. Do clubs not realise this? They most certainly do in other sports such as soccer and rugby, and this is reflected in the coverage these games get in the local papers. Also, the home club could probably advertise the games better in their own areas. It would not take a lot of effort to do out a few match notices and have them put up in the local shops and public houses. The local press could also help by giving the leagues a lot more publicity, especially in regard to previewing the games and perhaps featuring one game each week, and doing a comprehensive review. I am certain the ordinary club player would appreciate such coverage. All these measures would enhance the credibility of the leagues.

(8) **Referees:** Naturally we saw referees as being a vitally important part of the whole structure and we felt they should receive proper expenses for their time and expertise. We proposed that the expenses of a referee should be £15 per game, or £25 for two games at the same venue (it is now €30 per game). At the start of the season clubs were asked to pay £100 per team to cover the expenses of the referee, and the referees were to be paid on submission of their report to the GAA office. Other important regulations regarding referees were as follows: (i) If the official referee can't attend, he should first attempt to send a deputy, and failing to find a deputy, must give 48 hours notice to the Fixtures Chairman (or League Secretary), except in the case of sudden illness or other emergency. (ii) When the official referee fails to attend, if an official (i.e. one whose name is on the official list of referees) is present, prepared to referee and acceptable to both clubs, the game shall be played under him. If clubs fail to agree, no game takes place and the match will be refixed. (iii) When the referee fails to attend, without giving the proper notice, and is not covered by sufficient reason, he shall be fined £10. A couple of others have been added in the meantime: (i) Referees must notify clubs that they are being reported for late fielding on match day. (ii) When a referee fails to attend for an All County League fixture, and the fixture fails to go ahead, clubs are to be reimbursed by Wexford County Committee for legitimate vouched expenses incurred. These are to be reimbursed out of the fines collected during the All County League. Reflecting on these regulations, in general they have been adhered to well, but clubs should realise that referees are human like everyone else and sometimes can be unavoidably absent from a game at very short notice. Given the latter it can be very difficult to get a referee in time for the game. When a referee has failed to appear, clubs have, on occasion, tossed for referee and the game has gone ahead without incident. This is a common sense approach, as what is most important is that the players present are provided with a game.

(9) **Inter County Players:** The rule regarding inter-county players has been quite contentious and the subject of some controversy. It states that: *'all teams are required to fulfil their fixtures without their county players in the event of a clash with Inter-County Fixtures'*. In many instances this has been interpreted far too liberally by our inter-county managers, and has resulted in players missing a lot of games with their clubs, particularly at senior level. The intention of the rule was to keep the leagues going, even on weekends when the county teams were playing in the national league or championship, so as to ensure that the ordinary club player got games on a regular basis. It was an honest attempt to achieve a proper balance between club and county, but I would have to say, that it was not always kept in equilibrium by our inter county managers. For example, inter-county challenge games were sometimes fixed clashing with league fixtures. On occasion, players had to go training with the county team in preference to playing a league game with their clubs. In some instances, players were also told not to play with their clubs up to two and three weeks before the first round of the Leinster Championship and it wasn't just confined to the county senior team either. It's a pity the rule was abused, as it was a good accommodation between club and county and, in many respects, we were ahead of ourselves in Wexford in bringing it in. Perhaps the rule itself could be tightened up, as many feel it is too much open to interpretation, but I believe if there was give and take on all sides, the rule as it stands could be implemented quite successfully.

(10) Sportsmanship: When the leagues were first introduced there were some prophets of doom, who suggested that playing games on pitches that were not enclosed could lead to trouble or even riots! Thankfully such incidences have, to my knowledge anyway, been very rare indeed, if at all, and league games in general have been incident free. Clubs seem to have adhered to Rule 22 of the Official Guide, part of which states: "a club shall be held responsible for the conduct of its members and known partisans".

Undoubtedly, there is a lot of dissatisfaction, particularly among some senior clubs and some of our prominent inter-county players with regard to the current system. They would favour a return to a league-championship, many of them citing the example of Kilkenny, where such a system seems to work very well. But it is not a valid comparison, as Kilkenny don't really deal with football in a serious way, whereas we in Wexford make genuine efforts to cater for both games, as, under the auspices of the GAA, we are obliged to do. It would have to be said that the league-championship has its merits but, in my view, it favours the stronger clubs, those with greater playing resources etc. A new, developing club has a greater chance of making a breakthrough at senior level if there is a knockout or back door championship in operation. Fethard, St. Martins and my own Glynn-Barntown won senior championships for the first time in the mid to late 1990's when a knockout championship was in vogue, while St. Anne's pulled off an historic double in 2000 while the same format prevailed. In my opinion, the latter's wonderful achievement would have been highly unlikely in a league-championship set up, with the extra games and consequent risk of injuries, not to mention having to switch codes on a weekly basis.

I don't think people realise how far we have come with regard to fixtures in Wexford over the past ten years. Prior to 1995 the average club player was getting very few games annually and they were turning to other sports to get some action. Over the years we were ignoring hundreds who would have played our games, but we had no proper games structure in place for them. Leagues had been tried but with no proper rules and regulations in place they were generally very unsuccessful, and some were never even finished. We had also some very late championship finishes in the pre1995 period. I have already pointed out that when Starlights won the Championship in 1983, the final was not played until November 13th. In 1992 there were two county finals played in November, one in December, and one in January 1993. In 1993 there were two county finals played in November. In 1994 we had two county finals in November and one in December. Under the current system this has very rarely happened, with the exception of the All Ireland year of 1996, which, I suppose, was understandable in the circumstances.

This is in no way meant to reflect badly on those who were given the task of implementing fixtures during that period. They were all very honourable people doing their best for Wexford GAA. It is just that the system they were asked to implement was basically unimplementable.

The current All County Leagues now comprise almost a dozen divisions in both hurling and football. They give hundreds of players meaningful games (no game is meaningless and it is an insult to describe it as such) on a regular basis. They have been a major success particularly among Junior and Intermediate clubs who, I suppose, would not be so affected by county teams. Some senior clubs are quite critical of them because they seem to be without their county players a lot of the time, but this shouldn't always be the case with proper cooperation between club and county. What needs to be done over the next ten years is for the all county leagues to be built up almost in importance to the championship but without the "winning only" mentality of the latter. This can be largely achieved by increased sponsorship, more meaningful rewards for the players and greater publicity.

As mentioned earlier, an interesting aspect of the leagues has been their social element. Teams travelling long distances to play other teams have often received hospitality, and this has resulted in players and officials from various clubs getting to know each other. In the past, and not just in Wexford, hospitality for, and friendship among teams had often been sadly lacking, strange when you consider that one of the hallmarks of the Irish as a people is their generosity of spirit, warmth and hospitality.

There is no doubt that clubs are under threat from the increasing amount of games and training at inter county level, as they rarely see their county players for training, especially in the early part of the year. These players are often training up to five or six days a week with the county teams, and really, the rest of the time should be used as a recovery period, but naturally the vast majority feel they are obliged to give some time to their clubs. In the years to come one could reach a situation where players will be faced with a choice: play for your county (if you're good enough), or play for your club, and it would be a sad day if it came to that, as the club would undoubtedly be the big loser. The clubs simply cannot become subservient; if they do it will threaten the very existence of the GAA. Without question, the current fixtures system in Wexford has facilitated inter-county teams, which, of course, was its intention, but it was also our aim to strike a balance between club and county. We must be very careful to get that balance right as I believe, at the moment, it is being weighted more in favour of inter county activity. The Fixtures and Information Booklet, capably produced by the County Board Office each year, is a mine of information and gives players, officials and supporters valuable data concerning upcoming matches, but sadly, because of inter-county activity, the dates for matches in the booklet are not always adhered to, and this can be a cause of real frustration to players in particular, who for instance, have planned their holidays on the basis of information contained in the Fixtures booklet.

The recently published *'Strategic Review'*, which is basically a review of the GAA and how it is functioning at present, states that one of the major weaknesses within the association is *'the lack of a recognised fixtures programme for club players'*. I think that we have addressed that in Wexford, but we must continue to regularly evaluate our fixtures programme to ensure that players are getting enough games and on a regular basis. In a lot of counties this is still not the case, as inter-county managers seem to rule the roost during the summer months. Has the time come then for club fixtures to be administered by a central group, a national Fixtures body based in Croke Park? This body would then liase with a Director of games Development in each county, whose position would be full time. He or she would have to be given real power by county boards, and clubs would have to provide that person annually with a detailed account of the games they have played (i.e. the number of, the quality of, the benefit of etc.).

For all this to run efficiently, there would probably have to be uniform fixtures systems in all thirty-two counties, with a review of same every two to three years. Not every year, as I feel that a new fixtures system must be given a chance to run properly, and this may not happen if clubs feel they can change it, or aspects of it, each year. The ordinary club player will simply have to be looked after with regular games, even if that means setting up club leagues that would cross county and even provincial boundaries (something that is already beginning to happen in some parts of the country). I actually think this would be a great idea, if implementable, as it would give a new lease of life, and add great variety, to the life of the club player. It would have a great social impact too, as club players from other counties would get to know each other.

As I have said already the GAA was not set up to cater primarily for an elite, and it really should be doing something to divert some of the excessive amounts of money that are being put into the preparation of inter-county teams to real promotion of the games at club level.

Finally, I was glad that I, and the members of my fixtures sub-committee, were instrumental in bringing about change in Wexford GAA in 1995. Managing that change has been difficult, and has taken time, but I believe it has been beneficial to the county and its clubs, and the facts are there to prove it

PARIS TOUR 1998
We sent our current Bar Manager, Tony Butler, in search
of Myles Byrne's memories in the library in the Irish College in Paris!
Club members Anthony Whelan (seen pointing the way!)
and John Barron are in the background.

Chapter 7

A Chairman's Life

*"Some people see things as they are and say why?
I dream things that never were and say why not?"*
John F. Kennedy.

I became chairman of Glynn-Barntown GAA Club in December 1998 when I considered my playing career at senior level was coming to an end. There were certain things I wanted to do, things I wanted to achieve, and I was quite prepared to fight an election to secure the position. Before the vote the candidates had to say why we thought we should get the position. For my part I stated clearly that I wanted a modern, state of the art clubhouse built, with ancillary facilities. There was some mirth among those present (a record attendance of almost a hundred people) when I uttered those words, but I was deadly serious about my intentions and lost no time after my election in appointing John Barron, a great club servant, as Chairman of the Club Development Committee. John was given the go-ahead to handpick his committee, which comprised Cathy Atkinson (secretary) Shane Carley (Treasurer), Oliver Raftery, Fr. Pat Stafford P.P., Mai Doyle, Ambrose Madders and Christy Goggin. Jim McDonnell, a former Tipperary hurler, was also an initial member of the committee but had to step down due to other commitments. He did however lend a hand to filling out lotto applications etc.

Having been ratified by the Executive Committee, John's group got to work, exploring a host of different scenarios and visiting a lot of clubs around the country to find out what sort of facilities they had. Clubs called on included: The Sarsfields GAA Club in Cork, Kilmacud Crokes in Dublin, Ballygunner in Waterford and, within our own county, Duffry Rovers, Bunclody, Taghmon-Camross and St. Martin's. After much discussing and teasing out of possibilities, the committee eventually proposed that there should be three components to the proposed development:

1. A modern clubhouse which would include on the ground floor, a reception area, office, two large dressing rooms, external and internal toilets, first aid room, referee's room, bar store and shop. On the first floor there would be a bar, toilets, small kitchen and a large function room/club meeting room, which would open onto a balcony overlooking the entire grounds. The meeting room would be large enough to cater for our AGMs. The premises would of course be fully wheelchair friendly and accessible.

2. The second component would be the provision of two floodlit tennis and basketball courts to emphasise the community nature of the project and attract people who perhaps would never have been in a GAA club before. Many of those people would have children and perhaps in time they would become interested in Gaelic Games.

3. The third feature to be developed was aimed at improving hurling and football skills, namely a Hurling Wall.

The committee got this latter idea when a couple of its members visited the Sarsfield's GAA Club in Cork. They saw something they had never witnessed before – a basically simple structure, which the locals referred to as *'The Wall'*. It was about fifty yards long, 15 feet high and fully floodlit. Club officers told our delegation that it was in continuous use during the winter nights and was used regularly by the club's senior hurling team during the playing season. It was their view that *'the wall'* was excellent for developing ball control and wrist flexibility, in addition to improving coordination and reflexes. Some of their most dedicated players would spend part of their lunch break (or at other times) practising their skills and the beauty of it was they did not need anyone else to be available to puck the ball back to them.

Our delegation went away suitably impressed and reported their findings to the rest of their colleagues on the committee. After much deliberation a decision was taken to build 'the mother of all walls'. It would be 60m long and 4.5m in height, but it was also decided to expand on the Cork idea and extend the grit surface in front of the wall to provide a floodlit arena 60m by 30m with high secure netting right around the arena. This area could then be used for conducting full training and coaching sessions, playing six a side hurling, football and camogie. The club could run internal leagues during the winter months, and could also rent it out to other clubs and organisations, thereby generating extra revenue.

This was the main proposed development, but the committee also suggested that the following ancillary works be carried out in conjunction with it:

- A new entrance to the club would be provided.
- There was an urgent need to provide extra car parking and so the intention was to develop at least an extra 100 car parking spaces with potential for much more.
- Being community minded, the club wished to provide a safe area for walkers and joggers; to that end the committee proposed the provision of a fully lit 1000m walking/jogging path which, with its low level sodium lights, would be ideal for those wishing to exercise at night and, who for safety reasons, would have been reluctant to do so on the busy, unlit country roads.
- A fully stocked gymnasium was also proposed.
- A children's play area would also be developed.

These were the development committee's proposals, which were costed at about half a million euro. They had been teased out over months of debate, so no stone had been left unturned in their preparation. They were presented to the Executive Committee, and we in turn, discussed them at length before approving them enthusiastically.

The next step was to call an Extraordinary General Meeting of the club to present these proposals to the general membership for their approval or otherwise. The meeting was held on Saturday November 3rd 2000. I spoke to the very large crowd in the following terms: *"one of my chief aims on becoming chairman two years ago was the provision of a modern clubhouse and to develop facilities that would have wide community appeal.*

I believe that we must continue to plan for the future and that the future of the GAA in Glynn-Barntown and its continued prosperity will depend on how well it continues to integrate into the community.

Undoubtedly, the club has a strong community base already but I would like to see that base extended and developed much further, particularly in the Barntown area.

I think we should be giving a clear lead in the provision of community facilities. For us to remain purely as a hurling and football club there is a danger in us becoming isolated, and of the community at large passing us by in the years to come.

As a thriving GAA Club, without question one of the best in Wexford, with a very strong membership and very committed people working for the club, and with good basic facilities at present, we are ideally placed to give a strong lead in the development of community activities for all the people of the parish both young and old, male and female.

Development chairman John Barron will, in the course of his presentation, refer to several clubs (which members of his committee visited) throughout the country who have, with courage, vision, drive and imagination, strengthened their own position and support, and at the same time, contributed greatly to the unity of their communities through the common development of wide ranging facilities such as sports halls, tennis and basketball courts, crèches and playgrounds, walking and jogging areas and a new development, a hurling wall.

Finally, the GAA charter in the Official Guide clearly states that one of the main objectives of the organisation is and I quote: "to assist in promoting community development". While the Club Manual, published by the GAA a number of years ago to assist clubs with management and development states and I quote: "The Club of the future must cater for the sporting, recreational and social needs of its members in all age groups".

John Barron then made an excellent presentation of the committee's proposals, which were very well received and, after some discussion, were approved unanimously.

The next step was the Official Launch of the Community Development Project as it was now called. An imaginative glossy brochure was produced and sent to every household in the parish. Within it was contained an invitation to the official launch of the project, which was to take place on the first of February 2001 in the Ferrycarraig Hotel. And in due course it did, with Liam Griffin officially launching the project before a capacity attendance.

Part of my address on the night said that this was: *"the culmination of a lot of very hard work by a dedicated and professional group of people that comprise our development committee.*

Having attended some of their meetings, and having burned the midnight oil on a number of occasions as part of a sub-committee of the said committee, which researched and prepared the application for lotto funding, I can certainly vouch for a tremendously committed group of people who have given generously of their time in their willingness to serve their community in a selfless manner and, who have certainly left no stone unturned in bringing us to this point tonight.

It has become increasingly obvious to me that existing structures and facilities are totally inadequate to meet the current and future needs of our growing community. At present, many people go outside the parish to Wexford town, and other places individually for social and sporting activities. There is a very real danger of the area becoming a mere suburb of Wexford town rather than the close-knit community it once was. Consequently, Glynn-Barntown GAA club, as the major sports organisation in the parish, and indeed the only one currently catering for team sports, after much consultation, are now taking the lead role in the provision of community based facilities with broad appeal. In an era of increasing individualisation we believe it is important that we play our part in helping to recreate a real sense of community. In essence, we hope our new development will lead to a revitalisation of community life.

John Barron followed with a superb exposition of the project (his architectural skills were indispensable to its success), and all left the launch looking forward to the completion of the project in the not too distant future.

Of course the hard work was only beginning, what with lotto funds to be applied for each year, other fundraising, planning applications and of course the actual construction, but the load was lightened by the willingness of so many people to give so freely of their time to ensure the project would become a reality. And it became just that on

Sunday 1st August 2004, when GAA President Sean Kelly opened our new community facilities. An tUachtaráin was at an important match in Croke Park, so we had to fly him down by helicopter (we like to do things with a bit of style and panache in Glynn-Barntown!). It was a grand entrance and created tremendous excitement among the children. Much credit is due to one of our greatest benefactors, Paddy Kehoe, for being extremely instrumental in getting the President to the venue on time. In fact, after the main helicopter developed a fault and could not be used, three two-seater helicopters arrived in Killurin: one containing the President and his wife, another delivered Paddy, while a third subsequently landed with the President's daughter!!

So, after five years of very hard work by a very dedicated development committee, ably assisted by a myriad of helpers and voluntary workers, the project had been finally brought to fruition. The committee had worked tirelessly through thick and through thin and had been extremely resilient in overcoming many obstacles and setbacks. They had shown great vision, drive, imagination and courage throughout the project. Truly, it could be said of them that they were parish patriots and titans of the community.

We were delighted with the great contributions of the people of the parish, in particular those who paid their €635 for five year membership towards the project. We also had a very successful Commercial Committee under the chairmanship of John Doyle of Cleary and Doyle, which persuaded many local business people to pay €2,500 over five years for advertising signs at our main pitch – this has realised over €60,000 to date. Of course without generous lottery funding (€245,000 to date) the development would not have been possible at all, and we were grateful to our local politicians who worked in any way they could to help us achieve this. When I became club chairman I managed to secure the generous sponsorship of the Cleary & Doyle group, whom I approached as they were a successful company based within the parish. Their continued support of and contribution to the running of the club and the development project, was another major factor in our success.

The facilities are now in place and the challenge is to manage them correctly and ensure that they continue to be used into the future, and to improve and develop them as deemed appropriate. They were built for the community of Glynn-Barntown, a community that is increasing in size all the time. However, we cannot stand still or rest on our laurels as to do so would be to move backwards. My own idea would be to build, in the not too distant future, a good sized modern stand for the comfort of our patrons, and install state of the art floodlighting which could help relieve fixtures congestion among other things. Dream on, some might say, but as the 20th century American philosopher Oscar Hammerstein once said:*"you gotta have a dream, if you don't have a dream how you gonna have a dream come true?"* Well, Sunday 1st August 2004 proved that dreams do come true, so let's dream on further!

While rapid progress has been made in recent years, it would be only fair to point out that previous chairmen (and their respective committees) all played their part in bringing the club forward. One thinks of Micheál Kehoe who helped revive the club in 1930 and led it through much of that decade and the following one too, becoming President of the G.A.A in 1949. Then, there was the contribution of Bill Kehoe in the 1950's and early 1960's, the good work being carried on in latter decades by Pat Leacy, Jim Corcoran, Bobby Goff, Michael Laffan, the late Eugene Solan, John Wickham and Tom Rossiter.

Of course, there is more to running a club than development matters and chasing dreams; having successful club teams, and hopefully winning county championships has to be a primary aim as well. It's important that a club advance simultaneously in these two vital areas, as there is little point in having top of the range facilities if one is struggling to field teams, or is not competitive on the field of play. We discussed the idea of a full time coach at our AGM in 2004 and, while we didn't decide to go with it at present, I believe it can only be a matter of time before we embrace the idea. Of course voluntary effort will still be required to support such a person, who should ideally be available to all club teams. And this is where more parents should get actively involved, at least while their own children are growing up. And it's not just enough to get involved; they should also be properly trained in how to deal with the young players in their care. We developed a coaching philosophy in our club a couple of years ago, and I think it will stand us in good stead in the years ahead. At present, this philosophy is very much to the fore at our very well attended coaching sessions for young boys and girls on Saturday mornings.

And speaking of the girls, we are lucky to have a very progressive Camogie Club who won the county junior title in 2000 and the inter-mediate title the following year. Great work is also being done with several underage teams, some of whom have also tasted success.

Obviously, any person taking up chairperson of a club would love to see his/her club win a senior championship during his/her term of office, but sadly it was not to be for me. We did reach the senior hurl-ing final in 2003 and were in a great position 10 minutes into the sec-ond half, when we led traditional power Rathnure by eleven points to five; unfortunately we succumbed in the end, so we still await our first senior hurling championship title. But with good structures in place at underage, success may not be as far away as some people think. The pursuit of the elusive Holy Grail will continue relentlessly, and we certainly wouldn't turn down another senior football champi-onship title either.

I put my heart and soul into the chairman's job, being full of bound-less enthusiasm in my first year in the hot seat. In all, I held a total of seventy-four meetings during my first tenure, twenty-seven of those being meetings of the Executive Committee. I must say I had a very patient and forbearing committee with me, because we really worked hard in 1999 doing a lot of very useful groundwork such as getting an excellent sponsor on board in the shape of Cleary & Doyle, designing a club crest with the help of the children in the local national schools, working out a club motto (Le Chéile a Bheirimid Bua – Together We Will Succeed), exploring the whole area of sports psychology and doing a detailed study of our club constitution. There were also many other things to attend to, and I think the committee and myself were exhausted by the end of the year. I certainly did not maintain quite that pace in subsequent years; if I had I don't think I'd have had any committee to work with! Nevertheless the relentless stream of meet-ings, consultations and phonecalls necessary to the efficient running of a club take their toll in terms of time and energy. I have also had a great working relationship with my fellow club officers, secretary Bill Whelan and treasurer Celestine Fox, who have also done trojan work for the club over the past six years.

Sub-committees are a great way of sharing the workload and get-ting more people involved in the club. Over the past six years we had many of these bodies making a great contribution to club affairs.

These include the already mentioned Development Committee, the Finance Committee, whose primary duty it is to engage in fund raising (e.g. organising The Model County Development Draw, race nights, collection of membership fees, the Lotto etc.), Coiste Na N'og who do a great job with our young people and the Commercial Committee who have done such fantastic work in bringing in major revenue from the sale of advertising space.

Glynn-Barntown has become a very big club to run over the past few years and we now have a Bar Complex Committee in place to run the new development. So it's onwards and upwards, and hopefully over the next few years more of our goals will be realised and that elusive Bob Bowe Senior Hurling Cup, will finally come to rest in the parish.

Chapter 8

Glynn-Barntown on Tour

It was chiefly my experience as a student in the Irish College in Rome in the second half of the 1970s that got me interested in organising Glynn-Barntown's European Tours. As I stated at the outset, I was studying for the priesthood at the time in Maynooth College, and was sent to Rome after completing my degree by my bishop Dr. Cathal Daly (later to become Cardinal Daly). As I described in an earlier chapter, I had a bad experience with regard to gaelic football in St. Mel's College, in Longford and was really determined to make an impact when I came to Maynooth. I threw myself wholeheartedly into gaelic games at the college but also played other sports such as soccer and rugby, after, I hasten to add, I had eventually overcome a badly torn groin muscle that kept me out of action for a long time and threatened to wreck my sporting ambitions. In fact, the sheer frustration of being in a new college and not being able to play any sport was difficult to deal with at the time.

However, I was very serious about studying for the priesthood and when my bishop told me he was sending me to Rome I obediently journeyed to the *'eternal city'*. The only snag was that there was no Gaelic football there! Correction, we did have one annual outing against Aer Lingus of London, played on a rugby pitch in Rome, something I very much looked forward to. In between, apart from the occasional game of tennis, most afternoons were spent playing five a side soccer while the rest of Rome took its siesta. They say that Nero fiddled while Rome burned; well we played soccer while Rome slept!

We also played in an eleven a side soccer league against the other colleges such as the English or the Scottish College, but that was the extent of our involvement. We had a handball alley at the college, but it was not possible to use it, as it was full of rubble. With the permission of the Rector, Monsignor Marron, I decided to clean it out. It took quite a while, particularly when you only had a shovel and a wheelbarrow, but it was well worth the effort as I could now play a bit of handball, but, more importantly, work on my catching and kicking skills for when I would return to Longford in the summer, to play with my club St. Columba's of Mullinalaghta, in the Longford Junior Championship. We actually won that championship in 1977, and all the practise in that handball alley in Rome seemed to pay off for me, as I was adjudged to be the *'man of the match'* in the final. I might have got a call up from the county senior selectors after that, but it wasn't a runner, as I was on my way back to Rome to continue my studies.

There is a lot more football and hurling played in Europe nowadays than there was in my time but, surprisingly, given the amount of Irish people living and working in Rome, that said city still does not have a GAA club. This became very evident in 2003 when the Railway Cup final was hosted in Rome. A lot of people in GAA clubs around Europe took serious umbrage at this, pointing out, rightly in my view, that the final should have been played in a European city that had a GAA club in existence. Many saw it as an insult to the work of the European GAA Board. That was put right in 2004 when the Paris Gaels GAA Club hosted the Railway Cup Football Final. It was a welcome move, as it provided recognition and encouragement for those Irish people in 'the city of light' who have done trojan work in promoting and developing the games there.

The Paris club was in fact our first port of call in 1998 when we embarked on the first of our European trips. (The club had already visited the Fr. Murphy GAA club in London in 1981 where a great time was had by all apparently, but it was a once off at that time.) Paris Gaels had only been formed four years previously in 1994 but was now well established and well organised, catering for both hurling and football teams. Prior to their foundation, gaelic games had been played in an informal manner on the banks of the Seine for many years. We played the locals in exhibition games of hurling and football (on a rugby pitch) and emerged victorious, thereby starting an unbeaten European run that has continued to this very day. What a pity our home form cannot match our away form!

One of the local Parisian newspapers gave a very good preview of the games. With the title *'Les Celts débarquent'* (how's your French?) it stated: *'Les habitués de l'Athlétique Club de Bounogne-Billancourt assistèrent demain, sans le savoir peut-être, à une grande premiére dans la capitale. En l'occurrence, une rencontre sportive exceptionnelle organisée par la mairie du XVIe et le Paris Gaels GAA, une extension de la principle fédération sportive irlandaise.*

Plus de soixante joueurs de Wexford, l'une des meilleures équipes actuelles, seront en effet sur le terrain d'honneur pour faire une démonstration de hurling et de football gaélique, les sports les plus pratiqués en Irlande, loin, trés loin devant le rugby. Si le hurling, ce trés ancien jeu de crosse, ancêtre du hocky, est déjà décrit dans un manuscript datant du Xie siècle, les règles du football gaélique, à la frontière du foot et du rugby n'ont été codifies qu'à la fin du XIXe siècle.

"C'est presque une consécration", explique Anne Donnelly, une *des responsables du Paris Gaels GAA. "Nous espérons que ces joueurs exceptionnels permettront de mieux faire connaître en France ces deux disciplines, si populaires chez nous".*

C'est aussi l'un des objectifs de Claude Goasguen, adjoint au maire de Paris chargé des Sports, et de Pierre-Christophe Baguet, député de Boulogne, qui ont tous deux amorcé, cette année, an cycle de découvertes sportives aux jeunes scolaires de la région et sans lesquels cette rencontre n'aurait certainement pas eu lieu. L'équipe de Wexford sera également accompagnée de deux trophées tres convoités qui, jusqu' ici, n'avant jamais quitté les rivages de l'Irlande: la Bob O'Keefe Cup, des championnats de Leinster et la mythique Liam McCarthy Cup, qui récompense la meilleure équipe de hurling'. Praise indeed for our national games!

Apart from the games, which we greatly enjoyed, the other major highlight of our tour was a visit to the Irish College in Paris (Collége des Irlandais) on 5 Rue des Irlandais, in the famous Latin Quarter. It was a particularly nostalgic visit for me as I had spent a month there as a student in the summer of 1974, attending the nearby Institute Catholique de Paris, where I attempted to improve my French. Due to some sort of mix up I, and a few others, had arrived a day too early at tho college, and could not gain entrance, arriving as we did at night time. It took a few carefully lobbed pebbles at some of the top windows to alert the Rector of the college, a Polish priest, that we were there! The College was actually leased to the Polish hierarchy at that time but since 2001 has undergone a major transformation and now has a new role as the first, Irish government sponsored, Irish cultural centre in the world.

It was great to be back again, and we attended a very enjoyable function on the Friday night (6th February) and returned again on the Sunday morning for mass. Having been spiritually uplifted, we then sought some intellectual sustenance by visiting the library at the College, a very impressive sight containing as it did many rare and valuable items and books, some dating from as far back as the 15th century. One that particularly caught our eye was an original copy of Miles Byrne's 'Memoirs'. Byrne, from Monaseed in Gorey, was a hero of the 1798 Rising in Wexford. He managed to escape from the war ravaged model county, finally ending up in Dublin where he sought refuge from some relations and friends. He was quite involved in the planning of Robert Emmet's Rebellion in 1803, and was sent to France by Emmet, to brief the French government on what was happening in Ireland and ask for their help. Sadly, he was never again to return to his native shores, pursuing instead a career in the French army, as it was obvious to him that the cause was all but hopeless in Ireland. His 'Memoirs' were published in 1863, and are generally seen by historians today as probably the trustworthiest account of the Rising, written from the rebel's perspective. Miles Byrne, along with his devoted wife Fanny, are buried in Montmartre, Paris, and it was interesting to note that over their grave stands a prominent Celtic Cross.

Another book I found interesting was 'The Green Cockade' by Fr. Liam Swords, a former rector of the college. In it, he noted the association of Wexford 1798 priests Fr. Mogue Kearns and Fr. Michael Murphy with the Irish colleges in France. Indeed the case of Fr. Kearns was quite ironic. He was almost hanged from a lamp post by a mob during the French Revolution, managed to survive, but was then executed during the 1798 Rebellion in Ireland.

Before we left the College, we had a lovely reception in the courtyard hosted by the Manageress of the College, a Roscommon lady by the name of Roisin Dockery. I had worked closely with Roisin in the months leading up to the tour, to ensure that everything went smoothly and, as a token of our appreciation for her help, we presented her with a magnificent piece of bog oak sculpture commissioned from local artist Martin O'Rourke (that piece of sculpture sits proudly in the Irish College today). Returning thanks Roisin presented me with a comprehensive catalogue of the Library's books, which I plan to put to good use when I return to the college some day.

It was rather appropriate to be visiting France, and Paris in particular in 1998, given that it was the bicentenary of the Rising and being cognisant of the close links that have existed between France and Ireland over the centuries. My main claim to fame from that trip was that I sang *"Boolavogue"* in the Irish College to people of many nationalities!

Paris Gaels also treated us very well and we had an official dinner with them at which we also made them a presentation for their great hospitality. One of their most prominent officials was a Meath woman called Anne Donnelly and she worked extremely hard to ensure our tour was a success. Great credit is due also to one of our greatest supporters, Paddy Kehoe, who raised thousands in sponsorship to help defray the costs of our tour to this magnificent city.

Our trip to Paris really whetted the appetite for more, and in 2000, having received an invitation, I organised a trip to the GAA Club in The Hague, Holland. The Den Haag GAA Club, as it is called was set up in 1984, and is the backbone of the Irish Club in the Netherlands. Mary Gavin is the main driving force behind the GAA club, and she was extremely helpful with regard to every aspect of the trip. As with the other tours, dozens of phone calls passed between us in the eighteen months leading up to the trip. We stayed in Amsterdam but travelled to The Hague to play the matches, and had the use of the superb facilities of one of Holland's most famous hockey clubs, Kleine Zwitserland. We went in mid March, and celebrated St. Patrick's Day on Dutch soil. Hurling team manager Tom Rossiter and myself were invited to the Irish Ambassador's residence in The Hague for the official St. Patrick's Day reception, and later we all attended a lavish dinner at a nearby hotel. Again we made presentations, to both the Ambassador, John Swift, a Waterford man, and Mary Gavin, who hailed from Galway, and a great night was had by all.

We prepared to travel home in high spirits, but the return journey was full of adventure. What happened was, the bus driver brought us to the wrong airport! Instead of transporting us to Charleroi for our Ryanair return flight home, he brought us to Brussels International Airport so we had to make a mad dash to Charleroi and just about made the plane; it was really hair-raising stuff, but thankfully everything worked out well in the end. Almost sixty people travelled, and all were unanimous that they would undertake another trip in two years time.

Therefore when 2002 came round, we spent four nights in Barcelona at the invitation of the Barcelona Gaels, GAA Club. Cork man, Finbarr Barrett, was my contact in the Spanish city, and just like Anne Donnelly and Mary Gavin before him, was very helpful. It doesn't rain in Spain they say, well it did while we were there, buckets of it, so much so that the rugby pitch we were due to play our matches on, was waterlogged! Necessity being the mother of invention, we overcame this problem, by playing indoors. We were very lucky that the complex that staged the basketball and tennis competitions at the 1992 Barcelona Olympics was available. We played nine-a-side Gaelic football in this fantastic arena, against the local Gaels team and also against Den Haag, GAA Club, who had come down from the Netherlands for the weekend. It was really great fun and everyone enjoyed the novel experience of playing Gaelic indoors.

That night, in spite of all the rain, a number of us attended a Spanish League soccer game in the fabulous Nou Camp stadium, where Barca F.C. was hosting Deportivo La Coruna. The 120,000-seater stadium was only about half full due to the inclement weather, but we witnessed a cracking encounter with the home side winning by three goals to two. If my memory serves me right, Kluivert netted the winner. It rained for a lot of the game and we were quite miserable sitting up in the stands, but it was a great experience nevertheless, to witness, at first hand one of the leading sporting institutions in Europe.

One fascinating trip some of us took outside Barcelona was to see the ancient monastery of Montserrat. It is located 35 miles from the city and we went there by train. From the local train station we actually took a cable car to Montserrat itself. It was a really captivating experience; breathtaking or exhilarating might be better words, as we passed by the mighty, unique, rock formations. For over 700 years pilgrims have been climbing those rocks to the monastery. When we arrived, we went straight to see the Black Madonna statue, which is situated just above the Basilica's high altar. Another highlight of our visit was hearing the monastery's world famous choir, which performs at 1pm every day.

Barcelona itself is a splendid city. It is Spain's largest and its main port. It is very well laid out with magnificent avenues such as the Avenida de la Diagonal, the Gran Via de les Corts Catalones, the Paseo de Gracia and the ever popular Ramblas.

Next up was a trip to Munich in February 2004. We were guests of the recently formed, (2001), Munich Colmcilles GAA Club, and their chairperson Maria Lane, from Cork, was of tremendous help to us right from the word go. In recognition of her contribution and of our commitment to the GAA in Europe, we invited Maria to the official opening of our new Complex on August 1st 2004.

We had a great time in the capital of Bavaria and, as usual, played the local team in games of hurling and Gaelic football, emerging victorious again! That night we had a wonderful dinner in a Greek restaurant, which was actually one of the sponsors of the Munich Colmcilles' GAA Club. During dinner, we were entertained by a Greek musician playing classical Greek songs, while after dinner the official cheerleader of Bayern Munich soccer club regaled us with a splendid selection of tunes on his trumpet. We all sang and clapped along and it really was great fun.

Probably the major highlight of the tour for many, was a visit to Dachau Concentration Camp just outside Munich. It was set up by the Nazis in 1933, and became the model for the rest of the camps. There were many, many thousands of innocent people murdered there, particularly during World War II, and to see at first hand where they died, and the methods used to kill them, had a very sobering effect on all of us. It implanted in our minds in a very real way, that all those figures in our history books at school were actual human beings.

We also managed to take in a Bundesliga game featuring Bayern Munich and Hamburg in the famous Olympic stadium. The game itself was a dull affair with Hamburg most unfortunate to lose 1-0, as they had created most of the chances. However, Bayern were not at full strength and more than likely, had one eye on their Champions League encounter against Real Madrid a couple of days later. We were a good bit away from the action and I think this increased the boredom levels. In fact as the game wore on, one found oneself more interested in the magnificent architecture and layout of the stadium itself, (it hosted the 1972 Olympics), than the actual match. We also saw from a distance the apartments where the Israeli athletes were murdered at those games.

The following day, we also managed to see the Ireland v Wales rugby game in one of the many Irish pubs, that now proliferate in almost every European city. A visit to the famous Hofbrauhaus Restaurant was also a must, where we sampled a beer or two! This trip had everything, including snow on the day of our departure! And in spite of the very cold conditions, there was a carnival atmosphere in the city with people singing and dancing in the streets.

At this point, I think I should relate a brief history of the GAA in Europe. It is probably the least well known of the GAA county boards abroad and, to date at least, its youngest. The first written mention hurling gets on the continent is in 17th century France. Most historians are of the view that this would have been due to the so-called "Wild Geese" who sadly had to leave Ireland, and who subsequently fought for various European armies.

However, the game never really became organised apart from informal jousts in the parks of some European cities, but over the last twenty-five years or so, major progress has been made. All over Europe GAA clubs have been sprouting up and are now organised under the auspices of the European GAA County Board, which was set up in November 1999 in the Marriott Hotel in Amsterdam, with then GAA President, Joe McDonagh giving it his full support and guidance. The following clubs were represented at this inaugural meeting: Paris, Guernsey, Brussels, Den Haag, Dresden, Dusseldorf and Luxembourg, the latter being the first official GAA club formed in 1978. It was set up by Irish people working in the European Commission in Luxemburg, and the first team they played was the E.C. Gaelic Club from Brussels, a team comprised mostly of Irish people working at the European Parliament in Brussels.

The European County Board was fully ratified by Congress in 2000, and since then development has been steady with clubs being established in places such as Barcelona, Madrid and Costa del Sol in Spain, Brest and Rennes in France, Amsterdam and Gronegan in the Netherlands, Copenhagen in Denmark, Gothenburg in Sweden, Lahti in Finland, Vienna in Austria, Zurich in Switzerland and Budapest in Hungary.

Some of the clubs have only been formed very recently like the Copenhagan GAA Club, which was set up early in 2004. It now boasts well over twenty playing members, made up of expatriates, students and five enthusiastic Danes. They are in the process of looking for their own pitch, having earlier registered with the Danish Sports Authority.

Bremen Gaelic Football Club was also founded in early 2004, with the current Chairperson of the European Board, Paul Larkin, being the main driving force. Seven nationalities are represented on their team; they come from Scotland, Italy, Peru, China, England, Germany and Ireland.

The European Leagues are played on a tournament basis over eight rounds, with the best team over five rounds being declared the Champions. There are fourteen teams in the Men's European League with six teams comprising the Women's equivalent. Munich Colmcilles were Men's European Champions in 2004 while Luxembourg won the women's section. The Munich club hosted Round 4 of the League on the 17th of July 2004, and one finds in their excellently produced programme for the event that referees are frequently brought over from Ireland to officiate. For Round 4, Kieran McGuinness of Armagh and Brian Crowe of Cavan did the honours. One also read that their Guest of Honour was the Irish Ambassador to Germany, Seán Ó hUiginn. The Munich club were delighted that he was present, with Chairperson Maria Lane stating: *"Little does he appreciate the sense of pride we take in his attendance"*.

Playing the game can be an expensive pastime on the continent, and it is not unheard of for people to be out of pocket as they travel for weekend tournaments to the various European cities. In fairness, the GAA in Ireland have been supportive by supplying grants, and personally I have found Pat Daly, Head of Games at Croke Park to be very encouraging of our trips. Pat wrote the following letter to me (dated 6 Mean Fomhair 2001) in advance of our trip to Barcelona Gaels in February 2002: *"Dear James, The Central Council is fully committed to support the promotion and development of Gaelic Games – Hurling, Football and Handball in Europe. To date most of these efforts have involved expatriates, but in recent years, there has been a significant increase in the number of non-natives who have become actively involved in playing Gaelic games. We feel that your proposals will further enhance the work of a small but vibrant branch of the GAA based in Barcelona".* Leinster GAA Council have also been very helpful, supplying us with sports equipment for our last trip to Munich in February 2004.

One thing has given me particular food for thought and, it is, I believe, something the GAA should reflect carefully on in the midst of the on-going debate over whether Croke Park should be leased out to other sports. Clubs in Europe are more than grateful to be allowed the use of soccer, rugby, hockey and cricket grounds to play their games. Without this scenario, there would be little or no GAA in Europe and those interested in playing the games would be reduced to playing in parks again, or in handball alleys! This is not just hearsay on my part; I have witnessed it at first hand through our club trips to Europe. What if the people who loan out these grounds, and are so cooperative and friendly to our expatriates, hear that no soccer or rugby is allowed in Croke Park, it would certainly set them thinking. At the very least they would see a certain anomaly in the situation.

Just because you go to live in Europe should not mean that you have to give up playing Gaelic games, and those men and women who keep our games alive and often go beyond the call of duty in so doing, deserve tremendous credit. But keeping them alive is one thing, getting them flourishing is another, as recent surveys in Europe have indicated that only a small fraction of the possible numbers are playing the games, (although there is a growing interest among other nationalities), and a new strategic plan is being developed to be put in place for the future. As it now stands, underage games are being added in places like Guernsey, Rennes and Den Haag where we did a small bit of hurling coaching with some children on our visit there in 2000. Children from various European clubs, particularly Brussels, have represented the European GAA Board at the last few Féile na N'Óg in Ireland.

In October 2004, the Barcelona Gaels GAA Club staged TRI G, a unique underage event for teenagers from all over Europe. The main purpose of the event was education through sport, via the medium of Gaelic games. It was a seven day Gaelic youth event with teams of combined nationalities competing in the three Gaelic sports namely Gaelic football, hurling and handball and it was the first ever Pan European youth Gaelic Games event to be held. It is hoped that it will be repeated in a different city every year.

As our club has witnessed at first hand on our trips to Europe, it is essentially the clubs themselves that are the driving force behind the development of the games. As in Ireland, they are regularly fund raising, and often find that the locals are very generous in their contributions. On our visits to these clubs one found the same type of community spirit as would be evident in any club in Ireland. The ladies have not been forgotten either and they participate in the Women's European Tournaments, which are run in conjunction with the men's. It is hoped to get camogie up and running soon too. Handball actually is the most international of Gaelic games, and is played in various parts of Europe, often apparently in the racquetball courts of sports clubs and sometimes even on the gable end walls of houses!

Cultural activities are not neglected either with dancing and singing to rival any Scór night back on the *"auld sod"*. We witnessed this ourselves at first hand when we attended the St. Patrick's Day banquet outside The Hague on our trip there in 2000. The traditional Irish dancing was of the highest standard, their skills having been honed, no doubt, in the many Irish dancing schools on the continent.

As can be seen the GAA is developing at a rapid rate in Europe, and I believe there is a lot to be learned from the European experience. The first thing I've noticed on our tours is the large number of ladies involved in the various clubs. I'm thinking of people like Mary Gavin from The Hague GAA Club, Maria Lane from Munich and Anne Donnelly from Paris Gaels. There are many others too, and they tend to hold very prominent positions in their clubs. Women holding important positions in GAA clubs here at home still tend to be the exception rather than the rule, and that's a great pity because I think they have a great deal to offer the organisation, not just in terms of being administrators, but also because vitally, they are/will be the mothers of the children of tomorrow, children the GAA will want playing the games. Getting women fully involved also strengthens the community base, and would make them feel more appreciated and perhaps willing to contribute more to the promotion of the games, particularly lady teachers at primary and secondary level.

The GAA has been male dominated for far too long, but perhaps that arose from the fact that the organisation was founded in the late 19th century during Victorian times when, for many, a woman's place was in the home, though a very notable exception to this was the Ladies Land League, which did fantastic work while the male land league leaders were in jail, but which was abruptly dissolved by Charles Stewart Parnell on his release from prison in 1882 (two years before the foundation of the GAA). There was a lot of bitterness and resentment among women about this and ,perhaps, that was one reason why there was little women's involvement in the early days of the GAA (all the founders of the GAA were male). So basically the male dominated GAA got a head start, with the Camogie Association not being founded until 1904, while inter county competitions did not begin until 1932, and of course Ladies Football is quite a recent phenomenon, only getting up and running in the 1970s.

However, things are changing and there are on-going pilot schemes to integrate fully the Camogie and the ladies football associations into the GAA. In my view it should have been done long before now. Women can play a very full role in the association and, for me, the GAA in Europe has clearly shown that.

Another thing that struck me about the GAA in Europe is that there is a great social aspect involved. I am not saying that the games are not taken seriously, they are, but there is much more of a recreational element involved than at home. After all, sport is supposed to be an antidote to the stresses and strains of life, it certainly should not add to them, yet I do feel that here in Ireland the GAA is too success orientated, with a *'winning only'* philosophy very much to the fore. As a result I believe that we lose a lot of players who would otherwise be playing our games. They fall by the wayside because they are simply not able for, or want no part of this *'winning only'* approach. I have always considered that the average (club) player gets a raw deal in the GAA. Often he does not make championship teams in particular, and languishes in the subs most of the time, some eventually dropping out, disillusioned. When I put a fixtures working paper (with a proposal for an All County League) in front of Wexford County Board in February 1994, it was primarily players like that I had in mind.

Of course, championship competition at club and county level generates tremendous interest and excitement and one couldn't do without it, but one thing should be borne in mind, something then GAA President Peter Quinn alluded to in his address to the Wexford GAA Convention in 1994: *"Leagues are for playing, championships are for winning"*. We must endeavour to strike a balance between the two. Certainly the *'playing for fun'* concept should be very much a part of underage GAA but all too often, we find young children being put under incredible pressure by parents and mentors to win games. At times, we see these people half way in on the field almost getting in the way of the young players. On other occasions, we see linesmen and umpires giving decisions in favour of their team that should clearly be going the other way. This carry on is totally unacceptable and the GAA should be doing something about it, and it should also take a leaf out of the European GAA book and adopt a more recreational approach to its games; if it did I believe it could reach areas in Ireland (e.g. the inner cities) where it would never previously have had much of a foothold.

From talking to members of GAA clubs in Europe, there is no doubt that gaelic games give them a sense of their national identity in what is now very much a multi-cultural Europe. As I found myself when living abroad, the importance of the GAA as something uniquely Irish becomes much more pronounced to these people when they are living away from home. And another thing I found interesting was the fact that GAA clubs in Europe have attracted people (many of them women) who would have had little or no involvement with the games at home, something I believe the GAA here in Ireland should ponder on.

The growing success of the games in Europe and indeed elsewhere would seem to suggest that the Association is becoming much more sporting than cultural, and increasingly the games themselves represent the *'sine qua non'* of the whole GAA experience. I suppose it is a pity that the two do not go hand in hand, but that would be particularly difficult for the GAA in Europe who are working very hard to attract non-Irish people to the games and would have to operate through the medium of English rather than *'as Gaeilge'* to make themselves understood. Of course, bilingualism remains a key aim of the GAA but one certainly has to be realistic about it, particularly in the overseas context. However, I think the fact that both Irish and non-Irish people are increasingly embracing the games in Europe is a solid guarantee to the cultural survival of the GAA as an organisation. The Irish pubs, so numerous in Europe nowadays, do help in a cultural sense by sometimes having traditional Irish dancing, music and song in their premises.

Being Irish then on the continent and embracing gaelic games and culture does not mean that we are rejecting our increasingly European identity, nor is it any lessening of our commitment to a United Europe, but as it states in the GAA promotional video '*The Irish Game'*: "*in the modern global village where satellite TV and communications are in danger of devaluing national and local cultures, it's important for the survival of our distinctive identity that we continue to situate ourselves at the centre of our own creative world rather than at the margins of someone else's culture"* Of course, this was a huge factor in motivating Michael Cusack to found the GAA in 1884, and it continues to be a major reason for the '*raison d' être'* of the organisation today.

One hopes that the GAA continues to grow and develop in Europe, (and indeed Asia and other parts of the world), just as it has done in America and Britain. Perhaps in the not too distant future we will have a European team playing in the All Ireland Championship, just like New York and London do today. We often like to think our games of hurling and football are the best field games in the world, well maybe one day, through the efforts of dedicated people in Europe and elsewhere, they will become truly global sports.

Organising tours can be a very time consuming task but I believe they are very important for the '*esprit de corps'* of a club. After all the preparations and when the tour itself comes around, and I see the touring party enjoying themselves so much, it makes all the effort very much worthwhile.

Roll on Berlin in February 2006!

Chapter 9

Purple and Gold Stars

It had been in my mind for a number of years to found a scheme that would give due recognition to the efforts of the ordinary club player, and, in the process, also give a boost to the All County Hurling and Football Leagues. It eventually came to pass in 2002, when I put a motion to Wexford County Board to set up a *'Purple and Gold Stars Scheme'*. It was passed unanimously, and I was made chairman of a committee, which included Seamus Keevans (Gusserane), Johnny Cullen (Kilanerin-Ballyfad), Tony Kehoe (Rosslare), and Seamus O'Toole (Marshalstown).

This committee, having watched as many local league and championship games as they possibly could, set about picking the inaugural Purple and Gold Stars hurling and football teams. We got valuable assistance from David Williams, Donal Howlin, Alan Aherne and Ronan Fagan of the local media. After much extensive deliberation we came up with the following teams for 2002. A citation for each individual player is also included.

Hurling
Paul Carley, (Glynn-Barntown) – for the ever increasing assurance of his play and his consistent alertness.
Colm Kehoe, (Bunclody) – for his great dependability; his unobtrusive but very effective work in defence played a major role in his club lifting the Intermediate crown this year.
David O'Connor, (St. Anne's) – for his consistently high level of performance and his great versatility.
Dave Guiney, (Rathnure) – for the tigerish nature of his play and his ability to mark tightly without fouling.
Keith Rossiter, (Oulart-The Ballagh) – for the stylish nature of his play and his consistently good performances.

Declan Ruth, (Capt), (Rapparees) – voted captain by the selectors for his inspirational performances and his great leadership qualities.

Michael O'Leary, (Rathnure) – for the consistently classy nature of his hurling and his ability to inspire his teammates.

Paul Codd, (Rathnure) – for his considerable role in helping his club recapture the Dr. Bowe Cup. His wonderful scores, both from frees and from play, were a highlight of the year.

Rod Guiney, (Rathnure) – for the infectious enthusiasm he brings to the game, the swashbuckling nature of his play and his great versatility.

Michael Jordan, (Marshalstown) – for his admirable hurling style and his great ability to take scores.

Damien Fitzhenry, (Duffry Rovers) – for his great versatility in assuming an outfield position with his club, and doing so consistently with great distinction.

Michael Redmond, (Cloughbawn) – for his quick, incisive forward play. His scoring ability was one of the factors enabling his club to reach the senior hurling final this year.

Barry Goff, (Faythe Harriers) – for being a very reliable score taker and playing consistently well for his club all year.

Tom Dempsey, (Buffers Alley) – for proving conclusively that there is no substitute for class and that, if you're good enough, you're young enough. For running up some memorable scoring tallies during the year.

Frank Boggan, (Askamore) – for his score taking and general all round play, major factors in his club's march to the Intermediate final this year.

Subs:

Brian Ivers, (Rapparees) – for his great alertness and agility, qualities consistently shown for his club throughout the year.

Joe Mooney, (Rathnure) – for his very determined play and his steadying influence which were major factors in his club's triumph this year.

Tomas Furlong, (Cloughbawn) – for the consistently high standard of his play and his great ability to read the game.

Jim Doyle, (Cloughbawn) – for his wonderful attitude to the game, his tremendous work rate and never say die spirit.

Martin Kehoe, (Cloughbawn) – for showing great leadership skills; a key figure in attack for his club this year.

Fergus Heffernan, (Oylegate-Glenbrien) – for being consistently good for his club all year, shining in both league and championship.

Football

Jason Russell, (Starlights) – for inspiring confidence in his teammates as his club bridged a nineteen year gap.

Phillip Wallace, (Gusserane) – for maintaining a high level of excellence throughout the year.

Fran Fitzhenry, (Duffry Rovers) – for exhibiting many of the classical aspects of full back play as his club made a welcome return to the final stage.

Colm Morris, (Castletown) – for the earnestness of spirit and the adventurous nature he brought to his game this year.

Ken Furlong, (St. Martins) – for the notable and enterprising role he played in his club's advance to the Intermediate final this year.

David Murphy, (Rosslare) – for the manner in which he established himself as a brilliant centre back as his club made notable progress this year.

Leigh O'Brien, (Horeswood) – for the great inventiveness of his play and the unerring accuracy of his freetaking.

Willie Carley, (capt.), (Glynn-Barntown) – voted captain by the selectors for the range of his contributions to his club and his outstanding qualities of leadership.

Sean Whitty, (Adamstown) – for the elegance and style of his football and the influential role he played in his club's progress this year.

Diarmuid Kinsella, (Castletown) – for his undoubted class and the incisive nature of his forward play which brought him many fine scores.

John Hudson, (Starlights) – for his sheer scoring exploits and the maturation of his play, vital factors in his clubs ultimate success this year.

Patrick Naughter, (Realt na Mara) – for his tremendous accuracy which contributed so much to his clubs progress to the Junior title this year.

Derek Leonard, (Glynn-Barntown) – for his ability to seize on a half chance, and his lethal finishing.

John Hegarty, (Kilanerin) – for the subtlety and ingenuity of his forward play, and his perseverance in adversity.

Matty Forde, (Kilanerin) – for his inventiveness and wonderful scoring power, repeatedly shown both from open play and free taking.

Subs:
John Cooper, (Adamstown) – for continuing to turn in consistently high levels of performance with his club.
Tom Wall, (Starlights) – for his superb man-marking skills and his sheer versatility.
Philip McGovern, (Craanford) – for his very determined play and his indefatigable spirit.
Brendan Doyle, (Ramsgrange) – for his wonderful high fielding and his ability to inspire his team, qualities shown to great effect as his club marched to Intermediate glory this year.
John Mernagh, (Kilmore) – for the classy nature of his play, making a very notable contribution to his club's march to the county Junior final this year.
JJ. Doyle, (Duffry Rovers) – for the vital role he played in helping to steer his club to this year's Senior final.

These teams played Wexford selections on Sunday 29th of December 2002 at Wexford Park with the Wexford hurling selection beating the P&G Stars by 3-12 to 3-7, while the football game was a real cracker with the sides finishing level, (P&G Stars 2-15, Wexford 4-9) and being accorded a standing ovation by the close to 1,500 attendance. All proceeds from the games went to the Special Olympics 2003 Host Town Committees, (Ireland hosted the Special Olympics in 2003). A cheque for over €7,000 was presented to representatives from the Special Olympics at a County Board meeting during 2003.

Before the hurling and football games took place, each player received a specially designed Purple and Gold Stars jersey, togs and socks. At the commencement of each game the names and a brief citations of each Purple and Gold Stars recipient was read out, and they were also presented with a special P&G Stars Award at a function in White's Hotel (the chief sponsors of the event) after the games. We asked our most recent All Ireland winning managers to take charge of the teams on the day with Liam Griffin doing the honours for the hurlers, while the management duo of Kevin Kehoe and Aidan O'Brien who guided the Good Counsel senior footballers to All Ireland Colleges success in 1999, took charge of the footballers.

For 2003 the committee was expanded to include Joe Doran (Buffers Alley), John Whelan (Rathgarogue-Cushinstown), Michael

Doyle (Crossabeg-Ballymurn) and Larry Cahill (Ballyhogue). Journalists Alan Aherne and David Williams, from *The People* newspaper and Ronan Fagan from *The Echo* stood down and were replaced by Jimmy McDonald (The Echo) and Liam Spratt of South East Radio.

There were a few changes to the format from the inaugural year in that, firstly, nominations were introduced with seventy five players being nominated for hurling and football. Secondly, we decided to institute a new award for the player who was good enough to make both teams. Thirdly, we decided that the proceeds from the games (which amounted to €7,400) would be divided evenly between two very worthy causes: HOPE, the cancer support group based in Enniscorthy and Wexford Hospital, Accident and Emergency. Fourthly, we decided that the management of the teams would rotate between the Senior, Intermediate and Junior winners each year.

After many meetings and much consultation we came up with the following Purple and Gold Stars for 2003:

Hurling
Jim Morrissey (Rathnure)
Pierce Donoghue (Glynn-Barntown)
Eugene Furlong (Glynn-Barntown)
Anthony O'Connell (Rathnure)
Mick O'Leary (Rathnure)
Willie Doran (Buffers Alley)
Liam Dunne (Oulart-The Ballagh)
Paul Codd (Rathnure)
Tomás Mahon (Rapparees)
Paul Carley (Glynn-Barntown)
Trevor Hogan (Rathnure)
Matty Forde (Ballyfad)
Robbie Codd (Rathnure)
Tom Dempsey (Buffers Alley)
Rory Jacob (Oulart-The Ballagh)

Subs:
Stephen Doyle (Oulart-The Ballagh)
Enda O'Leary (Ballyfad)
Shane Carley (Glynn-Barntown)
Willie Carley (Glynn-Barntown)

Nigel Higgins (Rathnure)
Chris McGrath (Shelmaliers)

Football
John Cooper (Adamstown)
Brian Hughes (Kilanerin)
David Currid (Bannow-Ballymitty)
Phillip Wallace (Gusserane)
Páraic Curtis (Clongeen)
Pat Forde (Kilanerin)
Robert McGeean (Bannow-Ballymitty)
Seamus Hughes (Kilanerin)
Paddy Colfer (Clongeen)
Liam Murphy (Clongeen)
John Hegarty (Kilanerin)
John Hudson (Starlights)
Matty Forde (Kilanerin)
Aodhán Kavanagh (Kilanerin)
Stephen Sheehan (HWH Bunclody)

Subs:
Barry Hughes (Kilanerin)
Colm Morris (Castletown)
Leigh O'Brien (Horeswood)
Seamus Ryan (Gusserane)
David Shannon (Horeswood)
Scott Doran (Kilmore)

As per the previous year the teams played county selections, on this occasion at Glynn-Barntown's GAA Grounds at Killurin due to the unavailability of Wexford Park. We were very grateful to Ger O'Reilly, Joe Donoghue, Celestine Fox and all their helpers who worked extremely hard to ensure that the venue was in tip-top condition. Tea and sandwiches were provided right throughout the afternoon and were much appreciated by the attendance.

The games themselves were exciting affairs with the Purple and Gold Stars winning the football by 2-13 to 2-10 while the hurlers played a draw: Wexford 0-17, P&G Stars 1-14. Representatives of the county Junior Champions managed the teams on the day with Aidan Barden and Jim O'Connell (Bannow-Ballymitty) doing the honours in hurling, while Liam Pettit (Our Lady's Island) took charge of the football team. Matty Forde became the first player to be selected on both teams in the same year and it was something he richly deserved, since he had scored 5-28 for his hurling club Ballyfad in its march to the Skoda Intermediate Hurling Title, while he notched 2-40 for his football club Kilanerin, as it regained the Campus Oil Senior Football title. Who will forget his 0-13 point tally in the county final against Horeswood? And of course he also lit up the occasion at Killurin weighing in with a personal tally of 2-9.

We reverted to Wexford Park for the 2004 Purple and Gold Stars and they were:

Football
John Cooper (Adamstown)
Tomas Byrne (Ballyhogue)
Philip Wallace (Gusserane)
Mark Gahan (Starlights)
Darragh Breen (Gorey St. Enda's)
Michael Hanrahan (Sarsfields)
Paraic Curtis (Clongeen)
Paddy Colfer (Clongeen)
Denis Kent (Rathgarogue-Cushinstown)
Pat Forde (Kilanerin)
Shane Cullen (Gusserane)
Redmond Barry (St. Anne's)
John Hegarty (Kilanerin)
John Hudson (Starlights)
Matty Forde (Kilanerin)

Subs:
Tom English (Ballyhogue)
Brendan Mulligan (Sarsfields)
Leigh O'Brien (Horeswood)
John Harrington (Sarsfields)
Ollie O'Connor (Starlights)
Philip Cullen (Sarsfields)

Hurling
Jim Morrissey (Rathnure)
Anthony O'Connell (Rathnure)

Keith Rossiter (Oulart-The Ballagh)
Barry Kenny (Buffers Alley)
Willy Doran (Buffers Alley)
Liam Dunne (Oulart-The Ballagh)
Kevin Kavanagh (St. Patrick's Ballyoughter)
M.J. Furlong (Cloughbawn)
Darren Stamp (Oulart-The Ballagh)
Dessie Mythen (Oulart-The Ballagh)
Redmond Barry (St. Anne's)
Nigel Higgins (Rathnure)
Rory Jacob (Oulart-The Ballagh)
Michael Jacob (Oulart-The Ballagh)
Michael Jordan (Marshalstown)

Subs:
Noel Carton (Cloughbawn)
Mark Furlong (St. Patrick's Ballyoughter)
Garry Curley (St. Patrick's Ballyoughter)
Patrick Whitty (Adamstown)
Leighton Gleeson (Ballygarrett)
Keith Burke (Buffers Alley)

In bitterly cold conditions, maestro Matty lit up yet again, what was basically a dull affair, with some wonderful scoretaking as he led the Purple and Gold Stars to a one point win over the Wexford selection (2-6 to 1-8). The hurling match marked the start of Seamus Murphy's reign as Senior Hurling manager and it was a winning one too with his Wexford selection winning by 2-12 to the P&G Stars 2-10.

Redmond Barry became the second player to be selected on both teams and, like Matty Forde the previous year, received a special award for this distinction. The proceeds from the games, which came to €5,600, went to a cause dear to County Chairman Sean Quirke's heart, namely The Irish Guide Dogs For the Blind. The honour of managing the two teams on the day fell to the Intermediate Hurling and Football Champions, namely St. Patrick's in Hurling, represented by Mick Curley and Ballyhogue in Football, represented by Denny Tyrell.

Looking back on the three years of the scheme, I think the players are very appreciative of the awards they get, but would probably like to see the games played at a better time of the year, weather wise particularly. And one can certainly empathise with them on that score. But with a very full club and county schedule it's difficult to see what other time of the year they could be fitted in. Everyone is available around the Christmas period, with New Years Day probably the preferred date for the games. Of course, it's asking a lot of people to expect them to come out and watch matches in bitterly cold conditions yet attendances have compared very favourably (and even well surpassed on one occasion) the similar *'Blue Stars'* event in Dublin. These things can be explored in a thorough review of the scheme, and if they and a couple of others can be ironed out, I believe the Purple and Gold Stars can go from strength to strength, and become a much looked forward to event in the calendar year for GAA players and supporters.

Munich Tour
2004

The legendary Paddy Kehoe pictured with Munich Colmcilles
Chairperson, Maria Lane, Munich, Feb 2004

Chapter 10

Some things on my mind

The GAA official guide

This is our rulebook, our constitution if you like, and our guide as to how we should manage our affairs in the Association. And yet, having read it a few times, I find some of the rules vague, not specific or clear enough, open to interpretation and in a couple of cases almost contradictory. What we have to ask is: are all our rules still relevant to the modern age and can they still be effectively applied? Are some of them holding us up to ridicule – e.g. the mascot controversy in 2003 concerning Laois player Joe Higgins' sons (in fairness the rule was subsequently changed to allow one mascot per team) and what about the requirement for a two thirds majority on certain issues when the Constitution of the State requires only a simple majority?

Motivated by these concerns I put the following motion to our County Convention in December 2003: *"that the GAA set up a committee with some independent representation, to conduct a root and branch examination of the Official Guide, assessing its relevance to the modern age and presenting a report and recommendations to a special rules congress in 2005."* I must say I was surprised to be told that such a committee was already in existence as my club had heard nothing about it, it did not get any questionnaires etc, nor was it asked for any submissions. I thought that with a matter of such importance all GAA clubs would discuss it thoroughly and would make recommendations to Croke Park rather than the other way around.

The clubs are the backbone of the Association and I feel they should be more widely consulted not just in this matter, but in all matters. I have no doubt but that our overall structures need overhaul and that much greater power should be given to clubs in terms of voting rights and overall decision-making within the Association. I also feel that we should be big enough to study the constitutions of other major world sporting organisations to see if they have anything to offer us.

The Annual GAA Congress is basically an annual review of the association where there are motions down for discussion (that is if they haven't been ruled out of order first!). In addition to the top brass and officialdom, delegates from all the clubs in Ireland attend it. I have never been to one of these gatherings but if what went on in 2001 is indicative of how they do their business, I don't want to either. It was the year the government gave a €60m. grant to the GAA for the redevelopment of Croke Park, on the eve of the Congress. A motion to open up Croke Park to other sports was being debated at Congress that year and just failed by one vote to reach the required two-thirds majority. A lot of people feel that the Government's last minute largesse (which the GAA well deserved for its magnificent community work) clearly influenced the vote, but be that as it may, my main gripe was with how the vote was carried out. They decided to do it on a show of hands! Surely, with such an extremely important matter that would have widespread consequences for perhaps years to come, the only way to proceed would have been through a secret ballot, or at the very least a paper vote, particularly when you had several hundred people present. I also understand that there was only one count and no crosscheck, and that unbelievably, there were up to forty people out in the toilets while the vote was going on. Why weren't the doors manned to ensure that there was a full attendance for the vote? The motion itself only failed by one vote, a vote that could have easily gone astray in the count. But the powers-that-be refused a genuine and very reasonable request for a recount. When I heard this I just couldn't believe my ears, and I said to myself: *"the GAA prides itself on being a very democratic organisation but this is totally undemocratic"*.

The Quality and Quantity of Training at Inter-County Level
Training at senior inter-county level has become really intense in recent years, reaching virtual professional levels, yet we remain an amateur organisation (and should continue to do so) with all the players involved having to work for a living. In fact, it must be very difficult to be an inter-county hurler and footballer nowadays, because there is so much to juggle: job, family, parenthood, and of course, getting sufficient rest.

How can our players possibly get sufficient rest and relaxation when they have to hold down full time jobs? As the saying goes: 'you don't get fit when you train, you get fit when you recover from training'. There has to be a lot of stress involved in being a county player nowadays and I suppose, given the different make up of each individual, some can cope with it better than others. We have had some high-profile examples in recent years where players have simply walked away from the game because they have had enough; two names immediately spring to mind: Brian Corcoran and D.J. Carey, who obviously lost their appetite for playing, but thankfully returned to the game subsequently. In football, one thinks of Galway's All Ireland winning goalkeeper, Martin McNamara who retired from the GAA for a period a few years ago because he just found it too difficult to juggle his sporting, business and family commitments.

There is growing concern at the intense pressures being exerted on GAA players at inter-county level, with many people feeling (among them eminent doctor Risteard Mulcahy) that the physical demands of the game and the stress involved are leading to burnout.

I don't think the GAA is making a serious attempt to prevent burnout, particularly among our best young players. There seems to be very little co-ordination with regard to the use, or should that be overuse or even abuse of players. One really wonders does player welfare rate very high in the GAA's scheme of things, as it appears that the very best young players generally play far too many games and engage in far too many training sessions particularly during the months of January, February and March. These young players usually turn out for their Universities at that time of year in preparation for the Sigerson and Fitzgibbon Cups, but they can also be in demand at minor, U-21 and even senior level with their clubs and their county.

I have long advocated doing away with both the minor and under 21 grades and replacing them with an U19 competition. The under 21 grade (so extremely difficult to run) has, in my view, long outlived its usefulness and I cannot for the life of me understand why the GAA, if it is genuinely interested in the welfare of its young players, continues to persist with it. There is absolutely no doubt but that it has lost its *"raison d'être"*. The competition was started in 1965 (Wexford won the inaugural hurling title) to give players some badly needed games between minor and senior but most players now go to third level where they get more than enough games and they don't need the under-21 grade at all. In fact, having to play in it is putting them under incredible pressure at a time in their lives when they have enough to contend with, as they try to carve out a career for themselves. Some give up the game altogether in their early twenties as they become totally disillusioned with having to serve several masters, have chronic injuries that they cannot get to, or were never given a chance to heal properly, or simply because they are totally burnt out. It should surprise nobody that the training and match schedules that many of our best young hurlers and footballers are expected to endure would not be asked of professional soccer or rugby players. And our players are amateurs. Need I say more?

Do inter-county teams have to train five times a week to be successful? The success of Tyrone in winning the Sam Maguire Cup in 2003, training an average of twice a week and playing no challenge games, would seem to answer in the negative. I think the O'Neill County proved in no uncertain terms that cutting down on quantity does not sacrifice quality or limit success; for them less was more! And what about the extraordinary odyssey of little Fermanagh in 2004? They were annihilated by the said Tyrone team in the All Ireland Quarter Final in 2003, their manager resigned and close to a dozen players also pulled out of the panel. Nobody wanted the job until Donegal's Charlie Mulgrew had the guts to take it over and yet they almost reached the All Ireland final. They were relatively late in getting their show on the road and simply didn't have the time to undertake the arduous training other counties engage in. It should also be pointed out that, in GAA terms, Fermanagh is a very small county indeed and their County Board would have had great difficulty in financing huge preparations.

To maintain the amateur nature of our Association (we could never sustain professionalism) I believe that the GAA should confine inter county teams to collective training twice a week with a game at the weekend. I know this would be difficult to police or enforce, but if county boards were fined severely for non-compliance (e.g. €25,000 for a first offence, €50,000 for any further reoccurrence) it would soon bring counties into line. It would also help to bring about a level playing field given that the counties with major populations have far greater playing and financial resources than smaller counties such as Leitrim and my own native Longford. I believe that such counties, and others, will eventually go to the wall if they have to continue to compete financially against the bigger counties in terms of team preparation. They simply could not sustain it indefinitely.

What benefits would accrue from county teams training only twice a week? Well, primarily it would lead to less stress and strain on players, particularly those who have to travel long distances to training. It would help to prevent burnout and lead to the extension of inter county careers. County players would be more available to their clubs, not in a training sense necessarily, but by just being present at training sessions they would greatly help club morale. There would be financial savings by County Boards who could put the money into proper promotion of the game at local level, which, as I have said already, is in fact, their primary duty, not just catering for elite county teams.

County Boards should also be closely monitoring the quality and quantity of training being provided by managers of their county teams and not just from a financial point of view. And perhaps, given how incredibly demanding managing a senior inter-county team has become nowadays, they should consider turning the position into a full time one with a written contract as to what managers can and can't do, for there is certainly a perception that inter-county senior managers basically call the shots in counties during the Summer months while club players grow increasingly exasperated because of the lack of regular championship games. There is provision in Rule 12 of the Association for them to be made full time and perhaps it is the least that players deserve, given the amount of time they give and the fact that they are not being paid themselves. In those circumstances players certainly deserve to have a person in charge of them who can give his full attention to the job. And the farcical situation of appointing a manager for one year only, with a review at the end of that year should also cease. A manager deserves at least a two year period, as he is only getting to know the players in year one, while he would be aiming to make some serious progress with the team in year two. A minimum two-year period in charge gives a manager much greater security of tenure and it allows him to plan for success.

The Role of the Teacher in the GAA

Ever since the time national schoolteacher Michael Cusack founded the GAA, teachers have played a prominent role in the association. Since I am a secondary school teacher I will be confining my remarks to that area but I would like to acknowledge the fantastic work that is being done by teachers at primary level in turning out generally well coached youngsters who then pass on to second level. When you are preparing a secondary school team, it's certainly a big help that they already have the basic skills (of course credit to the clubs for this too).

The biggest problem I have found in preparing teams for school competitions is that I have little or no control over the amount of training and matches played by my players, and that is not just GAA games, which should, in any event, be over or very close to completion before the school year starts, to give us an opportunity to prepare properly for colleges competitions. The latter are probably of greater benefit as the student is often playing against students from other counties and would probably learn more.

Contrast this with the situation in top rugby schools where their students would not be playing any other rugby at club level and would have to get official permission if they wanted to. This would generally not be forthcoming as the teachers there would be very concerned about the dangers of burnout in their players.

In the light of this Coiste na nÓg in Wexford has to ask itself are there too many club games on, particularly during school's competitions and are we sacrificing quality for quantity? Are there too many divisions (Roinns) and is a county medal far too easily come by?

It seems incredible that in a proud GAA county like Wexford there has been no All Ireland minor hurling title won since 1968 and no Leinster minor football title since 1969. In fact, it's totally unacceptable. Why is it happening? It is hard to put one's finger on the exact reason but burnout may well be a factor. The young players, particularly the key ones, may well have gone stale from too many matches and training. It is something that has to be extremely well monitored, and consulting trainers at secondary school level has to be a vital part of the process. I am not satisfied that this is happening to any real extent at all. I trained the county minor footballers in 1992 and was in regular contact with teachers in the other schools to find out as much as I could about the players on my panel. I was not taking the player in isolation but wanted to find out about the whole person, what made him 'tick'.

That particular year was a good one for Wexford minor teams with the hurlers reaching the Leinster final and the footballers losing the Leinster semi final to Meath after a replay and extra time. About half the football panel were from St. Peter's College who had a wonderful run that year getting to the All Ireland colleges football semi final, but I've often wondered did that great run make them a little bit stale when it came to the Leinster Minor Championship; in addition to that quite a few of the lads were dual players and its quite possible that they had too much training and matches and had lost a considerable amount of their *'zip'*.

The dual player certainly can be a problem, but at that age I certainly would not put any young fellow under any pressure, implied of otherwise, to declare for one game or the other. At that period in their lives I think they have enough to contend with: approaching exams and their parents perhaps anxious that they would do further study would be two of their concerns. At that stage they would be playing sport for enjoyment and as a release from their studies, and the last thing they need is hassle over which game they should play, particularly when they enjoy both of them. However, I would certainly make allowances for the dual player in terms of training and matches, otherwise you may have a situation where the player is mentally and physically exhausted when you need him most.

In spite of a dramatically increased workload over the past ten to fifteen years, teachers continue to make a great contribution to the GAA. Not alone do they continue to train school teams but are also active at club and county level. Therefore, it was disappointing at the time of the teachers strike in 2001-2002 that the GAA did not come out strongly in support of the teachers, or at least acknowledge the work they were doing. It left a bad taste in the mouth of many of my colleagues. It seemed as if we were being taken for granted, and some people seemed to think that the extra curricular work we were doing in regard to games was all part of our job, which of course it isn't.

In fact, criticism of teachers got so bad and so vitriolic that I felt compelled to go on *'The Last Word'* to discuss the matter with Eamonn Dunphy in an attempt to set the record straight. I would have to say however that the Leinster Council of the GAA went at least some way towards recognising the contribution of teachers subsequently, by presenting all teachers involved in games in schools throughout Leinster with a fine selection of sportswear.

Facilities in schools to train teams and get pupils fit have often been sadly lacking and it's only been in the last few years that we in CBS Enniscorthy have got a gymnasium, but not all schools have that facility, something that would be seen as a basic requirement in most other countries. Is that one reason why these other countries do far better than us in the Olympics? The government simply must take sport far more seriously and ensure that every school in the country (primary and secondary) is equipped with a well-stocked gym and at least one qualified P.E. teacher. Local authorities too can play a major role in promoting sport in schools by providing and maintaining grounds where schools have no space to do so.

There is a real urgency about this as it would appear that thousands of young people are leading very sedentary lives, spending numerous hours sitting in front of the TV and playstation, doing little or no physical exercise and engaging in no sporting activity. While only a few can actually represent the school in sport, it is crucial that all students get the opportunity and encouragement to play at whatever level they can, as it is good for health and self esteem and encourages healthy living. We have a growing problem of obesity among young people, as those who do little or no exercise are likely to be eating far too much junk food. Could we possibly have a situation in years to come when children die before their parents because of health problems brought on by inactivity and obesity? Some health experts have already warned that this is a strong possibility if things keep going the way they are.

I have enjoyed my involvement with CBS teams down through the years, and you certainly see the students from a different perspective, which I have found can be quite a help in the classroom. Pupils who are academically weak often shine at games and it gives them an opportunity to be good at something and, in turn, raises their self-esteem. It is now well recognised that there is a "sport intelligence" as distinct from an academic one. It is also high time that pupils were recognised for their sporting abilities in the Leaving Certificate, and got points for their excellence in this area.

A major disadvantage we have in CBS Enniscorthy is that we do not have our own pitch beside the school unlike many other schools, which immediately rules out matches and training at lunchtime. We do have the use of the facilities in nearby St Patrick's Park and the Showgrounds, where long serving groundsman Mickey Lynch has always been most helpful. However, valuable time is lost going to and from these venues. In addition, many other teams, including county teams, use these facilities and due to overuse and other reasons, they are not always available.

Preparing a school team really eats into whatever free time you have. There is much more to it than meets the eye. For a start you have to run a series of trials to decide on your best panel, and this has to be done after school because, as I mentioned earlier, there just isn't sufficient time to do it at lunchtime. Having picked your panel you now have to train and coach them into a cohesive unit, and one has to be careful about overdoing it in this area, as the vast majority of them, particularly the most talented ones, are playing and training with their clubs and engaging in other sports. Some may also be playing with the county. Weight training should be an option with the senior teams as it is in rugby schools, but one is extremely reluctant to engage in it, as there is no guarantee that the students will get sufficient rest or recovery between sessions, which is vital for any lasting benefits to accrue.

Organising a match can also be very time consuming. The Leinster Council normally looks after the venue but generally the onus is very much on the teachers involved to get a referee and that can be a problem as, naturally enough, the vast majority of them work for a living and are not available during the daytime. Clubs are generally pretty good with regard to the use of their pitches but some are reluctant to give them, particularly if there has been very heavy rain, and one can understand why, as pitches can cut up very easily during such conditions. I should point out that most college's games are played during the very worst months of the year.

If you are playing at an away venue the players have to be transported there, and therefore a bus has to be booked; this can involve further phone calls and organisation. There are several other things you have to get ready before you can get on that bus. The vice principal has to be informed so that your classes are covered, and up to recently it was your colleagues who had to cover for you free gratis.

And of course when you are away at a match you are missing classes yourself, and since your primary duty as a teacher is to teach and get your courses covered this is not an ideal situation.

You must also ensure that you have sufficient jerseys and tracksuits, first aid and plenty of water. And if it is a wet and windy day, which is often the case at that time of year, you need good quality wet gear and even a pair of wellingtons. Otherwise you'll get a good drenching, and I speak from experience! In addition you have to make sure you have enough money in your pocket to pay the local groundsman and the referee (after the game!). You are of course always reimbursed by the school when you remember to ask for it. As in a club set up, you have to make sure that footballs are available properly pumped, and in the case of hurling, plenty of sliothars and hurleys. Also team lists have to be written out in triplicate, in Irish.

If a player is unfortunate enough to get an injury he must be looked after and given the best possible treatment. This may mean a visit to the casualty unit of the local hospital and often a long wait before the student is seen. But I or any other teacher in the school never had any problem in doing this as we have always seen ourselves to be *'in loco parentis'*.

If your team is doing well and they are willing to do so you might take them in to train once or twice during the Christmas or Easter holidays. If you get a very good turnout you know that these lads are serious about winning something with their school.

After a game everyone is in a rush to get back in time for the school buses, but sometimes when the match venue is a considerable distance from the school that is not always possible. Nowadays parents usually pick up their sons at the school when they return but over the years teachers have been known to drop students home also.

However, in spite of everything, I have enjoyed working with young people and get a great sense of satisfaction from it. It's great to see a young lad improve as he goes along. At the end of the day we are helping young people to grow and develop into fully rounded human beings, their involvement in sport being an extension of the classroom. The ancient Romans put it rather well: *'mens sana in corpore sano'*, a healthy mind in a healthy body.

The Current State of Wexford Football

I am thrilled to see the Wexford senior footballers going so well at the moment. They almost made a major breakthrough in 2004 with the suspended Colm Morris a huge loss in the Leinster semi-final against Westmeath. They allowed the Midlanders to get off to far too good a start (I was extremely impressed with the high tempo Westmeath warm-up and I wonder had that anything to do with their whirlwind start.) but eventually got into the game and had the Westmeath lead down to two points with about thirteen minutes to go (twelve points to ten). Now, my contention is that with twenty thousand supporters shouting the team on (a support the hurlers would have had) instead of the five or six thousand that were there, it's quite possible that it would have inspired the lads to victory. As it was, a couple of basic errors let Westmeath in for goals that really sunk Wexford, although in fairness to the lads, they fought to the very end only losing by four points (2-15 to 1-14). Laois man Pat Roe has done an excellent job and has instilled great self-belief in the team.

While things then are rosy enough at senior level, they won't remain that way for long unless we address immediately our very poor recent record at underage. Over the past few years we have received several bad beatings at both minor and under twenty-one level. A lot of good players don't seem to be making themselves available to the selectors of these teams. One has to wonder why? I think it's shameful that anyone would turn down a chance to wear the purple and gold jersey. Maybe with the increasing profile of the county senior team that will change over the next few years.

Apparently, there is a major problem trying to get people to take football development squads, and this would want to be addressed very quickly or the standard of our underage teams will plummet still further. However, there is some light at the end of the tunnel when you consider the performances of our colleges' teams. Over the period 1992-2004 several of our schools have won either Leinster or All Ireland titles. One thinks of St. Peter's in 1992, CBS Enniscorthy in 1995 and Good Counsel's marvellous triumph against St. Jarlath's in 1999. FCJ Bunclody have also been very successful in the same period, while other schools, particularly in the vocational sector have also made very good progress. Translating that into success at inter county level has proved rather elusive however.

I know I will be derided in some quarters for saying this, but Wexford County Board could do a lot worse than appoint current youth soccer supremo Mick Wallace to manage one of the county minor teams, both if he had the time. He has a proven record at managing underage soccer teams, and he certainly seems to understand young people, empathise with their concerns and get them on the right wavelength. He also takes the whole person into account, and is genuinely interested in helping young people grow and develop, not just become successful soccer players. Wexford's success in youth soccer in recent years (they have been in three of the last seven All Ireland finals) under the guidance of the man from Wellingtonbridge is in stark contrast to the failure of the county's hurlers and footballers to make a major breakthrough. I think he should be given the job of managing at least one of the county minor teams for at least a two year period to see what he could do with them. And what is most interesting is that the man himself is on record as saying that he would love a crack at trying to help the GAA in the county win a minor All Ireland. Michael Wallace is a proud Wexford man and a very successful one at that; a very interesting character who is passionate at what he does.

As in hurling, I believe we now have too many teams at senior level. Sixteen teams is too big a number and it's my view that that should be reduced to twelve if not ten. One way of doing it would be to have it based on championship (or indeed All County League) results over the past four to six years. Senior should be special, top of the range, but I honestly think that some of our senior teams would only be granted intermediate status at best, in some of the stronger footballing counties. It's something we will seriously have to look at very soon.

We will also have to get back to the basics of the game in our club competitions, i.e. catching and kicking the ball. That's what the game is supposed to be about, not running with the ball all the time. Now I accept that a certain amount of that is necessary in the modern game but Wexford was traditionally renowned for its high fielders, but sadly I have to say it's in scarce supply nowadays. And players are not going to get better at it unless they practise it on a regular basis. Of course, that's easier said that done when you consider that hurling has to be catered for as well. In fact, it is my long held belief that for skills to improve in both games, we will have to look at adopting a two season approach to playing our games in Wexford. A player dabbling in the two codes at the same time is not going to significantly improve at either. Whereas if a player could totally concentrate on one game for, say a three month period, I believe we would see higher levels of skill and better standards all-round in both games. With the recent impressive strides the footballers have made, we simply have to recognise that we are not merely a hurling county only, but a football one also, and plan accordingly. And *"plan"* here is the operative word because without meticulous planning for the future no long term success can be achieved. We are not producing enough consistently good players at underage and, as a result, our senior football and hurling teams lack real strength in depth particularly if they suffer injuries to key players

Over the period 1983-2004 the most dominant club team has undoubtedly been Duffry Rovers. To win seven senior titles in a row (1986-92) irrespective of the standard of play prevailing in the county at the time, is an outstanding achievement by any standards. We in Glynn-Barntown came closest to catching them in 1989, and have only ourselves to blame for not doing so. But any team that pulls back a ten point lead without scoring a goal has to be rated a very good one. I'm sure they will be disappointed that they didn't make a bigger impact in the Leinster club championship, though I do recall them turning in some very good performances against Baltinglass of Wicklow, Thomas Davies of Dublin and Portlaoise. I understand that, for a lot of the players, a county championship was the height of their ambitions and that seems a pity, as I felt that a fully focussed Duffry team would have won a Leinster Club Championship at least, thereby giving Wexford football a marvellous shot in the arm. Kilanerin stopped Duffry's great run in1993, but they were still good enough to come back and win one the following year, the sign of a great team.

The next most successful club in the period in question has to be the aforementioned Kilanerin. After their breakthrough year of '93, they won titles in '95, '97, '99 and 2003. Aside from the latter year they formed a habit of winning the title every other year, not quite being able to retain their title the following year. But it has to be pointed out that the standard of play would have improved from the period of Duffry dominance so theirs is still a very fine achievement. They were very much a unit, with their possession game very hard to break down and a lot of the credit for this must go to their trainer Gerry

Farrell. They also turned in some excellent performances in the Leinster Club Championship without managing to make a break-through.

Starlights would slot in next with titles won in 1983, 2002 and 2004. When we won in '83 we definitely had a team capable of winning three or four in a row. From a personal point of view our defeat to Sarsfields in the first round replay in 1984 continues to rankle with me. Still it's hard to believe that it took Starlights another nineteen years (2002) to win their next title. There were a lot of very talented players in the club over that period of time and I would have seen most of them on CBS teams.

For me the next most successful club would be St. Anne's who won two in a row in 2000 and 2001. They actually won the double (senior hurling and football) in 2000 which was quite an exceptional achievement in this day and age, though it would have to be pointed out that a straight knockout championship was then in vogue, which would have been a help with less games and less risk of injury or burnout etc. I saw the men from Rathangan et al give an outstanding performance in the Leinster Club Championship against the Westmeath Champions, Garrycastle in Athlone in 2001. They lost their two midfielders, Jack Berry and Richie Doyle through injury after only twenty minutes, a very serious setback for any team, but they recovered magnificently to record a decisive victory. They played some tremendous football in the process. They were, and remain, a remarkably big team, which I think is a decided asset in Gaelic football.

Bunclody would come next with two titles won in 1982 and 1985. They were an extremely consistent team appearing in thirteen consecutive senior quarter finals which must be a record. They have not been as prominent of late but a string of underage successes in recent years should translate into some silverware soon, but of course there are no guarantees.

Sarsfields won the centenary championship in 1984 and also appeared in the finals of '87, '93 and 2004, but they have not been the force I expected them to be. However, they have paid particular attention to underage over the last eight to ten years, and that should see them becoming a major force in years to come.

It was nice to see Fethard (1998) and my own Glynn-Barntown (1996) pick up titles during this period but both would soon want to introduce younger players to remain at or near the top.

Adamstown, Gusserane and Horeswood have all recently reached county finals, and they have certainly benefited from the success of Good Counsel College, but unfortunately all three lost some excellent players to emigration particularly Adamstown who, it is said, could currently field an even better team from those living abroad!

Its hard to credit that one of the most renowned clubs in Wexford, Castletown, has not won a county senior championship since 1981 while we have to go back even further to last find the name of another famous club, namely Ballyhogue, in the winners enclosure (1971). These clubs provided many outstanding players for Wexford teams over the years and I think it would be good for Wexford football if we saw a return to at least some of their former glories.

Clongeen, with whom Glynn-Barntown had many great battles in the late '80s and early '90s, has produced many fine players over the period we are dealing with, and currently have a fine young team that is not far away from county honours.

Gorey and Bannow-Ballymitty have also fine players within their ranks and, if they can hold their senior status for the next few years, they could well make a big impact.

Interest in other sports

Over the years I've got the impression from some people that I'm an out and out Gaelic football fanatic and I've no interest in, or cannot tolerate, other sports, but such is not the case at all. The reality is that I have a general interest in all sports and a particular interest in hurling, soccer and rugby. I greatly regret that I got no opportunity to play hurling growing up in Longford as, given the very skilful nature of the game, I know I would have worked very hard to master it. I found that I had an affinity for *'stick'* games when visitors to our farm guesthouse from Britain taught me how to play cricket and hockey. We used to play hockey on our yard with improvised sticks, while the same pertained with cricket out in one of our meadows. The nearest I came to playing hurling was, after a televised game, my brothers and I with a great burst of enthusiasm, would spend a couple of hours out on our lawn using makeshift sticks to puck a sponge ball over and back to each other, and we might even set up a makeshift goal to test our accuracy and shot stopping capabilities. We would continue until It was time to bring in the cows for milking.

It was not as if there was no tradition of hurling in Longford. In fact according to An Br. L.P. Ó Caithnia's book 'Scéal na h-Iomána' hurling was being played in my native area of North Longford (and other areas) even before the foundation of the GAA itself. It would appear that the game then was called *'Commons'* and the rules stated that you could not get the ball into your hands but had to strike it along the ground or in the air. Seemingly, the ball itself was made of cork tied around with woollen thread and covered with leather.

Longford actually competed in the Leinster Championship in hurling before it did in football. The year was 1903, the opponents were Wexford, and as might be expected, the purple and gold came out on top! Since then hurling has been very hit and miss in Longford, though in fairness they do compete manfully at inter-county level at the moment.

I've always had an avid interest in soccer dating back to the late '1960s and '70s when I was a keen follower of Leeds United and even though they are now out of the Premiership I still maintain an interest in their fortunes. My brothers supported Manchester United and Spurs so there was a lot of rivalry around. I have always liked playing soccer as I feel I can really express myself at the game and attempt the unexpected. As I've stated already I played a lot of the *'no hands game'* while a student at the Irish College in Rome but was also an avid follower of A. C. Roma attending their games regularly at the Olympic Stadium. Going to and from the games by bus could be quite an ordeal, particularly if it was a local derby match with Lazio. The sheer din on the packed buses was something to behold and I'd swear the driver used to jam on the brakes coming up to a bus stop just to get more in at the back. It gave: *'to be packed like sardines'* a new meaning!

I also attended a number of internationals there but undoubtedly the highlight was the European Cup Final of 1977 when Liverpool beat Borussia Munchengladbach by three goals to one, thereby winning the elusive trophy for the first time. We had queued for hours to get good tickets for the game, and I don't think we could have had better seats, being right in the centre and in a position to shake the hands of the Liverpool players, in particular *"man of the match"* Kevin Keegan, as they came up the steps to receive the Cup. I don't think I washed my hands for days afterwards! There was a terrific atmosphere in Rome after the game with Liverpool fans splashing about in the numerous fountains.

I've also attended soccer matches in the Nou Camp in Barcelona and the Olympic Stadium in Munich while I've been present at several soccer internationals at Dalymount Park and Lansdowne Road, where I've also gone to rugby internationals. In recent years I've also attended League of Ireland games involving Longford Town. My brother in law, Benny McGuinness, and his family are very much involved in the club, and I've gone along to a number of games at Longford's home pitch, Flancare Park. It is a splendid little stadium and a great credit to the Longford Town club. I didn't play much soccer or rugby in Wexford as I felt I had to specialise if I was going to make the grade. I certainly had no antipathy towards the games and would follow their progress in the local papers. At the invitation of Starlights colleague Nicky Sweetman I did attend several rugby sessions in the mid'80s at Enniscorthy Rugby Club but felt I was too advanced in age to learn the techniques of the game properly and take it up competitively. However, I read voraciously on the two games, being particularly taken by articles in the Sunday Times, Tribune and Independent. I have a great love of sports biographies and autobiographies as I am really fascinated by the life stories of great players. Currently I am reading the autobiographies of Nobby Stiles and Willie John McBride.

It doesn't bother me what sport young people play once they are engaging in a healthy activity, but to win and to make it really big, I do think you have to specialise at the end of the day.

Innovations in Wexford GAA 1983 – 2004

There have been a number of progressive developments during the period in question, some of which have been dealt with already, but I would like to focus on two in particular, the advent of the County Board Office, and the arrival of South East Radio. The former was first located at Murphy Floods Hotel in Enniscorthy and at present operates out of Wexford Park. For me this office has really helped to streamline the organisation within the county. It provides a very efficient service to the GAA public and great credit for this must go to county secretary Michael Kinsella, and his secretary Margaret Doyle and staff, who do a difficult, demanding job very well. I have not always seen eye to eye with Michael but that does not prevent me from saying that he and his colleagues do an excellent job and, in fact, they often go beyond the call of duty, particularly at ticket time when they work extremely long hours in ensuring that tickets for Wexford's championship matches are distributed in a fair, equal and transparent manner.

South East Radio has given a great service to the people of Wexford since its inception in the early 1990s. Of course the voice of Gaelic games on the radio is the inimitable Liam Spratt, who brings great passion and excitement to his commentaries of matches. Liam and his colleagues present a much listened to sports show on Saturday and Sunday nights. The same goes for the GAA programme presented by Pat Murphy and Margaret Doyle on Thursday nights. It also gives up to date information on club and county matters and deals with many other issues as well.

Of course, as I stated at the outset there have been other progressive developments with regard to the GAA in the county during that time, such as the much lauded Seanna Gael awards scheme, but the above two stand out for me because I believe they have had a major positive impact on the association and the Wexford community, and I am sure this will continue to be the case.

Chapter 11

My Best Fifteen

In picking the best fifteen I played with, against or saw playing over the period 1983 – 2004 there is of course a temptation to have a preference for the players of your own era. However, I will endeavour in my deliberations to be thoroughly objective if that is in fact possible.

The Goalkeeping Position

There have been many fine goalkeepers over the period in question. Obviously the first goalkeeper that caught my attention was Billy Morrissey of Starlights. Billy, an agile keeper, played an important part in our senior championship success in 1983, and got some games with Wexford. When I began playing with the model county, Vincent Murphy from the Davidstown-Courtnacuddy club immediately caught my eye, being the county goalkeeper at the time. He had a tremendous pair of hands, and I will never forget the league tie against Dublin in 1985, when he pulled down two or three dangerous balls from right under the crossbar. He quit the game soon after, but I've no doubt that had he continued he would have become a really great goalkeeper.

Other fine goalkeepers included George O'Connor and Pat Goff (Starlights). The latter was involved in an amusing incident in the Wexford/Wicklow championship game in 1983. The Garden County's full forward Tom Foley was involved in a bit of argy-bargy with his namesake the Wexford full back. Pat took the situation in hand by delivering a playful toe poke to the Wicklow man's backside. The whole episode was captured on camera and shown on the Sunday Game that night. Presenter Jim Carney, went to town on the incident, and it angered a lot of Wexford people who felt that the treatment a relatively trivial incident received was way over the top.

High on the list of goalkeepers one would have to name Ger Turner (Rosslare), John Roche (Geraldine O'Hanrahan's), Ciaran O' Leary (Sarsfields) and Ollie Murphy (Gusserane). Brendan Duffin of Gusserane was another really excellent goalkeeper with cat like reflexes; but for consistency and longevity the number one spot must go to Adamstown's John Cooper. I was part of a county minor football selection committee that gave John his first real taste of inter county action back in 1987 and while his kickout was a little suspect then (it has improved immensely since) he had all the other attributes to become a top class goalkeeper, and so it has transpired in the meantime. He is a tremendous shot stopper and brilliant in a one on one situation, never diving too early, thereby forcing the forward to make up his mind what he is going to do with the ball.

Full back line
My full back line has many worthy contenders and I will take the corner backs first. Two players who came into very strong contention were Padraig O'Gorman, a member of a famous footballing family from Taghmon-Camross and Tom Foley, originally of Geraldine O'Hanrahans but later of St Mary's GAA club in Sligo. Padraig was a very pacey defender with a great ability to carry the ball clear from defence . Tom was a great man marker who first made his mark with University College Cork in the Sigerson Cup, Others with strong claims included: Liam Kelly (Bunclody), Ger Halligan and Larry Roche (Sarsfields), Eddie Mahon (Glynn-Barntown), John and Paddy Fitzhenry (Duffry Rovers), Sean O'Neill and Sean Nolan (Starlights), Cormac Jevens (Glynn-Barntown), Eddie O'Connor (Gusserane), Arthur O'Connor (St. Martin's), Niall Murphy (Bannow-Ballymitty), Eugene Brennan and Brian Furlong(Rosslare), Michael Kavanagh (Castletown) and Richard Purcell (Adamstown). The latter looked to have a great future in the game, but went to work in the United States while still very young, and was a great loss to Wexford.

However, the two players I have chosen are Colm Morris of Castletown and Michael Caulfield of Gusserane. The former, in my opinion, is an outstanding corner back with a great sense of adventure, undoubtedly one of the best in the country. His consistently good form has been an important factor in Wexford's recent rise to prominence. Michael Caulfield gave sterling service to club and county over a long number of years. He was also a very consistent player and utterly reliable.

I have come up with eleven contenders for the full back position, all with varying claims for inclusion. I played with the classy Ed Doran of Starlights for several years, and considered him to be a brilliant player, giving several outstanding exhibitions of full back play. But for the fact that he was hampered by a persistent back problem, I'm sure he would have gone on to play for Wexford for many years and perhaps got even further recognition too. Michael Dillon (Volunteers and Kilmacud Crokes), Jay Mernagh (Duffry Rovers), Jack O'Leary (Blackwater), Sean Murphy (Clongeen), Larry Cahill (Ballyhogue), Tom O'Gorman (Taghmon-Camross) and the Gusserane trio of Liam Fardy, Kevin Kehoe and the current Wexford full back Philip Wallace, would all come into consideration, but the person I have plumped for is John O'Gorman of the Taghmon-Camross club. John gave many classic displays in the number three position, and during a career spanning almost fifteen years as an inter county footballer, was widely recognised as being one of the best full backs in the country. A lovely fielder and excellent on his feet, he had the uncanny knack of holding the ball out from him, level with his head, as he danced out through opponents to clear in fine style.

Half back line

The half back line also had a lot of worthy candidates and I will select my wing backs first. From my playing days at Starlights, I found Padge Courtney and Michael Millar to be two excellent, attack minded wing backs; both played significant parts in our championship win in '83. Paul Nolan (Starlights) a brother of Sean's was another fine player, and for me he has arguably been the finest footballer to come into the CBS in Enniscorthy in my time there. Others in contention included Ciaran Roche (Glynn-Barntown), John Casey (Duffry Rovers), Jack Swords (Bunclody), John Cullen (Gusserane), John Creane RIP (St. Mary's Maudlinstown), Donal Caulfield (Bannow-Ballymitty), Billy Walsh and John Curtis (Sarsfields) Bernard O'Gorman (Taghmon Camross) The latter (a brother of John and Padraig), was a much underrated player and, but for a chronic hamstring injury, would have played for Wexford for much longer than he did. I also gave serious consideration to present day inter county players Paraic Curtis (Clongeen), Leigh O'Brien (Horeswood) and David Murphy (Rosslare). But at the risk of an accusation of bias, I have gone for two players from my own playing era, namely, Liam Cullen of Gusserane and Noel Swords of Bunclody. Liam was a tigerish wing back who knew his first duty was to man mark and defend. Likewise with Noel who probably had an extra string to his bow, in that he was a beautiful striker of a football, and had the ability to score points coming forth from his wing back position. Noel was also a very versatile player who also excelled at midfield. For various reasons both players didn't play inter county football for as long as they should have, but for the relatively short time they did, they left an indelible imprint on me.

Those in contention for the centre half back position were, John Dunne (Bunclody), Garry Byrne (Ballyhogue), James O'Connor (Duffry Rovers), Darragh Ryan (St. Anne's), Padge *'Skinner'* Walsh (Starlights), Tony Walsh (Sarsfields), Michael Stafford (Clongeen), Barry Kirwan (Glynn-Barntown), Michael Carty (Castletown), Noel Barry (Kilmore) and present day inter county footballers Darragh Breen (Gorey) and David Murphy (Rosslare). All were/are excellent footballers and would have strong claims to the position. Had I been picking the team over twenty five years (1979-2004) I would have no hesitation in saying that Michael Carty, one of the most brilliant foot-ballers Wexford has ever produced, would be an automatic choice, but the Castletown man was past his considerable best during the period in question (the same would apply to Kilmore's Noel Barry). Undoubtedly too, had Darragh Ryan remained injury free and been able to concentrate more on football, he would have had very strong claims to the position. Garry Byrne was very good there as well but probably played more of his football, at least at inter county level, in the forward line. Padge Walsh, James O'Connor and Tony Walsh were excellent at club level in the position, but, at the end of the day it all boiled down to a choice between four players: Barry Kirwan, John Dunne, David Murphy and Darragh Breen.

Barry and John were tremendous servants of Wexford football over a long period of time, while Darragh and, in particular, David are rel-atively *'new kids on the block'* so to speak, with much service given, and I've no doubt much more to come. John Dunne was one of the hardest and fairest players to play the game during the period in question. He was an amazingly strong man who played the game with little or no fuss. In the county senior semi- final of 1983 I crashed into the Bunclody man when both of us were going flat out to contest a fifty-fifty ball. John came worst out of the incident but there were no complaints from him. Barry of course was a colleague with Glynn-Barntown for years. Like John, he was extremely wholehearted never giving an inch, and well capable of winning a *'sixty-forty'* ball. This position was very difficult to call but John Dunne just gets the nod on the basis of his sheer obduracy, effectiveness and longevity for club and county.

Midfield

I had the following players in mind for the two midfield positions; Pat Neville, a team mate of mine with Starlights, Eamonn Kehoe and Michael Mahon (Bunclody), Greg Waters (Fethard), George O'Connor (St. Martin's), Paddy Byrne (Kilmore), John Cullen (Gusserane) John Lacey (Shelmaliers), Louis Rafter (Duffry Rovers), John Harrington (Sarsfields), Johnny McDermott and Michael Carty (Taghmon-Camross, the former never really fulfilled his vast potential while the latter was an extremely wholehearted player), John Nolan (Volunteers), Joe White (Clongeen), unheralded but very effective, Seamus Hughes and Jim Darcy (Kilanerin), and present day players Willy Carley (Glynn-Barntown) and Paddy Colfer (Clongeen). I should also point out that I thought Nicky Sweetman and Pat Creane were a very good midfield partnership when Starlights won the Championship in 1983.

After much deliberation I went for two players I would have played with myself, Louis Rafter of Duffry Rovers and John Harrington from the Sarsfields club. Louis, over a long career, out -fielded some of the best men in the game, and he was also an excellent long range free-taker and distributor of the ball. John was also a dominant man at midfield for a long number of years and it could be argued that Wexford has still not fully replaced him (or Louis) in that area. Given the dearth of midfield talent available, I think his retirement was a little premature.

Half forward line

Taking the half forwards first, I saw the following men in contention: John Walker (Sarsfields), James Morrissey (Glynn-Barntown), Jim Byrne (Fethard), Tadhg Foran (Gusserane), Jim Rigley (Starlights), Seamus and Noel Fitzhenry (Duffry Rovers), Seamus O'Sullivan (Clongeen), a lovely languid style, Sean O'Shea (Blackwater), Garry Byrne (Ballyhogue), Billy Byrne (Gorey) and present day players Scott Doran (Kilmore), Pat Forde (Kilanerin) and Redmond Barry (St. Anne's). All these players had valid claims for inclusion, but for me, two stood out from the rest, namely Seamus Fitzhenry and Scott Doran. I played with Seamus, and I thought he was a gifted player who was extremely difficult to dispossess, especially while on a solo run. He would more than hold his own in any company. Towards the end of his career he left the footballers to try his hand at inter county hurling, and this caused a bit of resentment, but I suppose after such long service to the footballers, it was something he was entitled to do. Scott Doran was a free scoring forward with a wonderful left foot. He first came to my attention when I was in charge of the county minors in 1991. He was also on the team the following year, and played under twenty-one for three years, Liam Fardy (then senior manager) having brought him into the senior set up for the 1992-93 National League. He was also a very talented soccer player having had trials with English club Queens Park Rangers, but I'm delighted he decided to carve out a career for himself in the purple and gold jersey, but sad that it ended a bit prematurely.

Centre forward

The centre half forward position did not have, in my opinion, as many outstanding candidates as other positions. I did not consider Martin Quigley as I felt the Rathnure legend was past his considerable best during the period in question, plus the fact that he was focussing almost entirely on hurling. The following would have strong claims to the position: Pat Neville (Bannow-Ballymitty and Starlights), Pat Barden (Adamstown), Aidan Jordan (Duffry Rovers), a key but probably underrated member of the all conquering Duffry seven in a row team, John Roche (Gusserane), another underrated player and Mick Walsh (Glynn-Barntown), a player with great peripheral vision and quite influential, when fully fit! However, the person I have selected is somebody who I just was not able to accommodate at midfield but whose sheer natural ability dictated that a place had to be found for him somewhere. I refer to the great George O'Connor of St. Martin's. As I've said already I was thrilled for George when he finally got his just desserts in the form of an All Ireland senior hurling medal in '96 but he was also an exceptional footballer who would have stood out in any company.

Full forward line

I have now reached the final line of my team, and again I will select the corners first. I picked two from the following: Richie Neville (Bannow-Ballymitty), Michael McGee (Kilmore), Nicky Darcy (Kilanerin), Eddie Mahon (Glynn-Barntown), Billy Dodd (Sarsfields), Martin Fitzhenry (Duffry Rovers), Larry Murphy (Cloughbawn), Martin

Hanrick (Bunclody), Derek O' Reilly (Horeswood), and current inter county players Jason Lawlor (Adamstown), John Hegarty and Matty Forde (both Kilanerin). All twelve players had a lot to recommend them, with all capable of running up big tallies. But for me, two players clearly stand out, namely, John Hegarty and Matty Forde. I had John on the county minor panel in 1992, but having considered the matter very carefully with the rest of the team management, he didn't make the team for the replayed Leinster semi-final against Meath. However, he could have counted himself very unlucky. John, of course made up for that in the meantime, making the minor team the following year, and going on to have an illustrious career with Wexford. He also played on a fine UCD team during his university days, and mixing with players from other counties undoubtedly helped his game. What can I say about the great Matty Forde that has not been said already? All I will venture is, that, as someone who has been involved in Wexford football for a long time, it is great to see that at long last, we have produced a fully fledged All Star.

The selection of the full forward caused me a lot of difficulty, and initially I had trouble coming up with nominations. In fact I had to seek the further assistance of *'Mr. Football'* himself, Seamus Keevans to guide me. This man has made an absolutely enormous contribution to Wexford football since I came to the county in 1982, and I'm sure it was going on long before that too. He has an encyclopaedic knowledge of players, and I've lost count of the number of football competitions he has run, and continues to run in the county. The retired Garda Sergeant could only come up with two names: Ger Howlin (Dan O'Connell's) and yours truly. I saw very little of Ger but I gather he was an outstanding full forward who once scored three goals against that great Dublin team of the '70s in the championship but his best days were behind him during the period under discussion. I have debarred myself from selection. I eventually came up with the following names: Eamonn Kehoe, Michael Mahon and Martin Hanrick (Bunclody), Seamus Hughes (Kilanerin), J.J McCormack (Castletown), Seamus Cullen (Gusserane) and Jim Byrne (Fethard). I have gone for Martin Hanrick of Bunclody even though he didn't often play full forward. He was a class forward and I simply had to include him. On the 'Sunday Game' programme in June 1986 featuring Wexford and Dublin, presenter Michael Lyster referred to him in glowing terms, comparing him to his counterpart on the Dublin team, Barney Rock, for his scoring exploits.

So my team in full reads:

1.
John Cooper
(Adamstown)

2.
Michael Caulfield
(Gusserane)

3.
John O'Gorman
(Taghmon-Camross)

4.
Colm Morris
(Castletown)

5.
Noel Swords
(Bunclody)

6.
John Dunne
(Bunclody)

7.
Liam Cullen
(Gusserane)

8.
Louis Rafter
(Duffry Rovers)

9.
John Harrington
(Sarsfields)

10.
Scott Doran
(Kilmore)

11.
George O'Connor
(St. Martin's)

12.
Seamus Fitzhenry
(Duffry Rovers)

13.
John Hegarty
(Kilanerin)

14.
Martin Hanrick
(Bunclody)

15.
Matty Forde
(Kilanerin)

Without doubt, the really unlucky players not to make my team were: Brendan Duffin, Padraig O'Gorman, Tom Foley, Eddie Mahon, (an All-Star replacement in 1985), David Murphy, Padge Walsh, Garry Byrne, Michael Mahon and ace opportunist, Billy Dodd.

Epilogue

Wednesday, 4th May 2005

"Life can only be understood backwards;
But it must be lived forwards".
Sören Kierkegaard, Philosopher.

These are indeed heady days for Wexford football. I pen these final few words three days after the county contested its first national league football final in fifty nine years. Those of us involved in Wexford football over the years lived in hope of something like this happening but certainly, from my perspective anyway, I scarcely believed it would ever come about and I have to pinch myself at times to realise that it has happened. Oh you of little faith I hear you say! However, I honestly believe that we too could have made a major breakthrough in the mid 1980s but we just didn't have the faith in our abilities or the amazing self belief that manager Pat Roe has instilled into the current group of players. Laois man, Pat, has done a magnificent job and has produced a team that the county can be proud of. But let us also give great credit to his long serving selectors Michael Furlong, Declan Carty and Ger Halligan who saw real potential in the team many years back and stuck at it through thick and through thin. They richly deserve this marvellous breakthrough. Ger in particular deserves special mention as he stood down as manager when he felt he could take the team no further but was quite prepared to continue on as a selector under different managers. This was very noble on his part and showed his dedication to the cause of Wexford football.

I know Wexford was well beaten by Armagh in the final but the experience of playing in front of such a large crowd (46,000+) should prove invaluable for the championship. The players were intensely disappointed with their performance and this just shows how far they have travelled and how ambitious they have become. Moral victories or heroic defeats are no longer the order of the day but have been replaced by fully merited victories against the likes of Armagh (first league game) and Tyrone (league semi final), the 2002 and 2003 All Ireland champions respectively.

The league semi final against Tyrone at Portlaoise is a game I will never forget, as it was one of the most thrilling encounters I have ever experienced. It was a tense, see-saw battle all the way with the issue in doubt right up until the final whistle. And what Wexford supporter will ever forget the great calmness and composure shown by St. Anne's David Fogarty as he kicked that crucial winning score. And lets not forget that substitute Darren Foran of Rosslare showed great vision to pick David out with a fine pass in the first place. The score of course (registered well into injury time with little chance of a Tyrone response) led to absolute bedlam among Wexford supporters in the stand. I was sitting beside two Foley fellows from Horeswood and when the ball went over the bar they jumped up on their seats and started singing: *'football's coming home, it's coming home'!* I was almost joining them until I was engulfed in a bear hug by a past pupil of mine, Tommy Kelly of Davidstown-Courtnacuddy. Tommy is one of Wexford's greatest supporters and along with his friend Jason O'Brien (another past pupil) follows the team right around the country. It was a very special moment indeed and then we all went on to the field to greet the Wexford heroes and I met some former county colleagues like Mick Caulfield, Garry Byrne, Eddie Mahon and John 'Chairman' Dunne!

Being on the pitch we were able to experience at first hand the dreadful underfoot conditions that the players had to endure in the course of the match. And whatever about Tyrone, such conditions did not suit the Wexford style of play at all. There may have only been a point in it at the end but the model county men were thoroughly deserving winners and a wider winning margin would not have flattered them.

Hopefully Wexford is now back in the big time in football, but let me hasten to add that, if such is the case, it should not be at the expense of hurling, a game I also feel very passionate about. If we organise ourselves properly the county is certainly big enough and has the population base to support successful hurling and football teams. To that end I would like to see the standard improve greatly at club level. Long term (as I mentioned earlier), I believe that can only be achieved by the adoption of hurling and football seasons for our club games and I hope this will happen soon.

One thing Wexford County Board has done for 2005 is the appointment of a Secretary to the All County Leagues after an absence of more than three years. Dedicated Gael Jack O'Brien from the Buffers Alley club is the person in question and I'm sure he will see to it that the credibility of the leagues is enhanced and, in the process, take a weight of work off the County Board Office. Ever efficient County P.R.O. Alan Aherne is doing everything in his power to ensure that the Leagues run smoothly but he needs the full co-operation of all the clubs.

I also pen these lines four days after my school, St. Mary's CBS Enniscorthy, reclaimed the All Ireland Colleges Senior Hurling 'B' title after a marvellous match that went to extra time, on Saturday 30th April, at Templemore, Co. Tipperary. Their opponents were Charleville CBS from Cork and its not too often that a Wexford team beats a Cork team in hurling and, what made it even more pleasing was the fact that, due to a clash of colours, we donned the purple and gold jerseys with the Cork school pulling on the rebel red. It was 1-7 to 0-10 at the end of normal time but our lads dug really deep in extra time to emerge winners from an absorbing contest on a final scoreline of 3-8 to 0-13.

The Enniscorthy lads played with tremendous spirit all through; with some breathtaking saves by Ballyhogue's Niall Maher (a nephew of Damien Fitzhenry) being critical to the outcome of the match. Charlevillle had one quite exceptional player in right corner forward, Cathal Naughton and I'm sure we will hear a lot more about him in the future.

For CBS manager and coach Adrian Walsh, this success was a further string to his bow. Since arriving at the school in September 1994 Adrian has guided CBS senior hurling teams to five Leinster finals, winning four, and three All Ireland deciders, winning two. This is an outstanding record especially considering the fact that before his arrival we had not won a Leinster senior hurling title for over thirty years. An excellent trainer and coach and an astute tactician, I have no doubt that Adrian will be called upon to manage the Wexford senior hurling team one day.

I think the Annual Congress of the GAA in April showed great vision and maturity in allowing Central Council to decide on the future use of Croke Park, thus amending Rule 42. One thing I found truly ironic about the situation was that many of those who condemned the *'open vote'* in 2001 were looking for one on this occasion. But the lesson was learned and the vote was by secret ballot, and the result of it could have been more magnanimously received by some sporting bodies that may very well be seeking the use of Croke Park in the near future. Hats off to the GAA on a brave, courageous decision. It was a wonderful example of sporting ecumenism.

I have, at times, been constructively critical of the GAA in this book but that does not prevent me from saying it is still a great organisation, that makes a magnificent contribution to Irish society. In fact it provides us with something that, given the globalisation and increasing fragmentation of society, we very badly need nowadays and, that is, a close identification with our native parish and a real sense of belonging. Long may it continue to do so.